D1195768

THE ECONOMIC BASIS OF
ETHNIC SOLIDARITY

THE ECONOMIC BASIS OF ETHNIC SOLIDARITY

Small Business in the Japanese American Community

Edna Bonacich
and
John Modell

UNIVERSITY OF CALIFORNIA PRESS

Berkeley / Los Angeles / London

University of California Press
Berkeley and Los Angeles, California

University of California Press, Ltd.
London, England

Library of Congress Cataloging in Publication Data

Bonacich, Edna.
    The economic basis of ethnic solidarity.

    Includes bibliographical references and index.
    1. Japanese Americans—Economic conditions.
2. Japanese Americans—Social conditions. I. Modell,
John, joint author. II. Title.
E184.J3B68   305.8'956'073   80-51233
ISBN 0-520-04155-0

Printed in the United States of America

1 2 3 4 5 6 7 8 9

Contents

Preface

As this book was an outgrowth of the Japanese American Research Project (JARP) at the University of California, Los Angeles, we owe thanks to the many people connected with that project. In a volume utilizing the same data, though from a different perspective, Gene N. Levine and Robert Colbert Rhodes acknowledge at length the people who have contributed to the project as a whole. Those who directly provided research assistance for this volume include Michael Edlen, Sheila Henry, Michael Rudd, Darrell Montero, Ford Waite, and Robert Rhodes, to whom we extend our thanks. We are also grateful to Howard Aldrich, Joe Feagin, Ivan Light, Frank Miyamoto, and Bill Wilson for careful and critical readings of earlier drafts of the manuscript, as well as to Gary Hamilton, Barbara Laslett, Ivan Light, Jon Turner, Takuo Utagawa, Pierre van den Berghe, and Walter Zenner for their critical reactions to and very helpful comments on chapter 2.

To the principal investigator, Gene Levine, our debt is immeasurable. It was he who conceived of a three-generational survey and who devised the instruments (with the aid of Modell) to put it into effect. We are especially grateful to Dr. Levine for permitting us the opportunity to develop this volume, which selects a fairly narrow theoretical point from the broad range of issues the survey sought to cover. Without his generosity in allowing us full use of the data, the study could not have been conducted.

The research was financially supported by grants from the Japanese American Citizens League, the Carnegie Corporation of New York, and the National Institute of Mental Health (Grant No. 5 R01 MH12780-04). Computing assistance was provided by the Health Sciences Computing Facility at the University of California, Los Angeles, and sponsored by National Institutes of Health Special Research Resources Grant RR-3. In addition, the university's College of Arts and Sciences supplemented waning resources in the final stages of the project.

The JARP as originally conceived was a wide-ranging effort, incorporating an archive, an oral-history collection, a sociological inquiry touching upon three generations, and a variety of historical investigations. Over the years, the JARP has evolved somewhat independently in each of these directions. None of its many achievements, therefore, can be taken as representative of the initial intentions of the project's sponsors or directors. Considering these achievements as a set, on the other hand, one can see that JARP researchers have made the Japanese Americans as well documented an ethnic group as any in the country and that they are uncovering the significance of the Japanese American experience as a part of the history of the United States.

The present volume appears neither at the beginning nor at the end of JARP publication. Rather than being a report on a single ethnic group at a particular moment in time, it is an effort to develop and clarify a particular theoretical position. In turn, we hope to challenge some currently widespread beliefs about ethnicity in general and about the Japanese Americans in particular. We suspect that elements of our interpretation (and even aspects of our scholarly goals) are distinct from those of some of the JARP's original sponsors and, in addition, from those of many within the Japanese American community who looked to the JARP for particular kinds of enlightenment. We hope and expect that what these people have sought and continue to seek is or will be available elsewhere among the JARP's products. However, even as we produce a volume resolutely our own in purpose, we recognize—and gratefully—that in no small part it has been the commitment to scholarly inquiry and intellectual debate on the part of all involved with the JARP which has made our volume possible. We believe that the JARP will be enriched by it.

1

Introduction

Ethnicity is a communalistic form of social affiliation, depending, first, upon an assumption of a special bond among people of like origins, and, second, upon the obverse, a disdain for people of dissimilar origins. There are other important bases of affiliation besides communalism, among which is solidarity based on shared class interest. These two forms of solidarity, ethnicity and class, typically cut across one another in complex societies. They represent competing principles, each calling on people to join together along a different axis.

The sociology of ethnic relations grew out of a tradition that underplayed the importance of communalistic affiliations. The classic writers in sociology paid little heed to ethnicity, assuming it would disappear with modernization and industrialization. Indeed, the early grand dichotomies, such as gemeinschaft/gesellschaft, and mechanical/organic solidarity, had built into them a movement from affiliations of the ethnic type, based on "irrational" kinlike bonds among people, to affiliations based on the "rational" principles of mutual interest and need. Ethnic affiliation was considered a traditional social form. The exigencies of modern society would liberate people from these traditions (Blumer, 1965).

The obvious falseness of this premise, perhaps especially evident in the face of Nazi Germany, forced a reassessment. Clearly these traditional sources of solidarity were far more resistant to change than had previously been realized. Several authors began to call for revisions in our thinking. Criticizing earlier writers, they demanded that ethnicity be given prominence as a phenomenon that could not be ignored. Some—for example, writers of the plural-society school (Smith, 1965; Kuper and Smith,

1969)—suggested that we place ethnicity at center stage. As they correctly pointed out, almost every society in the world has some degree of ethnic diversity, and for most ethnicity appears to be a pivotal point of division and conflict.

The polemic against the obvious inadequacies of the belief that ethnicity would disappear has led to another extreme position: the view that ethnicity is such a "natural" bond among people that one need not question it—it is a primordial phenomenon. In other words, since ethnicity is rooted in common ancestry (or putative common ancestry), it is experienced in much the same way as kinship.

Accepting ethnicity as primordial leads to a certain logic of inquiry. Ethnic affiliation requires no explanation in itself. Rather, one concentrates on its consequences, either on the negative side, in terms of prejudice, discrimination, and intergroup conflict, or on the positive side, in terms of the meaningful, culturally rich social life and sense of identity it can provide for members of the ethnic group. Questions regarding the existence and persistence of ethnicity are not raised; these things are taken for granted.

Recently a new school of thought has emerged, a school that does not repeat the earlier errors of the founding classicists by ignoring the importance of ethnicity. Proponents of this school believe that ethnicity cannot be taken for granted as "natural." Instead, they lay down the challenge to treat ethnic affiliation and antagonism as phenomena that are neither natural nor inevitable, but variable, and therefore in need of explanation. Without ignoring communalistic affiliations, we can now ask: Under what conditions will they be invoked? Under what conditions will they lead to extreme conflict? And under what conditions will they subside as a major axis of social organization and conflict?

There are at least two reasons for questioning the primordial nature of communalistic ties. First, ethnic groups have boundary problems (Barth, 1969; Patterson, 1977:103-104). Because of the pervasive tendency for human beings to interbreed, populations of mixed ancestry are continually being generated. To consign certain among these people to an ethnic identity requires a rule of descent. A variety of such rules exist, including matrilineal tracing of descent (which is found among the Jews); recognition of the presence of any one particular ancestry (as with United States blacks); and treatment of mixed ancestry as a separate ethnicity (as is the case for South African Coloureds). The variability in descent rules suggests their social rather than primordial nature. They reflect social decisions, not natural, kinlike feelings.

Apart from mixed-ancestry problems, ethnic groups can redefine their boundaries in terms of whom they incorporate. As many authors have pointed out (Yancey, Ericksen, and Juliani, 1976), several of the European groups that immigrated to the United States, such as the Italians, had no sense of common nationality until they came here. And the construction of "whites" took decades to grow out of the enmity between old and new European immigrants. Today, similarly, a new ethnic group, Asian Americans, is being constructed out of previously quite distinctive, and often hostile, national elements. That such a creation is social and political rather than primordial seems clear.

A second reason for questioning the primordial nature of ethnicity is that shared ancestry has not precluded intraethnic conflict, including class conflict. If one considers the history of societies that were ethnically relatively homogeneous, such as France or England, one finds not only intense class conflict but even class warfare. Even in ethnically diverse societies such as the United States, within individual ethnic groups class conflict is not unknown. White workers have struck against white-owned plants and have been shot down by coethnics without concern for common blood. Chinese and Jewish business heads have exploited their ethnic brothers and sisters in sweatshops. Indeed, one of the biggest problems with primordial approaches to ethnicity is that they tend to ignore intragroup conflict; in focusing on vertical divisions, they ignore the horizontal ones.

We cannot simply accept communalistic groups as natural or primordial units. Ethnic solidarity and antagonism are all socially created phenomena. True, they are social phenomena that call upon primordial sentiments and bonds based upon common ancestry. These sentiments and bonds, however, do not just naturally exist: they must be constructed and activated. It is thus incumbent upon us not to take ethnic phenomena for granted, but to try to explain them.

It is our contention that economic factors play an important role in the retention or dissolution of ethnic ties. This is not to say that economic concerns are the exclusive forces at work, but it is upon them that we wish to focus here. Put another way, the basic theme of this volume is the relationship between ethnicity and social class. Our central thesis is that ethnic groups often act as economic-interest groups, and when they cease to do so, they tend to dissolve. Whatever else it may be, the primordial tie of ethnicity is a tool that can be used to invoke class action. Ethnic symbols can be rallying cries around which to mobilize interest group members. The relationship between ethnicity and class is not always unidirectional. Not only does common-class membership tend to promote ethnic movements, but ethnicity, with its bonds and obligations, has upon occasion been the vehicle by which groups have established common-class positions.

In a majority of empirical instances in the modern world, the class position of ethnic, and especially racial, minorities is one of economic and political subordination. Minority members are colonized peasants (and other precapitalist forms) transformed into an urban subproletariat. They are faced with poverty and powerlessness. They are a peculiarly disadvantaged sector within, or even beneath, the working class.

One category of ethnic and racial minorities, however, does not fit this pattern. Varyingly called "middleman minorities" (Blalock, 1967:79-84; Bonacich, 1973), "middleman trading peoples" (Becker, 1956:225-237), and "marginal trading peoples" (Stryker, 1959), these groups occupy a position, not at the bottom of the social structure, but somewhere in the middle, typified by a concentration in independent small business. For middleman minorities, the relationship between class and ethnicity takes on a character different from the one it has for subproletarian minorities.

In this book we explore the relationship between class and ethnic solidarity for one particular ethnic group: the Japanese Americans. It is our contention that the Japanese are an example of a middleman minority in the United States. Their history and current experience can be utilized to exemplify and develop theory regarding middleman minorities and to elucidate the relationship between economic adaptation and ethnicity for this type of minority. In focusing on this one ethnic group, we emphatically do not mean to single out the Japanese as having especially acted upon economic motives. We believe that class factors have operated similarly for other ethnic groups, although the nature of the relationship may vary from group to group. The Japanese Americans are being used as an illustration of some general principles, though we hope in the process to use the theory to help explain their unique experience as well.

The first part of the study presents some general ideas about middleman minorities, laying the theoretical groundwork for the study. We then trace the evolution of Japanese American economic and social adaptation before and through World War II. Based on secondary sources, this section is not intended as a new history of the Japanese experience in this country. Rather, it provides a reinterpretation of that history in the light of middleman-minority theory.

The rest of the book uses nationwide-survey data collected by the Japanese American Research Project (JARP) at the University of California, Los Angeles, to examine the postwar developments of this particular ethnic group. These data permit us to view the economic differentiation of the first native-born generation of Japanese Americans, the *Nisei*, from a national perspective, which is available in no other source. The nature of these data, and cautions to be observed in interpreting them, are discussed at length in Appendix A. Specifically, we look to these data to determine the degree to which prewar economic forms have been reestablished among the second generation and what this implies for their internal social organization and for their social integration with the majority community. In fact, we find that there remains division among the Nisei, with somewhat less than half of our sample engaged in small businesses reminiscent of prewar arrangements. The remainder have moved into a variety of occupations more directly integrated in the general economy of the nation. Given this division, we are able to explore some of its causes, and we also examine the ramifications of such differences for the perpetuation or disintegration of a solidary ethnic community.

Despite the fact that they are the products of different methods, the two sections of the book are linked by a common theme. This is the relationship between being engaged in middleman-minority economic activities and the retention of a strong ethnic community. We attempt to demonstrate that involvement in certain kinds of enterprise supports strong ethnic ties (and vice versa), while the absence of this class concentration leads to the weakening of ethnic solidarity for Japanese Americans and, presumably, for other middleman minorities.

The "Theory and History" section of this book develops, from a variety of perspectives, several discrete aspects of the background that the Nisei brought into the mid-1960s, the period to which our survey data pertain. At that time, we argue, elements of the Nisei generation had established a group economy based on self-employment which in some ways resembled the more substantial ethnic economy that their parents' generation, the *Issei*, had developed in the years between their immigration and the wartime evacuation. Thus, chapter 6, the final chapter in this section, examines the role of the war and relocation in bringing Japanese Americans from the full flowering of their ethnic economy to the modest version some of the Nisei developed. Most Nisei, however, had always been less committed participants in the ethnic economy than were their parents, and the nature of this position is the subject of chapter 5. Among the bounds placed upon the prewar growth of the Issei ethnic economy was the hostility of white America, the topic developed in chapter 4. Such hostility, we argue in chapter 3, was an element of the situation of the Issei, but not the cause of their characteristic economic form. Endogenous and exogenous explanations for this characteristic economic form are compared and assessed in this chapter, together with an analysis of the Issei small-business economy at its height. Chapter 2, which follows this introduction, lays out in some detail the evolving theoretical framework that has led us to focus our efforts here upon the nexus of economy and ethnicity—a theory of middleman minorities, which minorities, we believe, are a repeated and significant phenomenon of world history.

The second section of this book begins by developing, in chapter 7, some key dimensions of Nisei economic participation in the mid-1960s. We are especially concerned with the differentiation of the Nisei generation in this regard, and in chapter 8 we discover that the Nisei differ in the form of their economic participation so much according to date of birth that, we maintain, this dynamic factor must be taken into consideration if the nature and future of Nisei ethnicity is to be fathomed. Very nearly the same may be said about education, which is covered in chapter 9. In turn, date of birth and educational attainment are both closely intertwined with the occupational histories of the Nisei and with their family backgrounds, the subjects of chapter 10. Finally, area of residence and residential history, which are described in chapter 11, help to round out our analysis of the causes of Nisei economic adaptations.

At this point, we move from explaining the economic differentiation of the Nisei to exploring its consequences for aspects of ethnicity, in part III. Of these consequences, the first, treated in chapter 12, is the family, the most elemental connection between an individual and a social grouping so substantially ascriptive as an ethnic group. Chapter 13 takes up the informal and formal associations that in twentieth-century America form a large part of the behavioral content of ethnicity. We conclude our study of consequences with an examination of socialization, values, and religion in chapter 14. Here we consider the degree to which learned mental constructs that may be said to be characteristically Japanese American depend upon the maintenance of an ethnic economy.

Finally, we conclude the volume with two chapters offering brief assessments of the future of ethnicity among the Japanese Americans. Chapter 15 examines the *Sansei*, the children of the Nisei. Chapter 16, our conclusion, moves more generally to the topic of the future, considering what we have learned about the economic basis of ethnic solidarity and about trends apparent in the recent economic participation of Japanese Americans.

Our approach to the Japanese Americans should be distinguished from the "success story" approach of Petersen (1970) and others. The image of the Japanese American situation as a success story plays its part in a rather self-congratulatory version of ethnic pluralism much in vogue today. A warm glow surrounds the notion of ethnicity, centering on ethnic foods and festivals, the staples of human-interest features on the local television news and in the Sunday newspapers. In this view, distinctive ethnic behavior is assumed to be a carryover from the country of origin, testimony to the strength of "culture" in the face of abrasive modernity, freely elected, and a good thing. This view, as we shall argue, trivializes the very phenomenon it celebrates and distracts those who entertain it from the local and immediate circumstances in which ethnicity rises or declines.

The success-story, or "model minority," view of Japanese Americans has already come under attack by a growing generation of politically concerned Asian Americans (Okimoto, 1971; Uyematsu, 1971). One of the points they make is that the success image is used to make an invidious comparison with other racial minorities. It pronounces the openness of the American system, regardless of race, and helps to place the blame for their lack of success upon the shoulders of other nonwhite groups by implicitly raising the question: If the Japanese Americans can overcome racial discrimination, why can't you? (Ogawa, 1971:52-57; Tachiki, 1971:1).

Recognition of the peculiar economic role played by the Japanese in American history makes a comparison with other racial minorities in terms of so-called success completely inappropriate. The blacks, for example, have played a totally different role. They were introduced into this country for the express purpose of providing cheap agricultural labor in the form of chattel slavery. Emancipation did not wholly change their class position as the white South reorganized itself and established a white aristocracy of labor that kept black people exploited as a group. The great postwar migration northward has produced some changes, but there is not complete consensus on the status of blacks today.

The Japanese, on the other hand, while often starting as cheap labor in the employ of powerful white capitalists, were never in a position so completely dependent on that class. The majority of the immigrant generation were able to move out of this role and into the independent-small-business mode of which we have been speaking. Their class position put the minority into conflict with certain important and powerful classes in this country, sometimes with devastating consequences for the Japanese. It was a different conflict from that of black America, however, and it had different results.

Overall, this volume attempts to develop an analysis of a certain type of ethnic group, the middleman minority. The Japanese Americans are used to exemplify and elaborate the model, while the model is used to help explain the Japanese American experience. In the process we hope to increase our understanding of both the general and the particular. We would not maintain that our account constitutes a rigorous test of middleman-minority theory, although in our reading the theory has provided a parsimonious explanation for the data examined. We are therefore encouraged in proposing our findings more generally.

We hope that no subsequent interpretation of the Japanese American experience will overlook the arguments and empirical findings presented in this volume. In no sense, however, do we wish to suggest that we have presented a final, definitive account. The theoretical elements of our account, especially as presented in chapter 2, are quite obviously part of a more inclusive and ongoing effort to add to the literature, a process in which Bonacich is an active participant. The historical embodiment of these elements, as we are aware, implies a narrowing as well as a redirecting of the historian's focus, as an examination of Modell's previous writings on the Japanese Americans will reveal. Finally, the use we have made of the JARP survey, although an entirely appropriate application, hardly touches the vast possibilities its three-generational design suggests. Every intellectual effort, however, must cut into complex realities and employ evidence in its own way. The present volume represents our way.

Part I
THEORY AND HISTORY

2

Middleman
Minorities

Several authors have remarked that a set of ethnic and racial minorities, including the Jews in Europe and the Chinese in Southeast Asia, share a comparable position in the social structures of the societies in which they reside. These groups—called *middleman minorities*—occupy "middle" positions rather than the bottom-of-the-social-scale position in which we more commonly find ethnic and racial minorities.

The middleman-minority phenomenon received attention from some of the classic thinkers in sociology, including Marx, Weber, Simmel, and Toennies. For several decades, however, it dropped out of view, only to be recovered again in the last few years, perhaps gaining attention as a result of the publication of Blalock's *Toward a Theory of Minority Group Relations*, with its brief but stimulating treatment of middleman groups (Blalock, 1967:79-84; see Cahnman, 1957; Rinder, 1958-59; and Stryker, 1959, for a few earlier treatments).

The intention of this chapter is to review the principal ideas in the literature on middleman minorities, since it is our contention that the Japanese Americans can be fruitfully studied from this perspective. In the first sections of the chapter we consider the more abstract and comparative ideas regarding middleman minorities in general. At its conclusion, we briefly consider the appropriateness of the model for interpreting the Japanese-American experience.

Middleman minorities can be conceptualized in at least three ways. First, they can be seen as buffers between elites and masses, occupying a position somewhere between the two. In this capacity they act as go-betweens, playing the roles of rent collector and shopkeeper to the subordinated population while distributing the products of the elites and/or exacting "tribute" for them.

A second way to conceive them is to focus on their role as economic middlemen. They tend to concentrate in trade and commerce—that is, to act as middlemen between producers and consumers. Other economic roles they play, such as moneylender, rent collector, and labor contractor, also have this quality. Even the professional and bureaucratic government positions which they sometimes occupy, have a middleman aspect in the sense that they are interposed between the consumer and his or her immediate economic purpose. In other words, middleman minorities tend not to be primary producers; instead, they help the flow of goods and services through the economy.

Third, these groups can be seen as petit bourgeois rather than capitalist—they fall into the ranks of small business rather than those of the major entrepreneurs of modern capitalism. The petite bourgeoisie can be viewed as a kind of middle class between the big bourgeoisie, or capitalist class proper, and the working class. The petite bourgeoisie, moreover, often performs the role of economic middleman (as in our second conceptualization); its members engage in trade and services, including the professions, rather than in industrial production.

Despite a lack of precise conceptualization, there seems to be considerable agreement as to which groups fall within the category. These include the Jews in Europe, the Chinese in Southeast Asia, the Indians in East Africa, the Arabs in West Africa, the Armenians in Turkey, and the Parsis in India. Indeed, some groups, notably Jews, Chinese, and Indians, are regarded as middleman minorities no matter where they reside. (See Appendix B for a list of groups treated as middleman minorities by authors with a comparative focus.)

DISTINCTIVE TRAITS OF MIDDLEMAN MINORITIES

Middleman minorities possess a number of traits that make them stand out from both elites and subordinate groups. These characteristics, of course, are not universally found among all members of each group, nor are they found at all times. The commonly recognized traits can be divided into three broad categories: social characteristics, economic characteristics, and the surrounding society's reactions. For now, no presumption is made about the causal ordering of these characteristics, but some may be entirely the product of others.

SOCIAL CHARACTERISTICS

Middleman minorities originate in immigration rather than conquest. Typically they are either free or indentured immigrants, but not slaves (van den Berghe, 1975:198). As immigrants they tend to be sojourners, or "birds of passage," intending to return one day to their land of origin (Siu, 1952; Bonacich, 1973). This tie to the homeland is expressed in a number of ways, including the leaving behind of family members, the sending of remittances, and occasional visits.

Another common characteristic of these groups is that they tend to constitute a separate and distinct community from the surrounding society (Becker, 1956; Eitzen, 1971:134; Stryker, 1959). They often have a different religion or culture that marks them off from the rest of the community. They tend to be highly solidary within their own ethnic group, even though there may be important internal cleavages.

Ethnic solidarity is expressed in a number of ways. For instance, middleman groups typically have strong family ties. Often this is symbolized by ancestor worship or memorialization of deceased relatives (Zenner, 1976a:11), but in any case they tend to resist outmarriage and try to keep their offspring faithful to the preservation of group separateness and identity. Middleman groups often establish special schools to pass on the cherished tradition to the next generation. They are frequently ethnocentric, believing in the superiority of their own culture (Becker, 1940:31; Stryker, 1959).

Middleman-minority communities tend to have a large number of organizations representing suprafamilial ties but based on other ascribed statuses, such as locality clubs and surname associations. Indeed, the entire community may be organized from top to bottom with various voluntary and semivoluntary associations that enable it to conduct and control its internal affairs. These organizations include charitable and self-help associations, middleman minorities being noted for their ability to "take care of their own" and not rely on public charity.

Communal organizations support the maintenance of a separate group. People who are busy with community meetings and ceremonies do not have time for too much mixing with the outside world. In addition, the organizations create and sustain multiple, crisscrossing ties, so that even a fairly large ethnic community may suggest to its members that everyone knows each other. Perhaps as a consequence, members of these groups often emphasize the importance of maintaining a good name or preserving the family honor within the community.

The existence of internal cleavages within middleman minorities has led some authors to question the accuracy of the description. According to van den Berghe (1975: 198), "a group such as East African Asians is fragmented into so many linguistic, religious, caste and other subgroups as to constitute a 'community' almost exclusively in the minds of outsiders," while Zenner (1976a) devotes a whole paper to this question in regard to Jewish, Indian, and Chinese diasporas, concluding that solidarity is more intense at the level of kinship and locality of origin (and presumably at similar middle-range levels of organization) than at the level of the entire ethnic group. Be this as it may, there is in our view still a sense in which middleman ethnic groups present something of a united front to the rest of society.

Middleman groups have been noted for living in urban areas (Eitzen, 1971:137). They tend to be familiar with city ways and are not rooted in the life of the countryside. Their urbanity even goes so far as to take on a certain international flavor (Becker, 1940:33): often they know several languages, have traveled, and have contacts (of the same ethnicity) in other ports. Perhaps as a concomitant, they recognize the value of education and typically stress its importance to their children.

Finally, middleman groups are noted for not participating in local politics except as they impinge on the affairs of their own group. As with all the other traits listed so far, there are important exceptions to this generalization, especially among marginal or ex-members. The core of the community, however, tends to focus its political energies internally and to deal with the surrounding polity as a corporate entity, its main concern being the way in which that polity is treating the minority.

It is apparent, then, that middleman minorities are relatively solidary within the group and socially separate from the surrounding society. Admittedly, many ethnic groups display most of these traits to some extent, making the boundary around middleman minorities difficult to draw on the basis of this criterion alone.

ECONOMIC CHARACTERISTICS

We have already suggested that the economic position of middleman-minority groups is a major reason for considering them as a special type of minority. Middleman groups tend to concentrate in certain kinds of economic activity, notably trade, petty finance, and money handling. Not only do they show a fairly narrow range of economic specialization, but they often come to be very prominent in—and sometimes to dominate—their fields of concentration.

There are various ways to characterize middleman specialties. We choose to emphasize the form over the content of their businesses, but let us first examine what has been noted about the content of their lines of concentration.

One common observation is that middleman lines of business are not immediately productive. Neither peasants nor industrial proletariat nor industrial entrepreneurs who mobilize the productive labor of many others, members of middleman groups tend to concentrate their efforts in the circulation of goods and services (Cahnman, 1957).

Another common theme is that their lines are often marginal—in other words, that they concentrate in fields that others disdain to enter or never conceived of developing. This "disdain" theme is well developed in the literature. Medieval Jews entered moneylending because the field was proscribed for Christians by their church. Overseas Chinese and Indians entered trade in colonial territories in part because trade was despised in those societies (Stryker, 1959). Similarly, middlemen are often willing to serve as the shopkeepers and servicers of subordinated groups (Rinder, 1958-59). The classic middleman role of go-between for the elites and the masses is a marginal one because elites disdain contact with the subordinated population.

The fact that middleman minorities pioneer new fields gives them an enterprising image. They are said to be willing to take risks and open up new industries, and they are economically creative. Sometimes, though, their enterprises are in "morally questionable" lines, such as usury, pawnbroking, and the liquor trade (Zenner, 1976a:11). For instance, Chinatowns have often contained vice districts (Light, 1977).

With respect to the form of their enterprises, middleman minorities are found to concentrate overwhelmingly in small business. They tend to be self-employed or, if employees, to be on the way to becoming self-employed. This structural feature appears to transcend particular lines of endeavor. It is not uncommon, for example, to find members of middleman minorities who are artisans, such as goldsmiths, tailors, barbers, and launderers (Cahnman, 1965). These crafts workers, however, typically ply their trade in a small-shop setting, selling the wares they produce. Similarly, members of these groups frequently enter the professions but tend to favor the independent fields, such as medicine, dentistry, and the law, which can be run as small businesses.

Middleman-minority firms are typically family owned and operated. They make use of family ties and loyalty, enabling them to operate more cheaply than contractually based firms. The primordial meanings associated with the concept of family are often applied to wider circles of associates: extended kin, people with the same surname, people from the same village or province, and so forth. These ties may become the bases for forming partnerships, for securing loans, for obtaining employment, patronage, or credit, or for the establishment of any number of similar business arrangements (Light, 1972).

Common in these businesses is a tendency to practice thrift intensely (Waterbury, 1972:42). Especially during the early stages of establishing their businesses, middleman-minority members will carefully save and plough profits back into the businesses. They live frugally, often dwelling behind or on top of their shops; and they work long hours, involving the whole family in the enterprise if possible.

In general, then, we can say that middleman minorities concentrate in the petite bourgeoisie. They are able to run effective and competitive small businesses, in large measure because they can operate and sell with relatively low expense. Their effectiveness often enables them to "succeed" (with individual exceptions, of course), and their willingness to employ successful formulas once discovered may explain their tendency to dominate the lines in which they concentrate as well as their ability to pioneer new lines.

Middleman minorities typically face considerable hostility from the surrounding society. They are socially excluded by both the elite and the masses. Often they face discriminatory laws restricting their rights to citizenship, their places of residence, their freedom to intermarry, their rights to own land, and so on. Sometimes they are protected by elites, but such an arrangement is precarious since the middleman group lacks political power in its own right and is thus wholly dependent on its sponsors.

Middleman groups tend to face a common set of economic and social stereotypes (Eitzen, 1971:137). In the economic realm they are seen as ambitious and hardworking to the point of ruthlessness in pursuit of their goals. They are viewed as shrewd traders who are, perhaps, unethical in business. Another common stereotype is that of the parasite who is draining the country of its resources while returning nothing (Stryker, 1959:343). Above all, middleman-minority members are seen as mercenary, willing to do anything for money.

On the social side, two common stereotypes prevail: that they are clannish and refuse to assimilate, and at the same time that they are pushy and anxious to enter a social order in which they are unwelcome. They are thought to be disloyal to the country in which they are dwelling or to maintain a dual loyalty, splitting their devotion between their original homeland and/or ethnic culture and their new home (Eitzen, 1971:137). Even when they make efforts to assimilate, these are often interpreted as protective coloration rather than as serious attempts to become an integral part of their country of adoption. The theme of economic power and corruption thus combines with the theme of unassimilability to create a fear that these people are a dangerous alien power eager to take over the country.

Not infrequently, middleman groups face acts of open hostility. These range from discrimination in housing and economic opportunities to pogroms and riots, expulsion, and well-planned "final solutions." On the whole, these minorities occupy a precarious position in the social structure and may be subjected to outbreaks of antagonism.

CONNECTIONS BETWEEN TRAITS

The three sets of typical characteristics—ethnic solidarity, societal hostility, and concentration in small business—are interrelated. Figure 2:1 presents the various relationships possible among the three sets of characteristics. (Although the arrows are labeled 1 through 6, no implication of causal ordering is intended.)

Social solidarity within the ethnic group promotes ethnic small business (arrow 1) in that it leads to the availability, at relatively low cost, of resources of all kinds for group members. (For a fuller treatment of this link, see Bonacich, 1973:586-587). Trust, for instance, is maintained through the crisscrossing network of personal ties already mentioned and has a distinct significance in the economic realm: trust can, in effect, be capitalized on through such common middleman-minority institutions as low-interest loans and easy-to-obtain credit. Similarly, an employee of a small business may be willing to work for low wages and long hours because he or she trusts the employer to help later on in setting up his or her own business. Trust is generated, in part, by multiple and overlapping memberships in ethnic organizations, which provide people with reputations. Hence, "honor" becomes a vitally important issue within middleman minorities (Waterbury, 1972). Apart from trust, the high degree of organization among these minorities enables them to generate and distribute resources

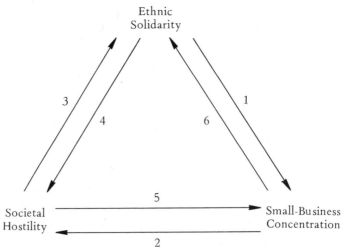

Fig. 2:1. Relationships among characteristics of middleman minorities

(such as capital, information, training, jobs, and labor) more quickly and efficiently than is possible among members of the surrounding society.

Success in business promotes societal hostility (arrow 2) for several reasons: jealousy over the wealth these groups sometimes amass, distrust of the shrewd business mind by clients who are afraid of being cheated, or hostility toward traders (or economic middlemen) as nonproducers.

Societal hostility promotes ethnic solidarity in the middle-man group (arrow 3), both as a defensive reaction in the face of a precarious situation and because the hostility is often expressed in legislation that builds walls around the ethnic community, keeping it separate. In other words, ethnic solidarity may be promoted by the surrounding society, either directly, by legal segregation, or indirectly, if the society establishes a climate in which the minority group feels that it is in danger and must turn inward to protect itself.

Social solidarity on the part of the ethnic minority provokes societal hostility (arrow 4). It leads to accusations of clannishness, unassimilability, disloyalty, and so forth. The relationship between middleman solidarity and hostility from the surrounding society is obviously a complex one, with roots that are difficult to pinpoint. The society blames the minority for being exclusive, while the minority either blames the society for excluding it or asserts its right to enjoy a certain degree of pluralistic separateness without having to face charges of disloyalty.

Societal hostility promotes small business (arrow 5) since it restricts the minority in what it can do (Hagen, 1962:247-248). Minority members face discrimination as employees and so tend to strike out on their own and become self-employed. Their precarious social status acts as a motivation for them to succeed in business, since no handouts are likely to be forthcoming from the state. In addition, certain of the typical features of middleman-minority business practices, such as the preference for easy-to-liquidate lines, can be explained by the dangerous environment in which these groups dwell. In some cases, the link between societal hostility and business is even stronger in that particular lines of economic activity are virtually dictated by societal policy. This phenomenon can be seen operating, for example, in the high concentration of Jews in moneylending and in the rag and junk trade in Europe. The middleman-minority characteristic of entering marginal fields is undoubtedly a product, at least in part, of being excluded from the central, more prestigious occupations.

Finally, concentration in small business promotes ethnic solidarity (arrow 6). The economic specialization of the ethnic group means that members are, first, in constant contact with one another for business reasons, and, second, separated from those outside the group except when the latter are clients, a relationship that does not foster close ties. Additionally, because the ethnic group provides multiple resources for small business, group members have an incentive to keep alive the source of benefits. In particular, since the business gains of ethnicity depend, in part, on trust, the individual must reinforce his or her image of trustworthiness by participating in multiple organizations and repeatedly meeting with community members. When group members no longer aspire to small business (or the independent professions), they do not have the same incentive to be active in ethnic associations, for then such activity is mainly socially and sentimentally, but not materially, motivated.

PROBLEMS OF DEFINITION

What we have sketched is a kind of ideal type. In reality there are problems of fit between any actual ethnic group and this picture, problems in establishing which or how many of the traits a population need have before it can be classified as a middleman minority. Another problem concerns the aggregate nature of the concept. Since it is extraordinarily unlikely that all members of an ethnic group conform to a set of traits, we can only speak of statistical tendencies among individuals in a group. How much must a group be overrepresented in a particular trait for it to qualify as a genuine middleman minority?

Some ethnic groups that are considered to be classic examples of the type, furthermore, go through periods when they do not exhibit many middleman-minority characteristics. Indians and Chinese often entered colonial territories as indentured or contract workers, taking at least part of a generation for numbers of them to move out of the subproletariat and into the petite bourgeoisie. Similarly, Eastern European Jewish immigrants in the United States began their residence as laborers before moving into self-employment. On the other hand, sometimes the children and grandchildren of immigrant small-business participants move into the professions. These changes over time, generation, and situation make it difficult to establish precise boundaries for the category.

Although a prominent characteristic of middleman groups is that they have a solidary ethnic community that resists assimilation, under some circumstances, many members of the ethnic group leave the community, intermarry, and shed their ethnic identity. This has been true for the Jewish community throughout its history. The problem is to decide whether these relatively more assimilated people are still part of a middleman minority. And if there is a high rate of assimilation, can even the core of the community be so considered?

In truth, there probably exists considerable variation both within so-called middleman minorities and among them (Schermerhorn, 1976). Within such groups not only is there individual diversity, based on age, generation, regional origins, economic position, and other such factors, but also each community, or locality, within a particular group is distinctive by virtue of its size (Zenner, 1976a), the nature of the surrounding society (Stryker, 1959), and probably many other factors. Among groups important differences also exist: Zenner (1976a) carefully documents dissimilarities in the social organization of Jews, Indians, and Chinese, while Eitzen (1971) notes that, although Jews in Poland and Chinese in the Philippines were very similar in many ways, some differences could be found, as in the use of a religious ideology to justify societal hostility.

Though Zenner (1976a:2) uses overrepresentation in trade, commerce, and banking as a heuristic definition, we prefer to use self-employment (and working for the self-employed within the ethnic group) as the key criterion. It is our belief that the essence of middleman minorities lies in the way they organize their economic activity. We consider problems of assimilation, generational change, and early history as laborers as not threatening to the model. For example, when people assimilate we no longer consider them group members, but the core of the group may remain in a middleman-minority position.

Problems of definition are inherent in the drawing of an ideal type. The fit will never be perfect, and there will be a range of cases that fall further and further away from the ideal. The tool is no more than a tool and therefore must be used with caution and sensitivity to exceptions. As knowledge now stands, the middleman-minority concept seems to us to be a useful sensitizer to a host of interrelated variables. The creation of such concepts is of value in that they aid comparative analysis and, indeed, force us to raise comparative questions. In particular, the middleman-minority idea makes us look at the relationship between an ethnic group and its societal context. Though the concept of middleman minorities is no substitute for tracing the historical development of a particular community in a particular context, the idea helps us ask certain questions that we might never think to ask if we were only looking at one group in isolation.

THEORIES

Many ideas and theories have been propounded to explain the middleman-minority phenomenon. The theories can be roughly divided into four types: pure prejudice, contextual, cultural, and situational.[1]

PURE-PREJUDICE THEORIES

By far the most common approach, *pure-prejudice theories* ignore the economic and structural aspects of middleman minorities and focus instead on the ideological level. Much of the work on anti-Semitism falls in this camp, as it looks for the roots of a disposition to hate Jews in such realms as religion, culture, or psychology of the surrounding population. Since we are primarily interested in the economic position of middleman minorities and the prejudice theories do not much concern themselves with this area, we shall not review those theories here.

CONTEXTUAL THEORIES

Contextual theories see middleman minorities as creatures of the societies in which they are found. They are concentrated in marginal trading activities, not because of any inherent group inclination or talent in this direction, but because the surrounding society makes them assume these positions. Van den Berghe (1975:198) probably makes this point as strongly as anyone: "Such similarities as exist [among middleman minorities] must be

---

1. For another review of this literature, see Zenner (1976*b*; 1977*b*).

sought principally in the *social structure of the plural society as a whole*, and only secondarily in the characteristics of the immigrant groups." Two types of contextual theories can be distinguished: those that see middleman minorities as arising in "traditional societies," and those that see the relevant context as societies with a "status gap."

The traditional-societies approach (Hamilton, 1978; Jiang, 1968) starts with the fact that trade is a despised activity in premodern societies. The pursuit of money, a characteristic of traders, runs counter to the dominant otherworldly values of such societies (Sjoberg, 1960:183-185). The hatred traditional societies have of traders stems from a broader hatred of modernization. Traders are seen as harbingers of the breakdown of the old moral order. They represent the city, cosmopolitan values, strange and foreign customs, and the decline of subsistence agriculture and home crafts. They stand for the creation of commodities out of goods that once had value only in use. The bearers of these changes are despised for what they bring.

Distinctive ethnic minorities come to occupy the position of traders in part because no one else in the society will do this particular form of "dirty work." Traders, moneylenders, and other middlemen must be imported from outside; outsiders will, of course, be culturally different. If they become assimilated, they will no longer want to play a role that is despised; they will accept the host society's values. On the other hand, because they are traders, they are treated as outcastes or pariahs, which makes assimilation very difficult. The result for the middleman minority is a state of equilibrium, in which engaging in trade and being a despised outsider reinforce one another.

A second reason for using a "stranger" group for trade and other middleman activities is that they are unlikely to be politically dangerous (Coser, 1972; Hamilton, 1978; Jiang, 1968). Traders may amass considerable wealth, and wealth is a ticket to political power. Native elites, therefore, have an interest in ensuring that trade does not fall into the hands of a potentially powerful rival, especially if they themselves do not want to engage in it (as they do not in traditional societies). Strangers serve the purpose admirably. They can be preserved as outsiders, disenfranchised, threatened with the possibility of expulsion if their economic power gets out of hand, and heavily taxed into the bargain.

An alternative contextual theory views middleman minorities as arising in societies where there is a status gap, or discontinuity between dominant and subordinate elements in a society (Blalock, 1967:79-84; Loewen, 1971:49-55; Rinder, 1958-59; Shibutani and Kwan, 1965:189-197). Such a gap is found in feudal societies between the aristocracy and peasants, in slave societies between free persons and slaves, in colonial societies between the colonizers and the colonized, and in racist societies between dominant and subordinate racial groups.

The status gap is a social gulf between the dominant and subordinate groups which is so wide as to make it difficult for them to interact—even commercially—on a face-to-face basis. Since those who engage in trade must be courteous to their clients in order to "serve" them, a third party, a group of outsiders who are not involved in the niceties of status in this society, may be recruited to perform the role of go-between. From this enterprise they may prosper, but because they engage in daily contact with the subordinate masses, they are not considered respectable and are treated as pariahs by the elite. These minorities are ideal scapegoats in time of trouble, serving as a buffer for elites against the anger of the masses (Blalock, 1967:81-83; Shibutani and Kwan, 1965:196).

The status-gap approach does not depend on traditional society's values regarding trade. Status gaps can be found in modern industrial societies as well—for instance, between blacks and whites in United States cities. The ghetto shopkeeper and pawnbroker are likely to be minority members, commonly of Jewish background but also of Chinese, Iraqi, and other origins (Rinder, 1958-59:257; Sengstock, 1974; Shibutani and Kwan, 1965:197; Charles Choy Wong, 1977). Similarly, the presence of middleman groups in colonial settings suggests a phenomenon that does not depend on a premodern set of values. Colonial rulers were themselves capitalists, well versed in commerce. That they subcontracted their internal trade out to foreigners, or permitted it to fall into the hands of these groups, cannot be accounted for by a disdain for trade itself.

Since contextual theories predict that middleman minorities arise only in certain kinds of societies, it follows that they should not often be found in environments that do not conform to the specified type. Middleman groups can disappear in two ways:

either they can be assimilated, or they can be expelled (including by extermination). Two specific predictions have been made in this regard. One, applied mainly to colonial societies, is that when the old elites are removed from power, middleman minorities are exposed to harsh treatment by the new nation (van den Berghe, 1975:202-203). The other, more general prediction is that middleman minorities disappear in modern capitalism. Since commerce and trade have become ubiquitous and lost their low status, there should no longer be a need for a distinctive pariah group to fill these roles (Hamilton, 1978; Leon, 1970).

CULTURAL THEORIES

Instead of explaining the phenomenon of middleman minorities by characteristics of the societies in which they arise, *cultural theories* focus on characteristics of the minorities themselves. For instance, in analyzing the Chinese and Japanese American propensity to be overrepresented in small business, especially in retail trade, Light (1972) stresses an institution that both groups brought from their countries of origin: rotating-credit associations. This cultural item made it possible for them to raise capital, despite discriminatory lending practices by banks, so that they were able to finance their enterprises.

Another version of the cultural hypothesis is that minorities with religious values similar to the Protestant ethic tend to assume middleman roles. The religious values are thought to promote thrift and hard work, which in turn aid entrepreneurship. For instance, in analyzing the concentration in the grocery business of Jerbans in Tunisia, Stone (1974) emphasizes their membership in an ascetic religious sect of Islam. Sombart (1951:191-251) makes a similar argument for the Jews.

A third variety of cultural explanation deals with the importance of internal group solidarity in promoting a concentration in trade. While several of the theorists in this tradition indicate that antagonism from the surrounding society supports the separateness of the minority, they see solidarity as primarily self-generated. A major proponent of this viewpoint is Max Weber, who used the concept of "pariah people" to describe the Jews and that of "pariah capitalism" to describe their economic adaption. Weber (1968:493, 614) argues that the Jewish religion, with its laws against commensality and intermarriage, cut the Jews off from others socially, contributing to their treatment as outcasts.

Their pariah status made it difficult for Jews to engage in industrial entrepreneurship, Weber (1968:614) explains, as "the legally and factually precarious position of the Jews hardly permitted continuous and rationalized industrial enterprise with fixed capital, but only trade and above all dealing in money." Furthermore, as pariahs, they developed a "dual ethic," with one set of moral standards for dealing with in-group members and another for dealing with strangers. Pariah groups can be "ruthlessly economic" in their dealings with outsiders and are thus useful for performing such tasks as tax collecting and moneylending.

Weber draws a sharp distinction between pariah capitalism and modern industrial capitalism. The former may lead to the accumulation of considerable wealth on the part of pariah groups, but it does not generate new wealth. The principles of industrial capitalism are, in many ways, the opposite of those of pariah capitalism. The former depends upon rationality—the treatment of everyone according to objective standards—while pariah capitalism relies on irrational attachments to ethnic-group members. Ironically, Weber explicitly rejects the Weberian idea that a Protestant-ethic type of value system explains Jewish (and presumably other middleman-minority) capitalism.

The relationship between internal solidarity and effective business practices is developed by Light (1972), who argues that strong ascriptive ties enable certain ethnic groups to succeed in entrepreneurial activities when their more "rational" competitors fail. Similarly, in a study of Indians in East Africa, Benedict (1968) shows that family businesses, using primordial ties of trust and loyalty, can be more viable than firms run on strictly universalistic criteria. Loewen (1971:37-39) analyzes the success of Chinese grocers in Mississippi in similar terms.

Cultural theories, then, attribute middleman-minority economic behavior to factors internal to the minorities themselves, although the particular cultural traits that receive emphasis have varied from theory to theory. They all, however, share the notion that these minorities are not simply creations of a particular environment; instead, the groups are seen as bringing to the environment characteristics of their own, which help account for the particular adaptation of the minority members.

SITUATIONAL THEORIES

A fourth set of theories, *situational theories*, tries to explain the middleman phenomenon neither by the features of particular environments nor by the cultural baggage a group brings to a situation, but, rather, in terms of the structure of the historical situation itself. In particular, these theories emphasize the situations of certain *immigrant* ethnic minorities which might lead them to concentrate in trade or small business. Two themes can be distinguished here: strangers and sojourners.

The concept of the stranger is associated with Simmel (1950). He defines the stranger as a social type, a kind of immigrant who never fully belongs to the society in which he or she settles and is always likely to move on, "the potential wanderer" (Simmel, 1950:402). According to Simmel (1950:403), "throughout the history of economics the stranger everywhere appears as the trader, or the trader the stranger." Strangers make good traders because they are able to be objective in the marketplace (Blalock, 1967:80-81; Fallers, 1967:7-13; Foster, 1974; Loewen, 1971:39-48; Toennies, 1971:308-312). Members of traditional societies are bound by social obligations that make it difficult for them to run viable businesses. It is hard to refuse credit to friends and relatives, and impossible to collect debts from them. A person who persists in businesslike behavior risks sanctions and reprisals for violating the norms. Nonmembers, or strangers, on the other hand, have different obligations.

The concept of objectivity in the marketplace is similar to Weber's dual ethic, though it need not have the same heavily moral connotations. Most authors treat objectivity in the market as morally neutral, or even desirable in the sense of being "rational." Strangers need not take "irrational" social demands into account, thus representing the most modern approach to trade. They are liberated from the bonds of custom which weigh most people down. In contrast to Weber, "stranger" theorists tend to support the idea that middleman groups are the harbingers of modern capitalism and are at the base of its principle of economic rationality (Sombart, 1951:176-177).

A second situational approach is to point out that often these groups are sojourners, or temporary migrants, who plan one day to return to their homeland (Siu, 1952; Bonacich, 1973). Authors in this tradition look for the historical roots of the "stranger" phenomenon in the initial orientation of a group towards its territory of residence. Sojourning is seen to promote concentration, both directly and indirectly, in trade and similar middleman lines. Directly, it encourages thrift and hard work for the purpose of amassing capital as quickly as possible; it encourages concentration in liquidatable lines; and it leads to placing a premium on risk taking rather than on job security. Indirectly, sojourning promotes the retention of ethnic solidarity, which, as cultural theorists have pointed out, aids business.

While sojourning can, and sometimes does, end in the realization of the sojourner's aspirations by return to the homeland, this goal is frequently not achieved. In some cases, homeland political conditions preclude immediate return. Even when return is feasible, however, sojourning creates a dialectic of success such that those segments of the group who are successful in business can no longer afford to go back to a poorer situation in the homeland. They thus retain an ambivalence toward their place of residence, both wanting to remain and wanting to go home. This, Bonacich (1973) argues, is close to the "stranger" orientation described by Simmel.

Overall, situational theories stress the peculiar circumstances in which some minorities find themselves, arguing that it is this situation, rather than culture of origin, that encourages them to develop a certain kind of economic adaptation. However, both situational and cultural theories contrast with contextual theories on the issue of the degree to which characteristics of the minorities themselves contribute to their economic forms.

DISCUSSION

It is not our purpose here to assess the validity of any particular theory or category of theories. Obviously, these theories are not necessarily mutually exclusive. A complete theory would undoubtedly have to specify the contextual, cultural, and situational factors that, in combination, help to account for the middleman phenomenon. This said, we still believe that some of the ideas are more useful than others.

In particular, in arguing that middleman groups are a product of a certain type, or phase, of society, some of the contextual theories presented here imply that such groups will not be found in other types of societies. They would predict that where such groups as Jews, Chinese, and Indians have entered advanced industrial societies, they ought not to have shown the same complex of middleman traits among them. Most cultural and situational theories, on the other hand, would predict that the propensity to engage in entrepreneurial activities would persist as long as the group retained those characteristics (religion or sojourning, for instance) that encouraged its concentration in business to begin with. One would still find middleman minorities in advanced industrial societies, according to these theories.

And there *are* many examples of what we would categorize as middleman minorities in advanced capitalist societies: Asians in Britain (Aldrich, 1977; Dahya, 1974); Koreans in Los Angeles (Bonacich, Light, and Wong, 1976); Arabs in Detroit (Sengstock, 1974); and Jews in Britain (Aris, 1970) and in the United States (Decker, 1977; Fauman, 1941; Koenig, 1942; Meyer, 1940; Platkin, 1972; Zenner, 1977a). Indeed, our task in the present volume is to explicate what we consider to be one such case. Although small commercial minorities in advanced capitalist societies clearly do not attain the kind of economic power that such groups reach when they monopolize the field (as in medieval and colonial societies), some minorities still tend to concentrate in trade and small business, to retain a separate and distinctive minority culture and community, and to face some hostility from the surrounding society. These three factors seem to form the hallmark of middleman minorities, and there is no denying that they arise within advanced capitalism, even if in a somewhat muted form.

We do not mean to suggest that contextual theories have no validity; obviously, societal antagonism plays a major part in the evolution of the middleman form. What we are contending is that a theory about this form will not be adequate if it assumes these minorities are totally (or almost totally) the creation of the societies in which they reside and that any minority group could have fulfilled the same role. There is ample evidence to suggest that only some groups, and not others, come to concentrate in middleman-type economic activities, regardless of context. An adequate theory, therefore, cannot ignore internal factors.

Despite the fact that they are found in modern capitalist societies, middleman minorities are not themselves modern capitalists in orientation. Rather, they are essentially petit bourgeois, failing to engage in the kind of activity that epitomizes modern industrial capitalism, namely, the hiring of contracted wage labor from which profits are extracted. Instead they work as a single unit, in which the distinction between owner and employee is blurred. Their shops depend on the use of ethnic and familial ties, not on impersonal contracts.

One consequence of the difference in organization between middleman petit bourgeois shops and modern industrial bourgeois factories is that they grow in different ways. Because of its reliance on impersonal contracts, there is no limit on the growth of the industrial plant. Armies of workers can be employed. In contrast, the petit bourgeois shop depends upon personal ties and loyalties, mutual trust and obligation. It is thus imperative that people know each other well and in many contexts, a requirement that severely limits the growth of the firm, for it can only encompass as many workers as the employer can know well enough to trust. Such firms tend to grow by splitting off and setting up new versions of themselves with new owners who can have personal ties with their workers.

It is sometimes pointed out that middleman stores are small because they lack capital. Indeed, as objects of societal antagonism, it is not unusual for many members of these minorities to be impoverished or able to command only small sums for investment. It is also the case, though, that occasionally considerable wealth may be amassed by members of these groups; yet (with some exceptions) they still show a proclivity to concentrate in small commercial establishments. Their social form dictates this and limits the size and nature of the firms they establish.

Given that middleman minorities are at least partially premodern in their economic orientation, how can we account for their apparent persistence in advanced capitalist countries? This question has been addressed by Light (1972), who points out that, ironically, the ascribed ties of a strong ethnic community can, in some ways, be more efficient than the contractual ties of modern, voluntary relations. Bonacich (1973) develops this theme, trying to show how middleman groups have been able to use communal resources to cut costs in numerous directions. Despite their tendency not to let the market dictate all business practices, these minorities are able to undercut modern-style businesses, although admittedly only in a limited number of spheres, such as retailing and services, which are not highly developed. Within modern capitalist societies, however, there are many lines of business which are not highly evolved and can be pursued at relatively low costs by middleman groups, which may account for the persistent survival of such groups.

ECONOMIC BASIS OF ETHNIC SOLIDARITY

All of the theories discussed above attempt to explain why middleman minorities arise. The economic characteristics of these minorities are taken as the major dependent variable. Another theoretical tradition, however, takes economic adaptation for granted and concentrates on the consequences of middleman economic specialization for ethnic identification and solidarity. Since our ultimate interest lies in explaining the retention or dissolution of ethnic solidarity, it is important that we consider this work.

In his study of Hausa traders in Yoruba towns in Nigeria, Cohen (1969) argues that ethnic groups are really political-interest groups that are able to make use of moral and ritual obligations to bind their members to act in the interests of the group. Like Light (1972) and others, he points out that the use of such ties is not economically irrational: "Indeed, it is specifically because he [the Hausa trader] is rational in the conduct of his business that he continues in the old traditional ways" (Cohen, 1969:7).

The majority of the study, however, focuses not so much on the uses of ethnicity for trade as on the importance of a concentration in trade for the creation and perpetuation of ethnicity. Hausa symbols and communal organization, particularly in the area of religion, have been enhanced by economic specialty. Cohen (1969:14) observes: "Hausa identity and Hausa ethnic exclusiveness in Ibadan are the expressions not so much of a particularly strong 'tribalistic' sentiment as of vested economic interests." Group members themselves do not articulate their ethnic solidarity in these terms, emphasizing instead the values that bind them to their distinctive culture; but Cohen (1969:15) suggests at least two reasons why this explanation is an inadequate one. First, Hausa in Hausaland do not display nearly as much Hausa ethnic culture as is found in the diaspora; and second, there are many Hausa migrants who are not part of the trading network and who also do not participate in the kind of organized community found among the traders. In other words, only where the economic interest (in trade) is present does one find a highly organized ethnic Hausa community.

Essentially the same point is made by Leon (1970) in trying to account for the persistence of Jewish ethnicity. He uses the term *people-class* to capture the coincidence between ethnic group identity and specialized economic function.[2] "Wherever the Jews cease to constitute a class," he points out, "they lose, more or less rapidly, their ethnical, religious, linguistic characteristics; they become assimilated" (Leon, 1970:81). What is the class position the Jews represent? In Leon's own words, "Judaism mirrors the interests of a pre-capitalist mercantile class" (Leon, 1970:76). Thus his analysis is not dissimilar to Weber's; the tie between small business and ethnic solidarity is an instance, not of modern capitalism, but of a premodern form.

These theorists are suggesting that there is a link between small-business concentration and the retention of ethnic group ties and, conversely, that when the class concentration disperses, ethnic ties tend to weaken. This prediction should be viewed within the larger context of the middleman-minority phenomenon. In terms of figure 2:1, it stresses arrow 6. We have argued, however, that all the linkages are present and should be seen as forming a patterned, interrelated whole. Still, if we can show a relationship between small-business concentration and the retention of ethnic solidarity, at least a piece of the pattern is given support.

APPLICATION TO JAPANESE AMERICANS

This volume uses a middleman-minority approach to interpret the Japanese American experience, and thus it becomes incumbent upon us at this point to assay the appropriateness of the model for this particular ethnic group. Several authors have mentioned or studied the Japanese in this context, notably Blalock (1967:81), Bonacich (1973), Kitano (1976*a*; 1976*b*:

2. Note that despite a similarity in the words, the concept is very different from Gordon's "eth-class" (1964). For Gordon, *class* means status group rather than relations to the means of production. Gordon's eth-classes are social groupings of people who feel comfortable together because of similarity in style of life. They are not political- or economic-interest groups. Gordon's concept is not associated with a theory of ethnicity; it takes ethnic affiliation as a natural state of affairs and does not look beyond sentiment or primordial tie to the more material foundations of ethnicity.

198-201), Light (1972), McElroy (1977), and Morrison Wong (1977). Most analyses of Japanese Americans do not, however, use a middleman-minority approach. By far the most common mode of analysis is to see the Japanese in the United States as a racial minority suffering racial discrimination (Daniels, 1966*a*; tenBroek, Barnhart, and Matson, 1954:11-67). In this approach, the economic position of the minority is not given any special emphasis. Those who do focus on economic aspects of the Japanese American experience tend to emphasize success rather than closely examine the peculiar concentrations of Japanese economic endeavor. This success is often explained as resulting from the congruence between the values of the Japanese and those of middle-class America (Caudill and De Vos, 1970)—or, to put it another way, it is said that the immigrants brought Protestant-ethic-type values with them from Japan (Petersen, 1970:176). An exception is the work of Modell (1977), who argues that what amounted to a middleman form of ethnic economy among the Japanese Americans before World War II was partially a response to the rapid growth of a new region.

It is our contention that the Japanese American experience fits the middleman-minority model in many ways and that the model can provide important new insights into that experience. Prior to World War II the Japanese Americans formed a highly organized, internally solidary community. The majority were at one time oriented toward returning to the homeland. They concentrated in self-employment and nonindustrial family businesses located in marginal lines of endeavor. They were able to be competitive because they could run their businesses inexpensively and efficiently. And they faced severe hostility from the surrounding society, in the form of denial of citizenship, exclusion efforts, laws prohibiting their ownership of land, and evacuation and incarceration during World War II. The Japanese Americans were branded with stereotypic labels—crafty, sneaky, unassimilable, disloyal, and so on (Ogawa, 1971)—similar to those found in anti-Semitism and other anti-middleman-minority movements.

Certain problems arise in terms of the degree to which the model fits the Japanese American experience. First of all, an important arena of Japanese enterprise was agriculture, a line very different from those of trading and commerce. Japanese American farms, however, approached the ideal type of petit bourgeois business more closely than they did the peasant holding or the family farm. Close attention to market conditions and frequent innovations characterized these enterprises. Market gardening, or truck farming, was their most common operation, a line that is not at all unusual among classic middleman minorities (Bonacich, 1973; Leon, 1970:46).

The middleman-minority model applies best to the first generation of Japanese Americans but much less neatly to the second generation, which has shown an important tendency to move out of small business and into the professions. While providing professional training for their children has been a common feature of middleman groups (Benedict, 1968; Maxwell, 1975; 1977), it is clear that the Japanese American community underwent a major shift away from the middleman form after World War II. This fact does not affect our characterization of the first generation's middleman position, but it raises the question of why we concentrate the largest part of this volume upon the second generation in the postwar period.

It is precisely because the second generation is divided in economic orientation that we are able to examine empirically within a single case study a central tenet of middleman-minority theory: that (regardless of the direction of causality) both external and internal group relations practiced by minorities are functions of their peculiar economic position within the general economy. We can examine the degree of retention of the small-business mode for the second generation of a middleman immigrant group within advanced capitalism and trace the consequences of such retention for the ethnic group. Variability in the second generation permits us to examine how the middleman form operates and when it may break down.

Our assessment, as the succeeding chapters will show, is that the JARP national survey captured the waning phases of what was once a nearly classic variant of the middleman minority form operating within advanced capitalism. Our historical materials establish a prewar base line conforming to this characterization; our postwar survey data show, both retrospectively and by projection from cross-sectional differentiation, the path away from this peculiar, but by no means unique, minority experience.

3

Issei Small Business prior to World War II

In this and the succeeding chapter we examine the Issei experience in light of the analysis presented in chapter 2. While no attempt is made to assess definitively which of the causal models best explains the Issei tendency to occupy a middleman-minority position, we do attempt to show how the dynamics represented in figure 2:1 operated in the Issei case. In this chapter we focus on the reciprocal relationship between ethnic solidarity and small business (arrows 1 and 6 in fig. 2:1), especially on the role played by ethnic solidarity in the establishment of small business. In chapter 4 we turn to the question of societal hostility, examining its relationship both to concentration in small business (arrows 2 and 5) and to ethnic solidarity (arrows 3 and 4). By this means we hope to provide some new insights into the anti-Japanese movement.

Although some Japanese immigrants came to the United States with capital for the purpose of engaging in trade, the vast majority came as laborers with little or no money. According to Ichihashi (1932:75-76), the average amount declared to authorities by Japanese on arrival in Hawaii and the continental United States between 1899 and 1910 was $41.29. In some cases the transportation costs were advanced by emigration companies, so that the immigrant arrived in debt. The period beginning in the 1890s, when Japanese began arriving on the continent in large numbers, and ending around 1907-1908, when the Gentlemen's Agreement with Japan essentially cut off the immigration of laborers, is characterized by Issei concentration in wage earning.

They first found work as domestic servants, as farm laborers who joined the "harvest labor market" (Fisher, 1953:24-31; Mc-Williams, 1971:81-116), or, in smaller numbers, as workers on the railroads, in the mines, and in the fishing and canning industries (Ichihashi, 1932:137-159). They entered the American economy in much the same capacity as did many immigrant groups, moving into occupations where labor unions were not yet well entrenched.

Within a few short years, however, the Japanese had become established in city trades and in agriculture had moved from the position of farm laborers to that of owners and operators of independent farms. Let us consider each of these in turn.

URBAN PROPRIETORSHIPS

From the start of Japanese immigration, there were a few people who engaged in urban small business. In 1890 in California, the majority of Japanese were laborers, sprinkled with a few small traders of "oriental" goods and a few who ran cheap restaurants and shoe-repair establishments. These did business with American patrons. In addition, some who dealt in Japanese provisions or ran boardinghouses catered to members of the immigrant community (Ichihashi, 1932:117). Most of these small businesses were located in San Francisco.

The Immigration Commission found that by 1909 there were 3,000 to 3,500 Japanese-operated businesses in the western states. Of these, 545 were in San Francisco, 478 in Seattle, and 473 in Los Angeles. Among the most popular trades were hotels and boardinghouses, restaurants, barbershops, poolrooms, tailor and dye shops, provision and supply stores, cobbler and shoe shops, and laundries (Ichihashi, 1932:118-119). Roughly 15 percent of the Japanese population in the West at this time was engaged in small business, either as owners or as workers in Japanese-owned firms (Ichihashi, 1932:120).

By 1929, Los Angeles had a Japanese population of about 30,000 and was the largest Japanese American settlement on the West Coast. Looking only at businesses that employed five or more Japanese, Kataoka (1929:54-55) found 292 groceries, 221 hotels, 203 fruit stands, 108 cafes and restaurants, 107 barbershops, 74 flower shops, 69 nurseries, 68 dyeing and cleaning establishments—1,849 enterprises in all. While it was not explicitly stated that they were Japanese owned, the types of businesses indicate that they were. If we assume that all of these businesses employed the minimum of five Japanese workers, then at least 9,000, or 30 percent of the entire Japanese population of Los Angeles (including children), were engaged in urban trades. The true figure is undoubtedly higher, since some of the enumerated businesses employed more than five Japanese workers, and also some additional Japanese worked in firms that were not enumerated because they employed fewer than five persons of this nationality.

By World War II, small business was the predominant economic mode of Japanese American urban dwellers. Writing of Seattle immediately prior to the war, Miyamoto (1939:70-71) found that 45 percent of the workers were in what he classified as "trades," while another 31 percent classed under "domestic and personal services" were also all working in hotels, restaurants, barbershops, laundries, and the like, enterprises indistinguishable from the trades (which included such businesses as grocery stores and public market stands) in general form. Thus about three-quarters of the community members were working in small businesses. As Miyamoto (1939:70-71) states, "In speaking of the economic activities of the Japanese in Seattle, we must take special note of the overwhelming dominance in their lives of the 'small shop.' . . . When we note the lack of any capitalist or upper-middle class in this community, and when we see the vagueness and the relative smallness of a true working class, we can understand the remarkable predominance of a single class interest."

Similarly, a high degree of small-business concentration was evident in prewar Los Angeles. Bloom and Riemer (1949:19) found that in 1941 approximately 36 percent of all employed Japanese were self-employed (table 3:1). For males the figure was 47 percent. The older, more established men were even more likely to be self-employed: over 60 percent of those over forty-five years old were employers and workers on their own account (Bloom and Riemer, 1949:20).

Even these figures do not indicate the actual degree of Japanese concentration in small business, since many of the wage and salary workers were employed in their parents' or relatives' businesses and participating (if only in futurity) in their benefits. Moreover, as table 3:1 shows, over 16 percent of the community's

TABLE 3:1

CLASS OF WORKER AND OCCUPATIONS OF
EMPLOYED JAPANESE AMERICANS, LOS ANGELES COUNTY, 1941

Class of Worker and Occupation	Males	Females	Total
Employers and own-account workers	46.7%	10.2%	36.4%
Professionals and semiprofessionals	1.5	0.7	1.3
Farm and nursery operators	13.5	0.8	9.9
Proprietors, except farm	18.9	5.5	15.2
Salesmen	0.4	0.2	0.3
Craftsmen	1.1	0.1	0.8
Operatives and kindred workers	0.4	0.7	0.5
Service workers	0.4	2.1	0.9
Laborers, fishermen	0.5	0.0	0.3
Laborers, gardeners	10.0	0.0	7.2
Unpaid family workers	9.5	34.2	16.5
Clerical, sales, and kindred workers	1.8	11.7	4.6
Operatives and kindred workers	0.6	2.1	1.0
Service workers	0.6	6.5	2.3
Farm and nursery laborers	6.4	13.9	8.5
Laborers, except farm	0.1	0.0	0.1
Wage and salary workers	41.5	54.8	45.2
Professionals and semiprofessionals	1.7	2.9	2.0
Farm and nursery managers	0.4	0.0	0.3
Managers, except farm	3.9	0.2	2.9
Clerical, sales, and kindred workers	13.2	20.3	15.2
Craftsmen, foremen, and kindred workers	1.8	0.5	1.5
Operatives and kindred workers	4.5	11.9	6.6
Domestic service workers	2.4	9.2	4.3
Service workers, except domestic	5.0	6.4	5.4
Farm and nursery laborers	4.9	3.4	4.4
Laborers, fishermen	1.6	0.0	1.1
Laborers, gardeners	1.5	0.0	1.1
Laborers, except fishermen or gardeners	0.6	0.0	0.4
Class of worker not reported	2.3	0.8	1.9
	100.0*	100.0	100.0
Total employed workers (sample)	2,515	985	3,500

SOURCE: Bloom and Riemer, 1949:19. Based on 20 percent sample of U.S. War
Relocation Authority survey.

  *As a result of rounding errors, figures may not total precisely 100.0 percent. This
is true throughout the volume.

workers were unpaid family laborers working in family businesses, a figure that Bloom and Riemer believe to be an undercount.

Other cities and towns, such as Stockton, San Jose, Fresno, and Sacramento, show a similar development (Ichihashi, 1932: 116-136). Thus we see a gradual rise in the concentration of Japanese immigrants (and their families) in small business, until by World War II the overwhelming majority of those residing in cities were engaged in this form of economic activity.

AGRICULTURE

Japanese Americans came to concentrate in another form of small business, namely, farming or market gardening. We consider Japanese farms to be businesses because Japanese farmers were producing almost exclusively for a cash market. They specialized in vegetables and fruits for the towns and cities of the West. Although by the war the average Japanese-run farm included only about 45 acres, compared to an average of 200 acres for whites (Poli and Engstrand, 1945:355), their orientation resembled that of commercial shipper-growers who ran large farms and produced for more distant markets.

The movement into farm proprietorship occurred in a series of stages: first came labor contracting (providing workers to other farmers), then contract farming (contracting to produce a crop for a fixed fee), share tenancy (like sharecropping), leasing the land, and, finally, ownership of the land (Ichihashi, 1932:178-191). Table 3:2 shows the growth of these forms (except for labor contracting) in California from 1900 to 1925. Hindered by the enactment in several states of Alien Land Laws, which tried to prevent the process (the effects can be seen in the 1920s), Japanese still moved rapidly into self-employment in farming, whether or not they actually owned the land.

Edward K. Strong's somewhat representative survey of California Japanese in the early 1930s included an item asking about the occupation of Japanese then in the United States for twenty years or more at five-year intervals from their arrival in the States. The progress of the Issei through employee positions into self-employment is indicated by our reworking of his data, shown in table 3:3. The net mobility rate declined rapidly, reflecting the

TABLE 3:2
GROWTH IN JAPANESE FARMING IN CALIFORNIA, 1900-1925

Year	Contracted	Shared	Leased	Owned	Total
		Acreage			
1900					4,698
1905	4,775	19,572	35,258	2,442	61,858
1906	22,100	24,826	41,855	8,671	97,541
1907	13,359	48,228	56,889	13,815	131,292
1908	26,138	57,578	55,971	15,114	155,581
1909	42,276	57,001	80,231	16,449	195,948
1910	37,898	50,399	89,464	16,980	194,742
1913		254,980		26,707	281,687
1914		268,646		31,828	300,474
1920		383,287		74,769	458,056
1922		279,511		50,542	330,653
1925		263,058		41,898	304,966

SOURCE: Ichihashi, 1932:184, 193.

TABLE 3:3
OCCUPATIONAL DISTRIBUTION OF CALIFORNIA ISSEI AFTER
FIVE-YEAR RESIDENCE IN UNITED STATES AND CHANGES FOR
FIVE-YEAR INTERVALS THEREAFTER

	Distribution after 5 Years	% Gain 5th to 10th Year	% Gain 10th to 15th Year	% Gain 15th to 20th Year
Employers				
Agriculture	6.7%	191	31	5
Business, trade wholesale, retail	5.2	86	38	14
Employees				
Agriculture	42.3	−28	−22	−8
Business, trade	15.2	−32	−36	−46
All other	30.7	+13	+7	−7
Total	100.0			

Source: Strong, 1933:118-121.

remarkably short period required by the Issei to accumulate the capital and skills necessary to gain entrepreneurial status.

THE CHARACTER OF ISSEI ENTERPRISE

As can be seen from the lists of businesses mentioned so far, the Issei tended to concentrate in a relatively narrow set of business lines, common among middleman minorities. As with other middleman ethnic groups, Japanese businesses tended to operate on a small scale (Thomas, 1952:29). They were likely to be family businesses, whether farms or urban proprietorships. Wage labor was relatively uncommon and, when present, almost never took the form of a large factory with hundreds of hired hands working on the assembly line. This may have been due to limits on the amount of capital available, but it also seems to have been a feature of the way Japanese Americans organized their businesses. When a shop grew large, it was likely to expand by the opening of a branch office rather than by internal growth.

Although some Japanese business has always catered to the ethnic clientele, once established many Issei enterprises were geared to the general market (Ichihashi, 1932:117; Kataoka, 1929:56-57; Thomas, 1952:29), as is suggested by the narrow concentration in a few lines. Thus, labor contractors provided gangs of workers to white shipper-growers, farmers grew produce for the general market, and many restaurants, grocery stores, and other small businesses serviced clients from outside the community. The Japanese minority filled a particular and specialized niche in the general economy and was very important to it, providing certain key products and services.

By way of summary, table 3:4 shows the structure of Japanese economic activity (which we call the *ethnic economy*) as it had developed by the time of the 1930 census, before the depression distorted it. The table takes advantage of the rather detailed occupational information on Japanese Americans provided that year and gives direct information on some of the typical Japanese occupations we have already discussed. While the table as a whole is self-explanatory, showing especially how highly concentrated and stratified by age the ethnic economy was, several details, which exemplify the kind of adaptation the structure represented, deserve comment.

TABLE 3:4
AGE AND SEX OF JAPANESE IN SELECTED OCCUPATIONS, 1930

Age	Agriculture			Urban Occupations						
	Owner-Tenant	Manager	Laborer	Retail Dealer	Whole-saler	Boarding-house/Hotel Proprietor	Restau-rateur	Sales Worker	Clerical Worker	Service Worker
Males										
10-24	3.5%	1.7%	7.8%	1.9%	2.1%	0.4%	0.6%	16.2%	8.4%	6.3%
25-34	12.8	15.1	16.5	16.6	20.0	6.3	9.0	29.9	24.5	13.0
35-44	23.8	30.1	18.9	33.7	45.4	20.9	31.5	20.5	24.0	25.2
45-54	43.7	43.8	31.7	33.1	26.1	32.2	40.8	12.4	13.4	25.3
55+	13.5	9.1	13.6	9.1	6.2	7.9	9.7	2.7	3.0	8.1
Females										
10-24	0.3	0.0	1.3	0.3	0.0	1.8	0.0	4.2	16.2	5.1
25-34	0.6	0.1	3.9	2.0	0.2	11.4	2.2	6.3	6.7	6.9
35-44	1.1	0.1	3.9	2.1	0.0	11.3	3.8	5.6	3.1	6.0
45-54	0.5	0.0	1.8	1.1	0.0	6.4	2.0	2.0	0.7	3.1
55+	0.2	0.0	0.5	0.1	0.0	1.4	0.3	0.2	0.1	0.9
Total	100.0	100.0	100.0	100.0	100.0	100.0	100.0	100.0	100.0	100.0
	(5,141)	(1,776)	(16,558)	(2,947)	(421)	(1,259)	(942)	(2,605)	(1,015)	(5,418)

SOURCE: Fifteenth Census of the United States, 1930, Population, vol. V, General Report on Occupations (U.S. Bureau of the Census, 1933), pp. 210-213.

In 1930 there was less than one Japanese American sales employee per Japanese retail dealer, a measure of how small indeed was the modal economic enterprise. At this point, the great bulk of employees were males, especially young ones; of those between the ages of twenty-five and thirty-four, more were employees than employers, but by the next age category, the opposite was the case. Similar age/sex contrasts are present in the farm sector, but it is noteworthy that the agricultural group was older than the urban small-business group. However, they were not older than those working in restaurants, an early urban trade for the Japanese Americans which was less demanding and elaborate than subsequent specializations. The typical farm proprietor was likely to be older and less likely to be female than the typical retail dealer or wholesaler. Likewise, while workers in each industry were younger (and more likely to be female) than proprietors in either, those in the shops were markedly younger than those on the farm. Women had two places of importance in this economy: as boardinghouse or hotel keepers, and in clerical occupations.

MECHANISMS BY WHICH JAPANESE MOVED INTO BUSINESS

Despite the fact that most Japanese immigrants came with little money and had to work as laborers, they did manage to move out of those positions and into the ranks of the petite bourgeoisie. How were they able to effect such a change, given that many other groups starting in a similar position were and are not able to do so?

The first feature to note about Japanese businesses is that, for the most part, a great deal of capital was not required to get them established. One example is the leasing of orchards. According to Ichihashi (1932:181), "leases were mostly annual, and while rent was sometimes paid at the time of leasing, more often it was paid 'out of the sale of the first crop.' " In other words, one needed virtually no capital to enter this line of business. The various forms of labor contracting in agriculture (described by Ichihashi, 1932:172-176) did not take much capital either. A "club," for example, could be established by an enterprising person for the cost of renting a house in the center of a farm labor market, such as Los Angeles. This person would "hire" a secretary, whose responsibility it was to find work for club members and who was paid a commission from the workers rather than a salary from the owner. The latter would collect annual dues from the members in exchange for the right to live and cook at the club when they were out of work. Sometimes the owner could make a little extra money by selling provisions to the members on the side.

In the city trades as well, the bulk of Japanese businesses did not entail major investments. An investigation into Japanese business establishments carried out by the California Bureau of Labor Statistics in 1909 found that "the capital invested in most of these establishments was, in most cases, very small, 68.7 percent of the total having a capital of less than $1,000." Already these tiny firms were dealing substantially in the general economy, slightly over one-third of their combined business being conducted with whites (California Bureau of Labor Statistics, 1911-12:604). The most common Japanese businesses as of 1909 were lodgings (often tied in with labor contracting) and restaurants, with about 300 concerns of each kind in California. Their average capitalization was $680 and $585, respectively; their work force was made up of 1.36 and 1.74 owners or partners and 0.38 and 0.73 employees, on the average. Running a boarding-house often meant little more than renting a large house, and most restaurants involved mainly an outlay for rent. Even laundries, a long-standing type of business that served non-Japanese customers and employed on the average 7.5 workers (with 2 bosses on top), had an average net capitalization of only $1,652 (California Bureau of Labor Statistics, 1911-12:613, 622).

Even when outside capital was needed, it could be obtained by Japanese Americans. In the early days, this did not include, to any significant extent, loans from formal lending institutions such as banks (Light, 1972:19-20). Rather, the sources were suppliers of material and equipment, the marketers of Japanese produce, and the owners of leased land. For example, Bloom and Riemer (1949:74) report that "in the early days the lack of capital was ameliorated by Japanese making contracts with commission merchants and Eastern distributors. Seed, fertilizer, packing materials, and cash were advanced to the Japanese grower, and he was under obligation to sell his entire crop to the distributor making the advance, at a price set by the distributor." This type of credit arrangement is not unique to the Japanese (Davis, Gardner, and Gardner, 1941:chap. 15 on blacks in the South; Furnivall, 1956: 293-294 on Malaysia). What is remarkable in the Japanese case is that despite individual failures, the Japanese were not reduced to debt peonage by these mechanisms, but instead were able to turn them to a profit.

Two major principles seem to be operating in the climb up to self-employment from these humble beginnings. They are *thrift* and *community cooperation*, and we shall consider each in some detail. Thrift is shown in a willingness to work long hours, in getting the whole family to work in the business as unpaid family labor, and in saving the proceeds of the enterprise for expansion rather than spending them on consumer goods, such as luxurious housing. Iwata (1962:35-36) reports that "the farm home of a Japanese, even of a wealthy farmer, is far below that of a home of a white man owning a similar piece of ground or of similar wealth. The neatness of the field . . . is in direct contrast with the flimsy, improvised condition of the living quarters of the Japanese." In urban businesses it was a frequent practice to live above or behind the store. This saved money and also made it easier to keep the store open long hours, with the help of family members. When detractors pointed to the shabbiness of these homes as an undesirable trait, defenders of the Japanese explained that the newness of the immigration accounted for the objectionable conditions, which would soon be alleviated. Nevertheless, by 1942, despite some sprucing up, the basic visual signs of thrift remained.

Japanese businesses were labor intensive, and since labor was relatively cheap for them, as we shall see shortly, this characteristic can be viewed as a form of thrift. In farming one sees this in the intensive cultivation of the land. As we have observed, Japanese-operated farms tended to be much smaller than the average, but every inch of the land was used and much labor poured in, so that they were much more productive per acre than the non-Japanese farms. For example, in Los Angeles County in 1940, the value of land and buildings per acre of all farms was $371.20; for Japanese farms it was $636.00 (Bloom and Riemer, 1949:74).

Community cooperation, too, was evident in many aspects of Japanese American business. It played a role in the accumulation of capital, in the acquisition and treatment of labor, in the passing around of other resources, in the development of vertical integration, and in the control of competition between Japanese firms.

Family, prefectural, and ethnic ties provided the basis for this cooperation.

The simplest form of cooperation to develop capital was partnership. Among farm tenants, "leasing was done in partnership, which was encouraged by the landowners because that meant their interests were assured by a joint responsibility of several Japanese in place of one individual" (Ichihashi, 1932:182). Iwata (1962:28) notes that such partnerships were generally not used by other groups to better their position in agriculture.

Another form of cooperative capitalization was the *tanomoshi*, or rotating-credit association. Light (1972:27-30) describes the essential features of this institution as the regular pooling of money by a group of participants and the lending of this larger sum to each participant, in rotation. The members tended to be persons who had come from the same prefecture in Japan, often belonging to a prefectural association, or *kenjinkai*. The use of communal ties meant that trust played a large part in the negotiations. In exchange, loans were easier and less costly to acquire than through formal lending institutions. Thus it was not necessary to provide collateral for a loan (Light, 1972:59-60), and interest, which was frequently "paid" as a gift, was lower than on the open market (Light, 1972:28).

Another factor in the rise of small business among the Japanese was their ability to make use of "cheap" labor from within the ethnic group by recruiting through communal channels. Japanese labor was "cheap" before it came to be utilized for the benefit of Japanese firms, and we shall briefly digress to demonstrate this point. It should be noted that the cheapness of labor does not depend only on the level of wages paid to workers, but encompasses the total cost of labor to the employer, including such factors as recruiting expenses, room and board (in some cases), and the cost entailed by strikes and labor unrest.

In the early period of immigration, Japanese labor was cheap for a number of reasons, one of which was the "acceptance" of relatively low wages. Millis (1915:45), though friendly to the Japanese, accepts the conclusion of the U.S. Immigration Commission on this point:

> The Japanese have usually worked for a lower wage than the members of any other race save the Chinese and the Mexican. In the salmon canneries the Chinese have been paid higher wages than the Japanese engaged in the same occupations. In the lumber industry all races,

including the East Indian, have been paid higher wages than the Japanese doing the same kind of work. As section hands and laborers in railway shops they have been paid as much or more than the Mexicans, but as a rule less than the white men of many races. ... As construction laborers they have usually, though not invariably, been paid less than the other races employed except the East Indians and the Mexicans.

Detailed figures for Oregon in 1919 indicate that Japanese industrial workingmen earned no more, and possibly less, than the wages paid to field hands, and at a rate about 10 percent below that for all unskilled male industrial laborers in the state. Japanese American women, of whom there were few receiving wages, and those mainly in commerce, were paid perhaps 75 percent of what white female industrial workers were paid (Oregon Bureau of Labor Statistics and Inspector of Factories and Workshops, 1919-20:10-11, 18-19).

The relatively low level of wages for Japanese reflects, in part, an effort to establish a foothold in the labor market. As Iwata (1962:27) points out: "Their willingness to accept even lower wages than laborers of other races enabled the Japanese to acquire employment readily." They occasionally served as strikebreakers with the same end in view, though there were exceptions to this pattern (Yoneda, 1971).

Perhaps even more important to white employers than wage differentials were a number of conveniences that Japanese labor offered. The United States Immigration Commission reported that of all labor available, the Japanese,

because of the position of the contractors, ... involved the least inconvenience to the employers. ... Almost without exception the Japanese employed in the industries of the West have been secured through "bosses," ... These contractors have had a supply of labor available; other cheap laborers must be "recruited," largely through employment agents in the cities of the Middle West, which involves competition with the industries more conveniently reached from these supply centers. This organization of the Japanese laborers must be emphasized above all other things in explaining the demand for them (cited in Millis, 1915:44-45).

Note that this is probably an overstatement, since many immigrants obtained jobs through more informal kin and prefectural connections.

The convenience of the contractor to the employer extended beyond ease of recruitment. The employer who had seasonal farm work did not have to be concerned about the welfare of the workers during the off-season: when the work was completed, the Japanese were able to disappear through the use of various boarding arrangements set up by contractors and through a system of transporting labor to areas of demand, also organized through a network of contractors.

Even when the middleman—in this case, the contractor—was not an important figure, as was the case on some large farms, Japanese workers were inexpensive to maintain. They were willing to live in bunkhouses, since most of the early immigrants were single males, and they were sometimes willing to work longer-than-normal hours, thereby saving the employer the effort of recruiting additional help. Millis (1915:155) provides an example of this last feature:

> The basket factory [in Florin] was established ten years ago. At first most of the employees were white women and girls of the community. They were found to be unsatisfactory in certain respects and were rapidly displaced by Japanese, who by 1909 filled practically all of the positions. It is said that the white women were difficult to manage, could not be depended upon to report for work regularly, and, though paid by the piece (for making grape and strawberry baskets), did not wish to work more than ten hours per day, or work overtime, or on Sundays, as it was thought the interests of the business required. In all these matters the Japanese were more acceptable to their employers, who are white men prominently connected with shipping firms in Sacramento. Paid by the piece, they formerly worked twelve to fourteen hours per day, and on Sundays, when the demand was such as to make long hours profitable.

Additional factors operated to put the Japanese (and other Asian workers) into the category of "cheap labor." Important among these was the fact that their race made them ineligible for citizenship. As a particularly rightless group, they were subjected to more severe predation by employers than were other groups, and making demands was far more risky for them. Because of their special status, they were discouraged from bringing their families to this country, at least at first, a factor that made it easy for employers to provide only minimal housing and other services. In addition, Asian workers were subjected to a vicious exclusion movement almost from the time of their arrival (Chiu, 1963; McWilliams, 1971; Saxton, 1971; Daniels, 1966*a*). Heavily supported by white workers, this movement severely limited the options of the immigrant workers, forcing them to accept poorer jobs at lower pay and encouraging collective responses—such as group undercutting—on the part of the minority group. Employers obviously benefited from these divisions in the labor force and may have actively recruited in Japan (and elsewhere in Asia) to foment them. Certainly this was the case in Hawaii, and while the importing of contract labor was strictly prohibited on the mainland, it may have gone on illegally anyway. In sum, the fact that Japanese immigrant workers were cheap labor was not their fault; they were victims of a competitive system and, for a period, were among the most exploited of all the workers in the West.

Regardless of the causes, the cheapness and organization of Japanese labor were important in the transition of the Issei from contractors to renters to owners of farms. Iwata (1962:28) writes that "in many instances California farmers resorted to leasing their holdings to the Japanese as a means of securing the nucleus of a labor supply and of transferring to the tenants the task of obtaining other laborers needed." By such means, contractors were able to increase their responsibility and control. Thus Japanese small business developed by the transfer of "cheap" immigrant labor from the employ, primarily, of Caucasian-owned enterprises to that of Japanese entrepreneurs.

The organization of Issei businesses contributed to maintaining the low cost of the labor force. A paternalistic relationship between employer and employee developed, so that the workers felt their interests to be more bound up with those of the firm than with those of other workers. They were loyal to their employers and did not join unions or engage in destructive strikes. They were willing to accommodate the demands of the business. Consequently they were less expensive to employ than the average "alienated" members of the work force.

The most heavily paternalistic arrangement existed in the case of unpaid family workers, where the loyalty factor and cuts in the cost of labor are obvious. Even among wage earners, however, paternalism was in evidence:

> In the Japanese economy, work was largely available only through the mediation of kin and kenjin. To receive a job in the Japanese-American

economy was to become the recipient of a benevolence bestowed upon one by virtue of social connections. ... By virtue of the intrusion of fraternal ties into the economy, matters of wages and hours were largely removed from the direction of the market and hinged on normative conventions, custom, and social obligation. ... An unjust or exploitative employer could be curbed only through social pressures. Such pressures constituted the only legitimate defense of the Japanese worker. Traditionalism and paternalism in employment relations imposed on the employer the duty of fair treatment for his employees in return for the employees' loyalty and submission (Light, 1972: 78-79).

One of the means of cutting labor costs was to provide board and lodging for employees. Millis (1915:71) reports that "living in" was a common practice: "The California Labor Commission found that 69.9 percent of the Japanese establishments provided lodging for their Japanese help."

That these kinds of arrangements led to substantial cuts in labor costs is illustrated in the case of laundries. Table 3:5 presents a comparison between white, French-style, and Japanese-owned laundries in San Francisco. That all employees in Japanese laundries received board and lodging while all workers in white firms did not indicates differences in the degree of paternalism in the two types of firms. It is evident from the table that not only did the Japanese employees work a longer day than their counterparts in other laundries, but also they were paid less for their labor.

TABLE 3:5

COMPARISON OF LABOR CONDITIONS FOR MALE EMPLOYEES
IN WHITE, FRENCH-STYLE, AND JAPANESE-OWNED LAUNDRIES
IN SAN FRANCISCO, 1909

	White	French	Japanese
Hours worked per week	49	50-63	60-72
Average monthly wage with board and lodging		$37.69 (32)	$28.90* (89)
Average monthly wage without board and lodging	$69.74 (140)	$48.56 (52)	

SOURCE: Millis, 1915:65-66.

*Estimated cost of room and board for Japanese owners was $8-$10 per month.

Clearly Japanese laundry owners had a cheaper labor source than their white and French competitors.

The relative importance of unpaid family labor in farming is discussed by Bloom and Riemer (1949:79). In a survey conducted by the Los Angeles Agricultural Commission in 1942, it was found that the average Japanese-operated farm depended on the labor of five full-time workers, or four workers in addition to the operator. Half was supplied by unpaid family labor, and the other half by paid labor from outside. For rural-farm California as a whole, the figures are equally impressive. Statewide, there was an unpaid Nisei family farm laborer for every two Japanese-run farms. Eliminating Nisei-run farms and adding Nisei who were numbered as paid farmworkers raises the ratio to 1.75 Nisei farm workers per Issei farm. In addition, half again as many unpaid family farm workers were Issei, almost all of them women (U.S. Bureau of the Census, 1943:107).

Employers preferred to hire Japanese Americans in these small businesses because loyalty could be used to reduce costs. Thus, in a census of the 901 Japanese-owned businesses in Seattle in 1930, 65 percent of the employees were Japanese American. Of the non-Japanese employees, over 55 percent are accounted for by five cannery labor contractors whose "employees" were really their clients (Miyamoto, 1939:70-73).

An illustration of the advantage Issei entrepreneurs gained from using ethnic-group members as employees comes from an analysis of data collected by the Oregon Bureau of Labor Statistics in the 1920s, a period in which the ethnic economy was more developed in some areas than others. Two counties, Clatsop and Multnomah (which includes Portland), provide an instructive contrast. Throughout the 1920s, the former remained an essentially nonfamilial, and nonentrepreneurial, settlement. Multnomah, on the other hand, saw a high concentration of entrepreneurs (about one for every two male Japanese wage earners) and a high and increasing concentration of families and children. Over the period for which data are available, the wages paid to Japanese in Multnomah as compared to Clatsop declined from an advantage of a few percent to a disadvantage of about 10 percent (Oregon Bureau of Labor Statistics, 1923-24:51-53; 1925-26:41-43; 1927-28:75-77). According to Davey (1920:6), who surveyed Oregon's "Japanese situation" for the governor of the state in 1920, "the white farmer who hires a [Japanese] to work for him gets only eight hours a day out of him, but his [Japanese] neighbor who hires the same fellow gets fourteen hours a day out of him at the same wages paid by the white man for eight hours."

Another advantage of drawing from an ethnic work force was that it enabled the small-business class to call on the loyalty of the workers in times of crisis. In 1933 and 1936, Mexican American farm workers on Japanese American farms in Los Angeles County went out on strike. The community was able to have Nisei youth temporarily withdrawn from the schools to act as harvest strike-breakers (Modell, 1977:121-126).

In exchange for providing Japanese employers with a cheap and reliable work force, less-independent members of the community found secure employment, even when jobs were very scarce. Table 3:6 shows the employment status of three ethnic groups in Los Angeles toward the end of the depression. The low unemployment among Japanese suggests the degree to which the community was willing and able to support its own members. Undoubtedly this often entailed sacrifices on the part of the business owners, who would have to squeeze still another job out of a struggling enterprise.

One important aspect of labor paternalism in Japanese American firms was that the community formed a kind of apprenticeship system. More recent immigrants would work in the businesses of their *kenjin*, or relatives, as a means of getting established. There they would learn the ropes of the particular business

TABLE 3:6

EMPLOYMENT STATUS OF PERSONS FOURTEEN YEARS OLD OR OLDER IN
THE LABOR FORCE IN THE CITY OF LOS ANGELES BY RACE, 1940

	Whites		*Blacks*		*Japanese*	
	Males	*Females*	*Males*	*Females*	*Males*	*Females*
Employed (except for public emergency work)	85.2%	87.4%	70.9%	77.2%	96.0%	96.5%
Public emergency work	2.7	1.8	10.8	5.0	0.1	0.1
Seeking work	12.0	10.8	18.3	17.8	3.9	3.4
Total	100.0 (446,775)	100.0 (190,354)	100.0 (19,460)	100.0 (12,800)	100.0 (8,118)	100.0 (2,896)

SOURCE: Bloom and Riemer, 1949:2.

with a view to setting up their own small firm (Miyamoto, 1939:74-75). They therefore identified with business and the interests of business rather than with labor. They had reason to abjure protesting long hours and low wages. The owner would compensate for the latter by later lending the apprentice some of the capital he needed to set up his own business, or by providing what was less tangible but equally valuable—training.

Park and Miller (1921:168) and other observers found the Japanese to be the most highly organized of all immigrant groups, and there is evidence to support this contention. For example, Light (1972:75) reports that in 1920 there existed a Japanese Association of Southern California, which had nineteen local affiliates. In addition, in northern and central California there were thirty-six farmers' organizations that were joined into the Japanese Agricultural Association and the California Farmers Cooperative; and every other line of enterprise had its corresponding associations. There was even a Southern California Japanese Physicians' and Surgeons' Association, which published a journal for its fewer than fifteen members. Overlapping the occupational organizations were prefectural associations and strong family ties. At the pinnacle was the Japanese Association, which coordinated the various associations. Modell (1977:67-93) details the workings of some of these intersecting organizations in Southern California. In his Oregon survey, Davey (1920:5-6) reveals his awe for the power and attention to detail of the organized community:

> Not long since, a white man who was working for a [Japanese] near Gresham obtained some sake from the [Japanese], got drunk and coming to Gresham in that condition was arrested. The Japanese colony, fearing the effect, called the society together and a peremptory order was issued that no [Japanese] should give any sake to a white man. ... In another case, a certain merchant had extended credit to a Japanese farmer, who turned out to be such a slow pay that the merchant announced his intention of forcing him by law to make settlement. Within a few days, the merchant was waited upon by the Japanese Association secretary, who told him he must not crowd the man; if he did he would lose the patronage of the entire Japanese colony; that the man would pay him sometime, but he must not crowd him.

Most organizations in the Japanese American community tended to be multipurpose, satisfying both social and economic ends. Indeed, satisfaction of social ends—which involved the building up of trust, connections, and so forth—served to further economic ends as well. As we have seen, these organizations played a part in the distribution of capital and labor; but they also were important in providing a means by which other resources could be shared. Iwata (1962:33) lists several functions of Issei farm organizations: assisting members in finding land, in purchasing supplies, and in marketing crops; mediating in landlord-tenant disputes; disseminating technical and marketing advice; and performing a variety of more diffuse social services, including publishing a newspaper and supporting a mutual-benefit society.

There were many other ways in which resources were effectively distributed within the Japanese community. One was the tendency to spend one's money on goods and services provided by the ethnic economy; in exchange, the consumer would receive a favorable credit arrangement (Miyamoto, 1939:78-82). Credit terms were also more favorable among businesses within the ethnic community than among those outside of it. Thus, through informal and formal organization, the Japanese community was able to distribute among its members capital, labor, patronage, credit, goods and services, jobs, welfare and other social aid, and information and training. These resources could usually be acquired more easily, inexpensively, and reliably within the ethnic community than outside of it.

The epitome of communal economic organization was the vertical integration that evolved in the produce industry in Southern California, with Japanese American growers selling to wholesalers, who in turn sold to retailers of the same ethnic group (Bloom and Reimer, 1949:92-93). Ethnic ties oiled this link. Japanese growers would obtain financing from wholesalers, instead of turning to the banks, where the interest rates were higher. The farmers also received from them, on a nonprofit basis, fertilizer, seed, and equipment. In exchange, these growers would promise their produce to the Japanese wholesalers, who thus assured themselves of reliable supply sources. As usual, multipurpose ethnic associations supported these negotiations (Bloom and Riemer, 1949:93-94).

At the other end of the industry, according to Bloom and Riemer (1949:96), "the main retail outlets for Japanese American produce wholesalers in the prewar period were members of the same ethnic group," and it seems reasonable to conclude that, again, ethnic-group trust played a part in these exchanges.

Besides aiding in the distribution of resources, prewar Japanese American organizations helped ethnic small businesses in another way: they acted to curtail internal competition. This curtailment took two principal forms: agreement about prices, so that Japanese did not underbid each other or unnecessarily push up purchase or rent prices; and agreements about spacing, so that Japanese did not impinge on each others' territories.

The U.S. Immigration Commission pointed out both of these forms of limitation in an early type of Issei enterprise, farm labor contracting:

> For years their "gangs" of pickers have respected each other's territory to a certain extent. A special agent of the Commission reports that at the time of his investigation "the smaller gangs" who pick small vineyards have the territory distributed among them and one gang will not take a job in the district belonging to another. At the same time the larger contractors have an organization designed, among other things, to control the prices to be charged for work and the wages to be paid to laborers. ... To eliminate competition, or at any rate, to prevent undue competition which would destroy profits while wages are rising, the Japanese bosses of this entire district in 1890 organized the Fresno Contractors' Association (cited in Fisher, 1953:28).

When the Japanese entered farming for themselves, these organizations continued to carry out their functions. For example, Iwata (1962:33) notes that the Japanese farm organizations "served to limit the competition for land by fixing a maximum rental that a Japanese should pay."

In urban trades, guilds were developed to limit internal competition in much the same way: "Guild organization of their trades enabled Japanese to regulate internal competition by discussion and collective decision making, rather than by individualistic competition" (Light, 1972:68). The Issei organized such guilds in most of the trades in which they were employed in any numbers. The U.S. Immigration Commission found that the Shoemakers' Guild, for example, fixed prices; controlled the location of shops, making sure they were at least 1,000 feet apart; maintained a common supply house; controlled apprenticeship to the trade; and maintained a system of fraternal benefits (Light, 1972:69).

We have seen, then, that before the war the Issei were able to shift their proletarian position to one of self-employment. This transition was effected through thrift and through reliance on community, or ethnic, ties, which enabled group members to distribute resources efficiently and to control internal competition. The highly specialized Japanese American economy had a kind of symbiotic relationship with the rest of the society: the Japanese ethnic community was culturally distinctive and socially segregated, yet it performed vital economic functions for the society as a whole. We should note that all of these features are not unique to the Japanese Americans, but are typical of middleman minorities wherever they are found. In looking so closely at this one community, we hope to reveal the general principles at work for ethnic minorities that develop similar specializations.

"SUCCESS" OF THE FORM

The life of the Issei small entrepreneur was often difficult. Businesses sometimes failed, profit margins were slim, people had to work hard and live frugally, and, as we shall see in chapter 5, they had to face considerable hostility from the surrounding society. Despite these problems, however, Issei enterprise was, in a sense, successful, insofar as the immigrants were able to escape from the ranks of laborers and establish themselves in individual businesses. The lives of many particular families were undoubtedly difficult, but the group as a whole was able to make a spectacular shift. One of the major reasons is that the economic form we have been describing had a competitive edge over its rivals. Japanese entrepreneurs were able to charge lower prices on the open market and offer higher bids on purchases and rentals of such assets as farmland. Consequently, Issei business was able to expand rapidly and even to move into a "monopolistic" position in certain spheres of the economy.

The use of this competitive advantage in the urban trades is described by Millis (1915:64-65): "The investigations made by the Immigration Commission established the fact that there was or had been some underbidding as a rule on the part of the Japanese proprietors of barber shops, laundries, grocery stores, cleaning and dyeing establishments, and shoe-repairing shops. This underbidding was made possible because of lower wages paid employees, longer hours sometimes worked, and willingness on the part of proprietors to accept less profit than their white competitors." In the case of laundries, businesses expanded rapidly, so that by 1909 there were seventy-five laundries in Seattle, Tacoma, Sacramento, San Francisco, and Los Angeles, employing altogether about 950 people, including the proprietors (Millis, 1915:65). As we have already seen, Japanese laundry laborers worked longer hours for lower wages than their white counterparts, which resulted in "the fact that the prices charged by Japanese [were] frequently . . . less than those charged by white laundrymen of various races and French hand laundrymen in San Francisco" (Millis, 1915:65).

The growth of acreage under the control of Japanese farmers is a product of similar forces. Japanese-operated farms were considerably smaller than others, as mentioned earlier, but the land was used more intensively: "Through interplanting, double cropping and the application of considerable hand labor, [they] got production and incomes on these small farms often comparable to those of farmers with larger acreages of similar crops" (Poli and Engstrand, 1945:356). For instance, as early as 1909, Japanese farmers produced 18 percent of the value of farm products in Los Angeles County, although they used only 1.5 percent of the improved farmland (Modell, 1977:96). Intensive farming meant that the value of the land was higher for Japanese than for others, as mentioned earlier. The result was that Japanese farmers were able to pay higher rents or offer higher prices for land. McWilliams (1971:113-114) reports that

> as farmers, the Japanese carried on the process already begun in California; they intensified cultivation even further than it had been done before them, raising the productivity of the land and its yield, and raising land values correspondingly. . . . The small farmers and tenants found it difficult to compete with the Japanese who consistently overbid them for leases. In 1917 the value of the crops produced on Japanese-owned or controlled acreage in California was three and a half times as much as that obtained by California farms in general. The Japanese were naturally able, not only to bid more for leases, but to pay more for land, than their competitors.

The result was rapid growth and a tendency toward ethnic-group monopolizing of certain narrow lines. Table 3:7 shows the degree to which various crops came to be the exclusive prerogative of Japanese truck farmers in Los Angeles before the war.

There is a certain irony in the competitive advantage of Japanese small business. Many of its features can be classified as

TABLE 3:7

PERCENTAGE OF ACREAGE OF SELECTED CROPS GROWN BY
JAPANESE AMERICANS IN LOS ANGELES COUNTY, 1941

Crop	Acreage
Celery	99%
Peas	99
Spinach	99
Beets	99
Broccoli	99
Radishes	99
Peppers	98
Snap beans	95
Strawberries	95
Turnips	95
Cauliflower	90
Lettuce	90
Green onions	90
Green lima beans	90
Eggplant	90
Romaine	90
Summer squash	90
Cucumbers	85
Cabbage	75
Carrots	75
Parsnips	75
Endive	75

SOURCE: Bloom and Riemer, 1949:85.

"premodern—for instance, the use of familial and ethnic ties, or ascriptive bases of affiliation, rather than contractual, or strictly "objective," criteria for making market decisions. Japanese enterprise used very little wage labor, and what was used was often tied to the employer by bonds that extended beyond those of the simple labor contract. Despite its premodern features, however, Japanese enterprise was able to compete effectively with more modern forms. Granted that the Japanese did not compete in many business lines and that those they were active in tended to be the least modern; but when they were active, they were effective. And the reason they were effective was because ethnicity (or communal support) could be mobilized to cut costs and further common economic interests.

It can be seen that Issei enterprise showed many of the features characteristic of middleman-minority entrepreneurship which were described in the previous chapter. They concentrated in a narrow range of lines, were overrepresented in commercial and service occupations, used the family firm as their main business form, depended on thrift and hard work, were able to utilize communal ties to generate multiple types of business aid, and were able to sell their goods and services inexpensively. As already noted, these features are not unique to the Japanese, but are found, with specific variations, among other middleman groups.

CAUSES OF THE FORM

In chapter 2 we laid out some common explanations of the middleman-minority phenomenon in general. Most of these ideas have been raised in one form or another to explain the Japanese American experience. For instance, Japanese concentration in small business has been accounted for by the racism emanating from the surrounding society. They became proprietors, it is argued, because racial discrimination prevented them from finding opportunities for advancement in the general economy. Independent small business was an alternative route to success that did not depend on white goodwill. For example, Daniels (1966a:11-12) argues that "because of the high degree of unionization in northern California and the anti-Oriental agitation which had been prevalent since the 1860s, no significant number of Issei were ever hired by white firms for factory or office work. The [immigrant], if he stayed in town, had to go into business for himself, or, more probably, go to work for an already established Issei." In other words, the Issei were pushed into small business by the surrounding society rather than by forces internal to the group.

Another contextual argument is put forth by Modell (1977), who points out that the Pacific Coast states were not fully developed at the time of Japanese settlement; some economic niches were available, and the immigrants were able to take advantage of them.

Cultural explanations also exist. One idea is that Japanese in Japan were accustomed to running small businesses. As this was the typical economic mode of the homeland, it was transplanted, unchanged, to the United States. Thus, among other factors, Kitano (1976b:21) mentions "the traditional expectation of many Japanese to run their own businesses." Similarly, Miyamoto (1939:74) points out that "the tradition of individual enterprise [was] well laid in the customs of Japan." We might term this the *direct-importation thesis.*.

Most of the cultural approaches do not assume such a direct link, however. Miyamoto, for one, introduces another, indirect factor. Noting that the immigrants were often inexperienced in business even if they aspired to engaging in it, he points to communal solidarity as an important cause of their success (Miyamoto, 1939:74-76). The high degree of solidarity is in turn attributed to the cultural heritage brought over by the immigrants, as "the collectivistic system of Japan gave a strong base to group solidarity" (Miyamoto, 1939:62).

Another common theme under the rubric of culture is that the Japanese immigrants were ready for capitalistic behavior because they carried with them the prerequisite values of hard work and thrift. These values were rapidly pushing the Japanese nation along the road toward industrialization, and the same values were set loose in its emigrants, so that they were psychologically ready to storm ahead in the economy. Peterson (1970:176) captures this orientation: "The Issei who came to America were catapulted out of a homeland undergoing rapid change—Meiji Japan, which remains the one country of Asia to have achieved modernization. We can learn from such a work as Robert Bellah's 'Tokugawa Religion' that diligence in work, combined with simple frugality, had an almost religious imperative, similar to what has been called 'the Protestant ethic' in Western culture."

A related idea is put forward by Caudill and De Vos (1970: 179), who maintain that "there seems to be a significant compatibility (but by no means, identity) between the value systems found in the culture of Japan and the value systems found in the American middle class culture." These shared values, which include politeness, cleanliness, respect for authority, and a stress on achievement, provide a basis for relatively easy adaptation to the American middle-class lifestyle, which presumably encourages success in small business.

Light (1972) challenges these approaches based on values, arguing that rather than having a Protestant-ethic value system, which implies an emphasis on individualism, the Japanese immigrants relied on collective and ascriptive ties to develop the resources for entrepreneurship. In particular he emphasizes the institution of the tanomoshi, which was important for raising capital and depended upon ethnically generated trust.

Finally, a situational argument is made by Bonacich (1973), who tries to show that sojourning was prevalent among the Issei. She argues that the desire to return to Japan explains a tendency toward communal solidarity and provides a motive for thrift and a preference for easy-to-liquidate lines, such as trade. These features are all conducive to concentrating in small business.

As suggested in chapter 2, the middleman-minority phenomenon needs to be understood in systemic terms, as a product of the interaction of many of these forces, and the Japanese American concentration in small business is no exception. While racism may have limited the opportunities of Japanese Americans, it cannot fully explain why other objects of racism (such as blacks) did not also seek out a small-business resolution. Similarly, the availability of economic niches on the Pacific Coast cannot alone account for the Japanese ability to fill them, although this approach goes a long way to explaining the particular lines the Issei pursued.

Cultural arguments of the Protestant-ethic type are, we feel, the most limited, since they confuse modern with premodern, or petit bourgeois, forms. Cultural theories pointing to the importance of collective traditions, however, are clearly of great importance in understanding Issei adaptation. Indeed, we have, in this chapter, given prominence to a close examination of how these collective traditions worked in practice.

Finally, situational theories, notably an emphasis on sojourning and its consequences, may help to explain some of the immigrants' early motives that might have propelled them toward a collective adaptation. This approach, though, tends to minimize the important part played by hostility from the surrounding society in limiting the options of the Issei and forcing them into rather restricted lines. Indeed, sojourning itself can be seen as a partial response to the racism the group had to face.

In general, then, theories of Japanese American entrepreneurship have been limited because they have examined only single causes. A comparative approach, as we have endeavored to develop here, increases our awareness of the interrelatedness of context, culture, and situation.

4

Societal
Hostility

So far, we have attempted to show that Issei economic adaptation conformed to the middleman-minority type in many significant respects. In this chapter we examine the implications of the group's position as a middleman minority for its reception by the surrounding society. (Admittedly, a middleman-minority approach is only one of many possible ways to interpret anti-Japanese sentiment and actions. Our purpose here is less to create a rounded picture of all facets of societal hostility toward the Japanese than to show the usefulness of this comparative approach in providing us with insights about the Japanese American experience.) Essentially, we provide an interpretation of the antagonism that the Japanese faced, drawing upon parallels to other middleman-minority experiences. It is our contention that the evacuation of the Japanese Americans during World War II bears comparison to Hitler's "final solution" or to Idi Amin's more recent handling of the Indians in Uganda. The particular actions taken in each instance may differ, but the structural circumstances behind them are strikingly similar.

The Japanese Americans faced antagonism in the United States from shortly after the time of the arrival of the first immigrants. Early agitation primarily took the form of concern that the Japanese were another "coolie" immigration, like the Chinese, who had been the objects of a considerable and successful agitation a generation earlier. Labor organizations were fearful that Japanese workers would be used to undercut their wages and undermine their standard of living. We might term this the "labor-conflict phase" of Japanese American history. Labor competition was the dominant theme in the agitation for exclusion of Japanese immigrants until about 1907-1908, when the Gentlemen's Agreement with Japan effectively cut off further immigration of laborers. Denis Kearney's Workingmen's party and San Francisco political boss Abraham Ruef's Union Labor party played a major role in the agitation against Chinese and Japanese, respectively.

As the Issei moved into small business, aided by families who joined them in the years following the Gentlemen's Agreement, the locus of antagonism shifted, and its intensity grew considerably. Not only did the immigrants compete with laboring groups, but increasing numbers of Issei now competed with established business interests. In addition, the increasing economic power of the Japanese aroused concern over the fact that they were aliens and were not integrated into the American community. A solidary, distinct, and separate group was becoming more and more essential to the economy of the Pacific Coast, and this fact was viewed with alarm.

The middleman form put the Japanese American community in conflict with several sectors of the surrounding society. In particular, segments of both business and labor felt themselves threatened by Issei small business and were able to unite temporarily in the movement to destroy the ethnic economy. Each class had a somewhat different conflict with the Japanese, and we shall consider each in turn. In addition, the theme of Japanese ethnic solidarity could be used to unite otherwise antagonistic classes in the surrounding society in a joint anti-Japanese movement.

CONFLICT WITH BUSINESS

The Japanese American ethnic economy had its strongest effect on small businesses involved in lines similar to those engaged in by the Japanese. The most vocal and active of this threatened class, probably because of Japanese concentration in their line, were the small farmers. This group felt itself unable to compete with the long hours, low standard of living, and unpaid family labor of the Issei agriculturists.

The competition between the American and the Issei farmers is described in *California and the Oriental* (California State Board of Control, 1922:116-117), a document sent by Governor William D. Stephens of California to the secretary of state in Washington, D. C., to urge total exclusion of the Japanese:

> The working conditions and living conditions of the Japanese farmer and farm laborers make successful competition by American farmers almost impossible. The Japanese farmers and every member in the family physically able to do so, including the wife and little children, work in the field long hours, practically from daylight to dark, on Sundays and holidays, and, in the majority of cases, live in shacks or under conditions far below the standards required and desired by Americans.... The presence of the Japanese in agricultural pursuits under such working and living conditions works the greatest hardship upon the small farmer, especially those farmers who perform the larger part of their own work. This impossible competition is emphasized by the fact that the Japanese are in large measure independent contractors, or land owners, and not ordinary laborers. American farmers can not successfully compete with Japanese farmers if the Americans adhere to the American principles so universally approved in America, including clean and wholesome living quarters, reasonable working hours, the usual Sunday rest and holiday recreation, and above all, refraining from working the women and children in the fields.

Not only was the structure of the Issei farm more efficient for production than that of the American farm, but highly intensive farming tended to drive up the price of farmland. Non-Japanese small farmers were thus forced into sitting on land whose sale value was higher than the value of what they were able to produce on it; they finally had to sell (McWilliams, 1971: 113-114).

Data from the British Columbia Department of Agriculture show clearly how Japanese expansion in small fruit and berry growing affected the shape of the farming industry as a whole (table 4:1). After an initial burst in the amount of new acreage placed under this form of cultivation, the competition came to resemble a zero-sum game. Steadily, the proportion of growers who were Japanese increased; at a more rapid rate, the Japanese proportion of acreage used for small fruit growing increased. Under this pressure, the size of white-run farms shrank, so that by 1934, the average Japanese farm was triple the size of the average white-run farm.

The intensive use of farmland also aroused charges of land

TABLE 4:1
JAPANESE INFLUENCE IN SMALL FRUIT AND BERRY PRODUCTION
IN BRITISH COLUMBIA, 1920-1934

Year	Total Acreage	Japanese Acreage	Japanese Farms	Average Acres per Japanese Farm	Average Acres per White Farm
1920	3,330	29.1%	19.5%	4.15	2.44
1922	6,202	25.2	14.1	4.66	2.26
1924	6,310	23.2	14.5	4.00	2.24
1926	5,201	27.1	14.5	4.10	1.86
1928	5,757	34.0	22.3	3.37	1.87
1930	4,813	36.6	21.8	3.99	1.93
1932	4,989	37.7	21.8	4.11	1.85
1934	6,160	45.4	22.0	4.89	1.66

SOURCE: Young and Reid, 1938:269.

mining or careless depletion of the quality of the land (Poli and Engstrand, 1945:362). This fear was exacerbated by the perception that the Issei were sojourners. Since they were only temporary residents, why should they be concerned with preserving the quality of the soil? It seemed only reasonable that a sojourner, and especially a tenant, would try to eke as much out of the land as possible, and be concerned only with short-term gains.

Not only small farmers but also some of the large, corporate concerns felt the pinch of Japanese competition. Poli and Engstrand (1945:357-358), writing after the war (hence the reference to the Japanese as "evacuees"), describe this situation:

An interesting characteristic of evacuee farming was the ability of evacuees to grow truck crops on small family operated farms and yet survive competition from large-scale grower-shipper vegetable producers. In the Imperial Valley, for example, most non-evacuee small farm operators contend that vegetable production for them is too risky, principally because of difficulty in marketing. The non-evacuee truck crop acreage in this valley, therefore, is controlled largely by large-scale grower-shippers. This same condition exists also in many other parts of California where vegetable crops are grown. This situation, however, was not true of evacuee farmers. Although their farms were small, they grew and marketed truck crops successfully. In the Southern California coast region, evacuee farmers, mostly with small farms, were such successful truck crop producers that the non-evacuee grower-shippers complained of being frozen out by evacuee competition.

In California in 1913 and 1920, and in other western states at around the same time, Alien Land Laws were passed to suppress aliens ineligible for citizenship in their efforts to farm the land. The second California Alien Land Law of 1920, designed to close loopholes in the first, was passed as an initiative measure by an overwhelming majority. Farmers' organizations, such as the Farm Bureau Federation and the Grange, led the challenge. For example, in 1920 the Los Angeles County Farm Bureau demanded not only that Japanese not be permitted to lease, rent, or own any land at all, but also that a constitutional amendment be passed to disqualify the Nisei from eligibility for American citizenship in order to prevent the second generation from acquiring land titles (Iwata, 1962:33-34).

The responses to an open-ended questionnaire item asking high-school seniors and college freshmen in the late 1920s about their reactions to Japanese Americans reveal the importance of economic anxieties. Of the unfavorable comments, over one-third were categorized by the analyst as directly relating to "unfair" economic competition: the Japanese were land miners, tricky, grasping, or too successful in gaining control of the land. An additional 20 percent noted "unfavorable" ways in which the Japanese achieved such successful competition: self-abnegation and women's and children's work (Strong, 1934:128).

Japanese Americans had a very different point of view on the issue of farming competition. They claimed that they had improved much land in California which had hitherto been unusable, engaging in back-breaking toil to reclaim semidesert areas and swamplands that other Californians had deemed worthless, and that they had found a niche that was reasonably well suited to an adaptation of their traditional forms of agriculture and family structure. Now that they were reaping a profit from these efforts, white Californians coveted their land and wanted to take it back.

The Japanese farmers also couched their arguments in terms of their having aided consumers by reducing the cost of agricultural products. The slogan of the Japanese campaign against the 1920 Alien Land Law was "Keep California Green," offered in

opposition to their antagonists' slogan, "Keep California White."
In addition, argued the Issei, they had contributed to the development of new crops, in particular rice. The charge of land mining
was denied, and it was asserted that the Japanese used highly
sophisticated methods of fertilization and irrigation. The Japanese
argued that they were resented because they were more efficient
than the Americans and that to be resented for their hard work
and efficiency went against the very heart of the American creed.
America stood for the principle of free competition, yet when a
group showed itself ready to meet the challenge and was able to
compete effectively, Americans became frightened and wanted to
push out their competitors. The contradictions in the positions of
those who opposed them were so striking to leaders in Japan, as
well as to Japanese Americans, that they attributed these positions
to the confused thinking of ignorant racists who somehow had
temporarily gotten the ear of those in power (Iriye, 1972).

The Issei perspective on accusations about their low standard
of living was that such adaptations were necessary in a land where
they were denied the right of citizenship and faced constant
hostility and discrimination. In order to survive, they had to be
thrifty, to save for an almost certain rainy day, to be prepared to
move at the slightest notice. In an unstable and hostile world, the
Japanese could not settle down to a comfortable life. It was, they
maintained, societal hostility that had forced them into their work
patterns, and not the other way around. The "official" Japanese
position, as it emanated from the Japanese Association and other
Issei organizations, was that if whites would be a bit more reasonable, already instituted Americanization efforts could succeed in
raising their standard of living to the American level and thereby
remove the problem.

The heart of the business conflict was that the Japanese,
employing a different mix of labor and capital investment, indeed
seemed more efficient, as their rapidly rising rate of land control
and the development of near-monopolies over various crops testified; both sides to the conflict would concede the point. However,
while the Japanese saw this as an ordinary competitive outcome,
Californian farming interests saw only a group of "foreigners"
coming in and taking over "their" territory, and in particular a
group of foreigners who used techniques that were felt to be
"unfair"—internal collaboration and maintenance of a lower stan-

dard of living. In fact, more than one Californian echoed the words of J. M. Howells of the Commonwealth Club of California. Howells saw the economic competition as a conflict between two different systems of civilization:

> Our system of education is partly responsible for our inability or unwillingness to compete with the Oriental. We educate our sons to be overseers of the labor of others and expect our neighbor to furnish a son who will not mind doing the hard work. . . . While the Japanese toils in the field we ride in a luxurious automobile and while thus frittering away our racial stamina, he is building up or at least sustaining the primitive rugged strength which has for generations furnished Japan, from her rural districts, with her strongest national figures. . . . By their ambition and activity they will ultimately bring an issue as to control of our country and therefore bring war (Howells, 1920: 210-211).

When Japanese American enterprise came into conflict with local business interests, in a sense, two modes of production, precapitalist and capitalist, were at odds. The precapitalist method may have been effective in the short run, but the Japanese lacked both numbers and a political base, and were therefore the less powerful of the two contending parties. The business interests in California emerged largely victorious; by political means, they were able to cut the Japanese agricultural base back to the size it had attained by the mid-1920s.

CONFLICT WITH LABOR

The issue of labor competition was present from the inception of Japanese immigration. West Coast workers felt that Japanese labor could be used to undermine the wage gains they had painfully attained over the years. The Japanese (like the Chinese before them) were seen as pawns in the conflict between the capitalist class, which wanted to make use of inexpensive Japanese labor, and local labor organizations, which wanted to prevent their own position from being undercut (King, 1908). In other words, there was a "split labor market" between Japanese and white workers (Bonacich, 1972; 1976).

Local labor tended to react to Japanese immigrants with movements to have them excluded, seeing this as a method of preventing capital from using the Japanese to local labor's detriment. As an alternative, local labor might have tried to organize the immigrants, bring them into their unions, and thereby eliminate capital's ability to play one group against the other. There was a widespread belief that this was next to impossible, however. According to Cox (1948:417-418),

> the cultural bar between the European and the Asiatic makes it difficult and at certain stages impossible for the two groups to reach that common understanding necessary for concerted action against the employer. Moreover, the first generation of Asiatic workers is ordinarily very much under the control of labor contractors and employers, hence it is easier for the employer to frustrate any plans for their organization. Clearly this cultural bar helped to antagonize white workers against the Asiatics. The latter were conceived of as being in alliance with the employer. It would probably have taken two or three generations before, say, the East Indian low-caste worker on the Coast became sufficiently Americanized to adjust easily to the policies and aims of organized labor. Eventually, however, they would have been organized.

Whether local labor's perception was accurate can be questioned, but that this was indeed the common view is not in doubt (Meister and Loftis, 1977:8; Daniels, 1966a:19-30).

The nature of this conflict was neatly realized in British Columbia (at a somewhat later date than in the United States) in the lumbering industry. There, as a consequence of political bargaining between white-owned business interests and their white laborers, a split labor market was recognized by provincial law. Before regulation, Japanese employees typically received about three-quarters the amount of pay that whites received for the same work. When major employers strenuously objected to a labor-supported provincial law of 1925, which set the industry-wide minimum wage at forty cents an hour, sufficiently above the usual rate for Asians to achieve the end of destroying their competitive advantage, the law was modified. Under the modified law, one-quarter of the lumber workers could receive wages of twenty-five cents an hour, and this group could include Asians. Still, some Asian workers were displaced, their proportion being reduced from 45 to 34 percent of the work force (Young and Reid, 1938:48-50).

As Japanese moved into small business, the nature of the labor conflict shifted somewhat. Now white capitalists were not employing inexpensive Japanese labor, but Japanese family firms were, and while the Japanese and whites were competing for the same jobs just as much as before, the vigor of the white economy as a whole, and therefore the likely return to white labor, was seen to be threatened by the growing Japanese American ethnic economy. The basis of this conflict is easy to understand. When organized labor on the West Coast tried to improve its position vis-à-vis management (with which it had an institutionalized conflict), it had to face the possibility of pricing itself out of the market because of the less expensively run Japanese firms. (The same dilemma arises today in competition with enterprises in foreign countries where labor is cheaper, but such conflict can be dealt with more obviously by such governmental devices as import tariffs and currency devaluations; the boycott is used against both foreign and domestic undercutting).

As we have seen, white management, too, had some interest in opposing the inexpensive labor of the Japanese firms, but management could also use that very factor as a weapon in its struggle with its own work force, arguing that if labor insisted on higher wages and better work conditions, both labor and management would lose. Labor was caught in a bind: it could either improve its position in the short run and accept the possibility of losing work altogether, or accept a lower standard of living and Japanese-style work conditions. To avoid both horns of the dilemma would mean to organize the Japanese workers and convince them to accept a conflictual class relationship with their Japanese employers, a tack that most white labor leaders thought had no chance of success.

The conflict between organized labor and Japanese American small business surfaced early in San Francisco and other cities where Japanese businesses were first established. Millis (1915:68) describes the situation among barbershops: "Underbidding by Japanese barbers troubled their white competitors in some places. . . . This was notably the case in Seattle, where the union prices usual in the West had to be lowered to meet Japanese competition at lower prices."

In reaction to the low prices of Japanese restaurants, members of the Cooks and Waiters Union attacked a restaurant in San Francisco in 1891. In 1906, the same union, assisted by other labor unions, set up pickets around Japanese restaurants, urging that they be boycotted by whites (tenBroek, Barnhart, and Matson, 1954:33-34). The boycott was successful in reducing the number of Japanese American restaurants serving American meals from thirty to seventeen by 1908 (Thomas, 1952:30).

"Anti-Jap Laundry Leagues" were formed in a number of cities by employees of white laundries. Millis (1915:67-68) describes some of their tactics:

> In order to diminish the patronage of the Japanese establishments, lists of their patrons were prepared, and appeals were made in person, by card, or letter to them, to discontinue sending laundry to the Asiatics. Extravagant billboard advertising, making appeals along the same lines, were also resorted to. At the same time, these leagues were active in preventing the granting of the necessary permits to Japanese to operate steam laundries, and by appeal or threat of boycott, the cooperation of some of the laundry supply houses was gained, with the result that some of the Japanese proprietors experienced difficulty in securing needed supplies.

Again, the basis for the agitation lay in the fear that "the longer working day, the advantages of group organization, the paucity of wage laborers, and the perquisites provided made it possible to undercut on the prices charged the consumer" (Thomas, 1952: 30-31).

Working-class antagonism to the Japanese is revealed in the 1920 Alien Land Law initiative. Model (1977:47-51) analyzed voting patterns in Los Angeles County and found that the poorer areas were generally more in favor of the initiative than the wealthier sectors of the county. Anti-Japanese sentiment ran highest in the industrial sections of the city.

Labor opposition played an important role in settlement patterns. San Francisco was a prolabor city—it had even elected a Union Labor party mayor. According to Thomas (1952:31-32), "largely because of the effectiveness of labor opposition, San Francisco became a dead-end area for most Japanese enterprises, [whereas] the San Francisco pattern of restraint was applied only sporadically and far less effectively in Seattle and Los Angeles, where the relative weakness of their labor unions made it difficult to organize latent opposition against the Japanese."

When white organized labor tried to persuade the Japanese

workers to join their unions, the latter were generally reluctant to do so, and with good reason. The Japanese unpaid family workers regarded themselves, not as employees in the narrow sense, but, rather, as people having a personal stake in the future of the business. They identified with the business and its goals and did not see a conflict between their interests and those of management. Even Japanese wage earners did not see themselves in class conflict with owners, who often treated them like family members. Generally, they were preparing to enter small business themselves, using the wage-earning period as an apprenticeship.

Modell (1969; 1977:127-153) describes an attempt by the Los Angeles Retail Food Clerks, Local 770, to organize the grocery-business sales forces in 1937, reporting that "since white-run concerns could not concede a substantial advantage in labor costs to their Japanese competitors without suffering losses in trade, Local 770 believed that, if it was to organize the white portion of the industry, it could not ignore the Japanese" (Modell, 1969:198). Certain elements among the Japanese fruit-stand workers reacted by forming their own "union," which emphasized its responsibilities to the ethnic community and avoided all mention of strikes or collective bargaining. To its "Dear Brothers and Sisters"—Nisei fruit-stand workers to which the ethnic "union" was appealing—Local 770 argued in an open letter in the vernacular press that only the bosses would gain from their segregation. Nisei workers were challenged to place class interest first and ethnic interest second: "We believe that the Japanese and white workers should unite and work together. We recognize no national or racial difference. The 'Company Union' that your employers have asked or told you to join, . . . has been for the purpose of isolating and segregating the Japanese workers from the white . . . that they may, and can keep you under their thumbs, . . . that they can, and will, work you longer hours for less pay. . . . We have not set up a separate wage and hour scale for the Japanese worker, while the 'Company Union' proposes to do this very thing. If you are real Americans, why don't you fight for the American standard of living?" (cited in Modell, 1977:143). The wary Nisei workers could not respond wholly favorably to this appeal, and as a result, white workers blacklisted and picketed Japanese-owned stores.

Again, however, the conflict had two sides. Not only were Japanese workers less interested in unionizing than white workers, but also they had reason to distrust the whites and their unions. The American Federation of Labor in the Pacific Coast states had agitated against Japanese immigration and immigrants for years. Their approaches to Japanese workers now seemed opportunistic in the extreme; white "brothers and sisters" only turned to the Japanese when it was to the whites' advantage, and they seemed to have little interest in the actual welfare of the Japanese workers. What if, for example, Japanese workers did unionize and raise ethnic-economy wages to the point where the small businesses would lose their price advantage and might possibly be forced to go under—would white unionists guarantee an end to job discrimination in white-owned businesses? It seemed highly unlikely. Far better to stick with the ethnic economy, which had proven itself willing to support its own workers, even in hard times.

CONFLICT OVER SOLIDARITY

Business and labor shared a source of conflict with the Japanese community over the issue of solidarity. The Japanese were accused of being clannish, self-segregating, unassimilable, and disloyal. Pluralism, to be sure, was not the most easily grasped notion in the polyglot America of the period around World War I; but the arguments that the aliens were unusually solidary, an unfathomable lump in the body politic, perhaps even malignant, were especially persistent in their application to the Japanese.

A number of charges relating to solidarity were leveled at the Japanese. One was the question of dual citizenship. Because of their race, the Issei were not permitted to become United States citizens, a legal provision that interested parties made sure was applied. The second generation were automatically American citizens because they were born on United States soil, but whites hostile to the Japanese maintained that there was an ambiguity about where the true loyalty of the Nisei lay, their distrust initially fostered by Japan's citizenship laws. These laws ultimately were altered to make it easier for Japanese citizens born overseas (the Nisei, according to Japanese usage, fit into this category) to renounce their Japanese citizenship, but many did not.

More important than citizenship per se were the efforts of Japanese parents to keep their children actively involved in Japanese culture. Californians objected to the practice of sending children back to Japan as *Kibei* for part of their education in highly nationalistic Japanese schools. They objected to the Japanese language schools, which imported textbooks and instructors from Japan and were purported to teach loyalty to the emperor to the large proportion of Nisei who attended after school. And they objected to the continual intervention by the Japanese consulate or by the Japanese Association, which often acted as its agent (Millis, 1915:248-249).

The immigrants had retorts to these charges. The Issei were not permitted to become citizens and were thereby put in a tenuous position in this country. They had to maintain ties with the Japanese government, the only one that represented their interests. In addition, at the urging of the Japanese Association, Japan had made every effort to ease the problem of dual citizenship. That the Nisei did not all rush to renounce their Japanese citizenship should not, according to the Issei, be understood as an affirmation of loyalty to Japan; it was, rather, a matter of their not bothering to make the effort.

Language schools were a justifiable institution. They were essential in order for parents to be able to talk with their children and teach them to be responsible citizens. It was also argued that the schools played a positive role in Americanizing the Nisei (Svensrud, 1933; Tsuboi, 1926). Besides, many ethnic groups had language schools for their youngsters and were not accused of disloyalty.

The Japanese saw the self-segregation charge as fundamentally incorrect. Admittedly, there existed among them some preference for mixing with those of similar background, but this was not unusual for immigrants. However, the major impetus for segregation came, not from the Japanese community, but from the surrounding society, which cut them off, refused to sell them real estate, and prevented them from assimilating. Societal hostility was, according to the Issei, the cause, not the result, of communal solidarity.

Here again we seem to have a conflict unresolvable within the political values and economic system dominant in the United States at the time. Before the wartime evacuation, Japanese and whites would have agreed that the Japanese community was solidary, but they would have evaluated this fact in different ways and would have disagreed about its causes.

Conflict over solidarity combined with conflict over economic matters. Assimilation—or the lack of it—would not have posed such a problem had the Japanese been economically isolated. Groups who have preserved cultural distinctiveness but combined it with a relatively limited group economy—the Amish, for example—have not provoked the same kind of concern as did the Japanese. As we have seen, though, the Japanese had developed, and were continuing to develop, considerable economic power, and this in a country where they were seen as and felt themselves to be alien. The combination was deadly in the eyes of the white population, who felt that "their" country was being taken over by an alien group.

The economic power of the Japanese Americans enabled them to evade many of the efforts to displace them. Boycotts foundered because of the need for Japanese products and services. In Seattle, for example, the number of Japanese restaurants grew despite a boycott called against them by many of the labor unions (Thomas, 1952:32). In Los Angeles, says Thomas (1952:33), "attempts to restrain Japanese competition were similarly ineffective. For example, the Immigration Commission reported a 'Gentlemen's Agreement' between laundrymen and machinery-supply houses 'to the effect that the latter shall not furnish equipment of any kind to the Japanese,' but the boycott had little support, and several of the laundries soon became mechanized." During 1941, Japanese wholesalers in Los Angeles produce markets grossed $26,500,000 (Thomas, 1952:35). Clearly, their economic power was considerable and not easily dislodged. In farming too, the Alien Land Laws were largely ineffective, as Issei farmers, able to hire lawyers, found various loopholes in the law and were able to make use of covert allies among the whites, who looked the other way. This resistance intensified the determination of hostile groups to use the government to abate the so-called Japanese menace. Exclusion followed the Immigration Act of 1924; finally, war with Japan provided the Pacific Coast with the excuse for finding what many hoped would be a "final solution."

The fears that laid the stage for the wartime evacuation were present long before Pearl Harbor, as shown in an exerpt from *California and the Oriental* (California State Board of Control, 1922:107), under the heading "Menace in Alien Fishing Fleet":

It is very significant to note that the increase in Japanese fishermen . . . from the license year 1915-16 to the license year 1919-20 was 168 percent or 825 persons, while all of the other nationalities combined increased but 2.07 percent or 88 persons. . . . For the fishing fleet, operating off our coast, to be manned by an alien people involves several factors vital to the best interests of this country, amounting, in fact, to potential dangers. (1) Is it good public policy at any time, whether at peace or in war, to have so important a food as the fish supply monopolized by peoples of an alien race? The growth of the fish industry has made it one of the principal sources of food supply of the state. (2) The fishing boats in their daily and constant travels in and out and up and down the coast acquire an intimate knowledge of the coast line, harbors and defenses, which is not only exceedingly valuable if used for the benefit of our country, but would be extremely dangerous to us and serviceable to an enemy during a period of war.

The report goes on to cite two other dangers associated with an alien fishing fleet: the loss of a potential coastal patrol in time of war and the use of such a fleet in illegal immigration. (Note that these concerns were being voiced in 1920!)

THE WARTIME EVACUATION

The evacuation of all persons of Japanese ancestry from the Pacific Coast states has received various interpretations. One major school of thought is that it was the culmination of a tradition of racist thought in the West (tenBroek, Barnhart, and Matson, 1954; Daniels, 1971). The Japanese immigrants had been subjected to hostile stereotypes almost from the time of their first arrival. As Daniels (1971:xiv) states: "The evacuation. . . grew directly out of the American experience. Although it affected only a tiny segment of our population, it reflected one of the central themes of American history—the theme of white supremacy, of American racism."

We concur in Daniels' rejection of the idea that the evacuation was merely a "wartime mistake." The racism interpretation of the sorry event, however, by no means exhausts its significance. The Japanese were evacuated, in part, because of their peculiar position in American society. As a middleman minority, they were both economically concentrated and socially isolated; the war provided an opportunity for concerns arising from these two factors to be acted upon.

Of the two themes, concern over Japanese American social isolation, stemming from society's fear of alien disloyalty (as would be expected in view of United States wartime propaganda) was more immediately obvious. Even those who advocated evacuation, however, recognized that there were differences in degrees of loyalty within the Japanese American community. That they nevertheless pushed for evacuation of the entire ethnic group reflects, in part, their belief that this community was more solidary than most, could not be categorized by outsiders as loyal or disloyal, and was too solidary for those Japanese loyal to the United States—even if a substantial majority—to cooperate in handing over the disloyal to the proper authorities. Attorney General Earl Warren of California made this point to Congress' Select Committee Investigating National Defense Migration—commonly known as the Tolan Committee—which was examining the necessity for evacuation:

> I had together about 10 days ago about 40 district attorneys and about 40 sheriffs in the State to discuss this alien problem. I asked all of them collectively at that time if in their experience any Japanese, whether California-born or Japanese-born, had ever given them any information on subversive activities or any disloyalty to this country. The answer was unanimously that no such information had ever been given them (U.S. Congress, House, Select Committee Investigating National Defense Migration, 1942:141).

This fear was exacerbated by the social isolation of the ethnic group and the lack of familiarity with its internal politics. S. W. Spangler, vice president of the Seattle First National Bank, was one of the witnesses who voiced this concern before the Tolan Committee:

> We here on the coast—I think I am correct in including the whole coast—are more disposed to consider the Japanese as a problem for the reason that they, differing from the Germans and Italians, remain in blocs, so to speak. They preserve a group identity which you will not find generally to be the case with the other nationalities. Therefore, I think that we are more disposed to think of them, not only in terms of numbers, but in their adhesiveness as groups. I would be very loath to think a vast number of friends of mine who are Japanese, who have been living here for many years, some of them—and many of them are

citizens—I should be very loath to believe that any considerable number of them lack loyalty to the extent of being a dangerous element to the Government. At the same time, I perhaps should confess that I have very scant, and perhaps not sufficient, basis for knowing which is the correct interpretation; that is, whether or not you can rely upon them (U.S. Congress, House, Select Committee Investigating National Defense Migration, 1942:143).

Economic motives behind the evacuation are harder to uncover because, in the context of a grave national emergency when selfish interests are supposed to be suspended, almost nobody wanted to admit them. For the economic-interest groups that had wanted the Japanese removed from the Pacific Coast well before, however, the war provided and opportunity to implement this desire. Grodzins (1949:19-61) describes the activities of a number of economic pressure groups, including the Western Growers Protective Association, the Grower-Shipper Vegetable Association, the California Farm Bureau Federation, and various labor groups, most of whom were affiliated with the American Federation of Labor.

A representative of the Associated Produce Dealers and Brokers of Los Angeles testified before the Tolan Committee:

I have talked to many wholesaler growers of vegetables for the local market who have either gone out of business in the past 10 years or greatly reduced their operations due to Japanese competition of a type which they could not meet and who are willing to plant increased acreage especially for the local market if they have any assurance they would not have to meet the competition of the Japanese family. . . . In small acreages planted primarily for local markets the Japanese grower has had an advantage over the white grower that has pretty well driven the white grower out of small-scale vegetable production in many parts of Los Angeles County. These farms will average around 10 acres and the Japanese farmer can and does use his wife and children for practically all his labor requirements giving him a production cost substantially below that of a small white farmer. A comprehensive system of associations set up for these small Japanese farmers has enabled them to regulate market supplies, and reduce prices at will, to the point that the competing white grower has been forced out of production. However, there is a vast reserve of skilled white farmers who will resume the production of vegetables whenever they have any idea that it can be done without going up against this type of Japanese competition (U.S.

Congress, House, Select Committee Investigating National Defense Migration, 1942:145).

Herein lies an important precondition to the evacuation.

The evacuation itself was considerably more complex than these immediate motives of the Pacific Coast population would suggest. A history of deteriorating international relations and of struggle for hegemony in the Pacific arena by two competing systems of national interest contributed to suspicions regarding the Japanese American minority and the plans of Japan for that minority. Our point is not that the middleman-minority position of the Japanese is the sole explanation of the wartime tragedy, but that it was an important—and neglected—component.

It is clear, then, that a conflict between the Japanese community and the surrounding society had developed long before World War II. The antagonism faced by the Japanese drove them back into a segregated and self-protective community, where they maintained their ethnic economy but at the same time continued to run into conflict with the surrounding society. As is suggested in figure 2:1, a self-perpetuating cycle, of societal hostility and leading to communal solidarity, then leading to successful ethnic small business, and, once again, societal hostility, had been established. In farming, the cycle was perpetuated through the Alien Land Laws and farm tenancy. The existence of such laws, according to Poli and Engstrand (1945:355), "probably deterred many eligible persons of Japanese ancestry from acquiring permanent tenure status, particularly ownership of farm land, in areas where local attitudes were not favorable. Because of this uneasiness, many may have preferred tenure of land which would permit them to move on short notice if necessary—and a type of farming that requires a minimum of capital investment for permanent farm structures and perennial crops." Societal hostility had reinforced one of the economic patterns that had aroused it in the first place.

The antagonism toward the Japanese American community has manifested itself in ways that are not unique to that group. Other middleman minorities have been faced with similar hostility. The Jews in Germany are, perhaps, the most extreme example, but more recently the expulsion of Indians from Uganda was accompanied by a familiar set of accusations: they controlled certain business lines by using "unfair" business practices that made it impossible for locals to compete; they resisted assimilation, setting ethnic-group interests above national interests; and so forth. The similarity in reaction, apart from cultural differences, suggests that there is an underlying structure or relationship common to all these situations. Another commonality is that middleman minorities are typically small minorities who—despite considerable economic power—lack political power. In the long run they are likely to lose the conflict with the surrounding society, often at great personal, as well as group, loss.

5

Nisei Prewar
Position

By 1940, 42 percent of the Japanese American labor force on the Pacific Coast was Nisei (Bloom and Riemer, 1949:12). Most of these minority members were, of course, young and fairly recent entrants to the labor force. It is our purpose in this chapter to try to indicate the way in which the Nisei were involved in, and thereby attached to, the ethnic economy.

By the time of the evacuation, a number of Nisei had become independent small businessmen in their own right. Thus Bloom and Riemer (1949:80) found that 27 percent of the native-born Japanese American males engaged in agriculture in the three Pacific Coast states were farmers and farm managers, rather than employees or unpaid family workers. In Los Angeles County, Nisei were in at least nominal control of a slight majority of Japanese-run farms and three-fifths of the acreage. Nisei who had attained their majority were waiting in the wings in an additional 40 percent of the Issei-run farms (U.S. Congress, House, Select Committee Investigating National Defense Migration, 1942:11671-11672). Another area of Nisei concentration in self-employment was produce retailing; in fact, "there was a higher proportion of native-born proprietors in retail produce than in any other trade" (Bloom and Riemer, 1949:97). Nisei made up about half of the proprietors and managers in this line of work in Los Angeles County.

More typically, the Nisei before the war tended to be workers in the ethnic economy, rather than self-employed. As we pointed out earlier, the small-business economy constructed by the Issei depended heavily on unpaid family labor and paternalistic relations with employees. It was Nisei who made up an important element of this labor resource, though a shift toward including more females of both generations in the Japanese American labor force is a noteworthy trend throughout the prewar period. For instance, by 1940 no less than 39 percent of Issei women were members of the labor force, a proportion higher than that for black women at the same time.

An illustration of the importance of the Nisei contribution to the ethnic economy is provided by Broom and Kitsuse (1956:10), who, in describing the typical prewar Japanese American farm, point to "the degree to which economic activity was woven into the fabric of family life. Where the farm activity was concentrated in a few acres, it was, for the greater part of the year, strictly a family enterprise in which the activities of its members were adjusted to the demands of the work. This joint effort was coordinated by the parents so that farm duties were associated with obedience."

In the cities, too, Nisei were concentrated in jobs in the ethnic economy. In a sample of wartime evacuees who in 1940 had been working in wholesale or retail trade and personal services in San Francisco, Los Angeles, and Seattle, Thomas (1952:605) found that almost all the Nisei were either self-employed or working for Japanese employers. In San Francisco, for example, among Nisei who were not Kibei, 7 percent were self-employed and 86 percent worked for Japanese businesses. Among the Kibei, the figures were 25 percent and 68 percent, respectively. Thus, only about 7 percent of both groups of Nisei worked for non-Japanese employers. The self-employment rate was higher for Nisei in Los Angeles (16 percent) and Seattle (26 percent), but the vast majority of Nisei employees still worked for Japanese businesses.

Clerical and sales workers in Los Angeles County provide another example of the way in which the Nisei were integrated into the ethnic small-business economy. About 30 percent of the Nisei workers in Los Angeles in 1940 were classified as clerical and sales workers by the census (Bloom and Riemer, 1949:13). Among the males so classified, 13 percent were working in wholesale produce, 52 percent in retail produce, 8 percent in retail groceries, and 6 percent in other retail trades, such as cleaning and dyeing establishments (Bloom and Riemer, 1949:18). At least 79 percent of male Nisei clerical and sales workers, then, were employees of businesses that were almost certainly owned by Japanese. Within retail produce, which was one of the most important entering occupations for urban Nisei and a major source of part-time employment, Nisei made up about 85 percent of the sales clerks. One-fourth of all the sales clerks in this line were unpaid family laborers, including wives of the proprietors, while single male Nisei constituted the bulk of the paid labor force (Bloom and Riemer, 1949:97).

Altogether, it is fairly evident that most of the Nisei who were old enough to have entered the labor force were working in the ethnic economy before World War II. It is also of critical importance, however, to understand how they felt about their economic position. Were they reluctant employees in their parents' businesses, aspiring to join the nonethnic economy but pushed back into ethnic small business by racism? Or were they contentedly following in their parents' footsteps, pursuing an economic mode that held for them promise and satisfaction? The answer is important in two respects. First, it will help us determine the degree to which the ethnic economy and the link between class interest and ethnic solidarity were the result of personal choice, cultural factors, external pressures, or contextual forces. Put another way, we are trying to assess the relative importance of the impact of societal hostility and of ethnic solidarity on small-business concentration (arrows 5 and 1, respectively, in fig. 2:1). Second, it has implications for the behavior of the Nisei after the war, when, as we shall see in the next chapter, societal hostility diminished.

Extensive evidence suggests that the Nisei were dissatisfied with their role in the ethnic economy. Indeed, this dissatisfaction is what the prewar Nisei meant when they talked and wrote of the "Nisei problem." The picture was drawn as follows: the Nisei were highly motivated to obtain college education, and they hoped, after thus training themselves, to secure white-collar positions, particularly in the professions and at managerial levels in general-community concerns. On attempting to gain employment in the nonethnic world, however, they faced racism and discrimination. Consequently, they were forced back into seeking work in the firms run by their parents and their parents' colleagues. Now, not only were they overeducated for the menial jobs available, but they were forced to remain in unfortunate dependency to the same people upon whom they had always before been dependent. The paternalistic labor relations of the ethnic firm, its low pay, long hours, and expectations of loyalty, would seem suffocating to a Western-educated young person who hoped to become a doctor or an engineer. It was only because they had no choice—or so the argument ran—that the Nisei entered the ethnic economy.

Evidence of racist employment practices outside of the Japanese small-business economy is easy enough to come by. Ichihashi (1932:356-358) cites case after case in which university spokespersons point out that employers did not want Japanese graduates. For example, officials at Stanford University stated: "It is almost impossible to place a Chinese or Japanese of either the first or second generation in any kind of position, engineering, manufacturing, or business. Many firms have general regulations against employing them; others object to them on the ground that the other men employed by the firms do not care to work with them" (cited in Ichihashi, 1932:357).

Conditions within Japanese small business were also, according to the Nisei, clearly unsatisfactory in many ways. For instance, it was galling for them to be subjected to wage discrimination by Japanese employers, a not unusual practice: "In 1935 there were 76 Japanese wholesale produce houses in Seattle in which many Nisei were employed. For the same kind of work in these concerns, the Caucasian workers received from $25 to $30 per week, while the Nisei received $15 to $18. If an Issei produce merchant is questioned about lower wages for Nisei, his immediate response is that he cannot afford to pay more wages. . . . Some of the Nisei claimed that when they started working for a Japanese business, they did not even know what their wage would be" (LaViolette, 1945:80-81). This dual-wage system prompted many Nisei to try to open their own produce houses and other independent small businesses.

Dissatisfaction with these kinds of work conditions is evident in a quotation from a Nisei young man: "We had to put up with this sort of thing because jobs were so scarce and there were family obligations. My employer was a fellow church member and a friend of the family so he took advantage of me and honestly felt that he was my benefactor. The Japanese employers figured that the Nisei workers were part of a family system and that is why they took advantage. It may have been the system in Japan, but I could not take it" (cited in Light, 1972:79). (It bears repeating that this kind of labor paternalism linked with exploitation was not a peculiarly Japanese trait, but is common among all middleman minorities. Immigrant Jewish labor relations in the garment district of New York's Lower East Side are but one striking example.)

Kawai (1926:165) describes a Nisei friend who became self-employed in the ethnic economy as a fruit-stand owner. He had been an outstanding student in high school, but now saw no use in continuing his studies. His attitude was: "What's the use of going to college? I have a little fruit-stand, and I give the American customers the kind of service they want. I have a comfortable income. I am happy. But you go on to college and get a lot of theories that make you dissatisfied with the conditions of the Japanese here. You want to change things. But just the same, after graduation, you fellows come around to my fruit store begging for a job." It was with this kind of disillusionment that the Nisei were driven into ethnic small business.

Constraints on Nisei choices did not come only from racial distinctions made by the white majority; the Issei exerted pressure on their sons to work in the family businesses and eventually to take them over. One of the reasons that the first generation sent their sons to college was to bolster the family firms. Thus Ichihashi (1932:255) cites a fairly common Issei argument: "Intelligent farming requires a scientific knowledge, and successful marketing of its produce necessitates a technical commercial knowledge; the first generation are good producers, but miserable marketers, and they have to compete with educated American farmers." Similar considerations must have operated upon urban proprietors, inducing them, too, to send their sons to college.

It is quite common for middleman minorities to provide education for their children—Jews, Chinese, and Japanese, for instance, are all noted for the educational achievement of their progeny. Efforts have been made to explain this phenomenon in terms of values and beliefs, but it seems more than fortuitous that a small-business concentration and education of the second generation so often go hand in hand; the emphasis on education seems to be at least partially a product of an attempt to prepare the younger generation for independent enterprise. Thus Benedict

(1968:5-7) describes how Indian businessmen "invest" in the education and training of their sons and daughters with the express intention of seeing them return the obligation by applying their newly acquired expertise in their family's businesses. In a somewhat different vein, Maxwell (1975:485) finds that children of Chinese small-business owners in Thailand are unusually apt to receive training in the medical profession. Although such training would not be directly useful in their parents' businesses, they are being prepared to enter another independent, or self-employed, line.

Dotson and Dotson (1975:218) describe the mutal expectations of parents and children in Indian businesses in Central Africa: "In making the heavy investments in the education of its offspring, the paternal generation always thought familistically; they hoped that the young people so trained would be integrated in some fashion into a continuing extended family enterprise. The young people themselves, on the other hand, were inclined to see these opportunities as avenues to independence and respectability." Almost the identical statement might be made for Japanese Americans prior to World War II.

It was obviously advantageous to the Issei to make use of Nisei labor, and their putting pressure on the Nisei to continue within the ethnic small-business mold is perfectly understandable. These benefits sometimes clashed with Nisei interests, however. As one Nisei stated: "[The Issei employers] expected us to put in this overtime because it was supposed to be our duty to the store. Their idea was that it was the employee's responsibility to come to the aid of the company when it was busy. They certainly had funny ideas about a worker's duty to the company" (cited in Light, 1972:79).

But the desire on the part of the Issei to have their sons continue in the ethnic economy was not simply selfish. Those of the first generation had worked long and hard to establish their businesses, and naturally they did not want to see this effort go to waste by their sons moving into other lines of work. A heavy price had been paid to establish an economic foothold; one would not want it to go down the drain. After all, for whom had the price been paid if not for one's children?

Related to this was a desire on the part of the Issei to see their children stick to the ethnic community and not assimilate into American society too fully. Efforts to keep the Nisei close to the community were made through such institutions as the Japanese language schools and the practice of sending Nisei back to Japan for part of their education (the Kibei). Too, fresh memories of societal hostility (and, in the American blacks, a vivid example of the situation of a deprived minority without an ethnic economy) made their enterprises seem a bastion for the Japanese American group. Ethnic small business, ethnic identification, and ethnic community were closely aligned.

Typically, the so-called Nisei problem is seen in terms of their being squeezed by two external forces—the racism of the white community and the demands of their parents—both forces being exacerbated in the 1930s by the Great Depression. The educated Nisei were pictured as unhappy with this situation, desiring to move into the corporate or public economy. This was the analysis of the prewar situation by Nisei intellectuals (Modell, 1973), and this analysis has affected the way others have viewed it. Broom and Kitsuse (1956:7-8) summarize this perspective: "The incongruity of college graduates taking employment in produce markets, gardening routes, and small shops with scant prospects of advancement led to a growing pessimism in the Japanese population. The Issei pointed to this state of affairs as evidence that the Nisei must maintain their Japanese identity.... When the Nisei were rebellious, they were reminded that despite their education they had failed to surpass the Issei's economic achievement."

It is our impression that, in one crucial particular, this picture of the Nisei problem may be somewhat overdrawn. It is unrealistic to assume that all, or even most, of the Nisei saw the menial jobs in the ethnic economy as lifelong careers, however much Nisei intellectuals bewailed the situation. The utilization of inexpensive Nisei labor was, after all, part of an exchange process. On the job, the Nisei young man received training in how to run a business. It was often understood that he would either take over the business in the long run, or be aided in establishing a branch office of his own.

Strong (1934:8) and Ichihashi (1932:356) contend that the small size of the community ultimately limited the extent to which Nisei could advance in the ethnic economy. This view forgets, however, that Japanese American small business serviced primarily the large surrounding society, so that smallness of the minority community was no major hindrance to growth. Thus in the 1930s, for example, Los Angeles Japanese broadened the scope of their food retailing even to the point of operating one of the newly introduced supermarkets.

It is more likely that at least part of the Nisei pessimism of the 1930s stemmed from the fact that the depression inhibited the growth of ethnic businesses, as it did the growth of all business, and also coincided with the bulge in Nisei entering adulthood, a product of earlier Issei fertility patterns. In economically stable times, the Nisei might well have expected to strike out on their own fairly quickly. The problem now was not so much being stuck in the ethnic economy as it was being limited, by economic conditions, from advancing within it. Even Nisei who were dissatisfied with work conditions in the family firm did not necessarily see engaging in wage labor for a corporation as the best alternative. LaViolette (1945:80-81) points out that Nisei were dissatisfied with being paid less than white workers: "This dual wage system is one of the reasons why the Nisei are trying to push into their own produce houses or other small businesses." The situation they sought to escape was dependency, not ethnic small business.

Evidence suggesting that the Nisei were not entirely averse to active participation in the economy of their parents comes from studies on the vocational aspirations of the Nisei. Portenier (1947: 59), for example, finds that in the Heart Mountain Relocation Center in Wyoming, among those Japanese American high-school seniors who made a choice, the greatest proportion showed a preference for commerce over other vocations. Strong (1934:218) reports that the subject most preferred by Japanese American college students in California was business, including economics, with 38 percent favoring this area, while the small-business-like independent professions, including medicine, dentistry, and pharmacy, were second, with 14 percent preferring these fields. Comparing the occupations preferred by white and Nisei college men, Strong (1934:221) finds that 22 percent of the latter favored becoming a wholesaler or retailer, as compared to only 5 percent of the whites, while 34 percent of the Nisei expressed a preference for "business," as compared to 23 percent of the whites.

Another, less direct indicator of Nisei attachment to the ethnic economy is their reluctance to leave the Pacific Coast where it was based. When California Nisei fourteen years old or older were asked if they would move east, "say, to Columbus, Ohio," if their monthly income were to be augmented by a sure $50, fewer than half said they would do so, and even this figure may be

upwardly biased by embarrassment in front of those of the interviewers who were Caucasian (Strong, 1934:225-229). Absence of a
good alternative was not the only thing that tied the Nisei to their
parents' economy; prospects for the future may have also played
a part.

It will probably never be possible to ascertain fully the degree
to which Nisei involvement in the ethnic economy was a matter of
choice and the degree to which it resulted from external pressure.
As Broom and Kitsuse (1956:7) point out:

> The flow of Nisei into the occupations developed by the Issei was a
> result of the convergence of several factors: the depression, which
> limited occupational opportunities that normally would have been open
> to Nisei; the inability of the Nisei to break away from the ethnic
> community, and the concomitant availability of relatively secure
> employment in ethnic occupations; and the pressures toward ethnic
> coherence in a period of crisis. Viewed in this light the apparent choice
> for the Nisei of staying in the ethnic community or breaking away was
> in fact no choice at all.

Nisei involvement in the ethnic economy had implications for
their social integration. Broom and Kitsuse (1956:8) explain that
"the flow of Nisei labor into ethnically defined occupations had
important consequences for the group's adjustment to the society
at large, for it restricted interethnic participation." In other words,
the solidarity–ethnic small business–societal hostility cycle described in the previous chapter for the Issei actually continued into
the second generation before the war. Whether motivated by
internal or external forces, the Nisei were tied to the separate and
conflicting world of their parents. This is an important fact to
remember when trying to understand why native-born American
citizens were included in the wartime evacuation.

It was not solely because of their heavy involvement in their
parents' small-business economy that the Nisei were included in
the blanket evacuation order, however. Other considerations
included the facts that most Nisei were minors and that for those
who were not, removal of the Issei would destroy their ethnic-
economy base and create a substantial welfare problem (Modell,
1977:183-189). Still, Nisei participation in the ethnic economy
and its social correlates of ethnic solidarity and separateness
undoubtedly added to the anxieties that dual citizenship, language

schools, and the presence of Kibei educated in Japan had already created among Americans. It was feared that despite American citizenship, second-generation Japanese Americans would be more loyal to the ethnic group and, ultimately, to Japan than to the country of their birth. The fact that the Nisei were entrenched in the ethnic economy did nothing to alleviate these fears and, indeed, supported them. The Nisei participated in the middleman-minority situation of their parents. Upon this foundation, war with Japan set the stage for the evacuation of American citizens of Japanese ancestry.

6

The Effects
of the War

From its inception in 1942, one of the principal explicit goals of the War Relocation Authority (WRA) in the United States was to resettle the Japanese Americans in various sections of the country outside of the evacuated zone. It was believed that dispersal of this tiny minority would lead to their acceptance and rapid assimilation. The first people to be permitted to relocate out of the WRA centers tended to move to the intermountain states, especially to Denver and Salt Lake City, but they soon began to experience antagonism from both non-Japanese and Japanese residents of these communities. The latter felt their relations with the surrounding community would be threatened by a large influx (Spicer et al., 1969:278-279). In response, the WRA tried to disperse the resettlement still further by setting up field offices around the country.

While some Japanese Americans appeared in every nonevacuated state in the country, the relocation did show some concentration. Chicago in particular became a major area of resettlement, with over one-fifth of those relocated intending to move there (Bloom and Riemer, 1949:38). Chicago emerged from the war with a Japanese American community of about 20,000 (Spicer et al., 1969:280).

Those who relocated before December 1944, when the evacuation order was rescinded and the Japanese were permitted to return to the Pacific Coast, tended to be young, single Nisei. Seventy percent were between the ages of fifteen and thirty-five (Thomas, 1952:115), and over 80 percent were from the second generation (Bloom and Riemer, 1949:36). Bogardus (1945:219) describes them as follows: "In many cases the younger and more courageous have sought resettlement first. They have gone in ones and twos, and later if opportunities have opened they have sent for other members of their families. In the early stages their resettlement has been largely a youth movement. They have been able to act as a liaison for parents or other relatives and friends, and have eased some of the adjustments of the latter."

After December 1944, evacuees were permitted to return to the Pacific Coast, and most did. On arrival, though, they faced a number of problems, including an acute housing shortage and a need to turn to public assistance for survival. In addition, some of the agitation that had preceded their removal was renewed. Daniels (1971:159-161) describes various incidents of harrassment of returnees, primarily in rural California. More important, perhaps, were renewed efforts to enforce the Alien Land Laws and to ensure that Issei not regain their prewar position in farming.

The early hostility toward those who returned did not last very long, however. Daniels (1971:162-163) attributes this to a number of factors. First, many governmental leaders now tried to ease tension rather than whip it up, as they had at the start of the war. Second, West Coast cities had grown dramatically during the war, and because many of the new migrants were black or Mexican, the Japanese "problem" now seemed minor. Third, the younger generation of West Coast residents seemed to be growing up with less anti-Oriental prejudice. And finally, numerous white organizations aimed at actively aiding the evacuees to get reestablished emerged.

One might add to this list the fact that the military defeat of the Japanese nation had removed the long-standing and tension-provoking possibility of Japan establishing a frontier on the Pacific by expanding into the coast states. And once this defeat had been accomplished, officials and citizens alike could look back on the evacuation through different eyes, with some guilt and a renewed concern over the abrogation of the Constitution. They became aware of the incongruity between the fact of the evacuation and the stated war aims of the United States. The Japanese American Citizens League's strategy of unremitting wartime cooperation pointed this out more sharply. In addition, the formation of segregated Nisei fighting units (Murphy, 1954; Shirey, 1946) and their valorous contribution to the war effort, which received WRA publicity, helped increase tolerance of the Japanese Americans. They were now seen as an abused minority, not the vanguard of a potential invasion.

On the national scene, racial discrimination had become increasingly discredited, in part because of the realization of its potential consequences in Germany and in part because of changing foreign-policy goals after the war. The United States, which had emerged from the war as the dominant world power with widespread influence in nonwhite countries, could no longer afford to sustain an embarrassing race problem at home. The trend was distinctly away from the previous overtly racist policies, especially those toward blacks, and this set the tone for a shift in the treatment of other racial minorities as well, including Japanese Americans.

All these factors may have played a part in the postwar drop in antagonism, but of critical importance in our view is the fact that, at least immediately after the war, the Japanese American prewar relationship with the surrounding society was not recreated. Their position as a middleman minority was, at least temporarily, destroyed, and thus one of the important bases for societal hostility was not reestablished.

OCCUPATIONAL CHANGES

In the years immediately following the evacuation, the ethnic economy was basically not recreated. Bloom and Riemer (1949: 39-43) describe the changes in the predominantly Nisei community of Chicago in 1947. Looking at the 46 percent of the Japanese American labor force in Chicago who derived from Los Angeles County before the war, these researchers found that 8 percent of the males were proprietors in 1947, compared to 36 percent in Los Angeles in 1941. These proprietors mainly operated boarding-houses for Japanese and were not servicing the general community. The decline in unpaid family labor was even more precipitous: over one-quarter of those who came from Los Angeles had worked in that capacity before the war, but in Chicago only 1 percent were so employed.

Some of the Nisei who moved to Chicago entered the labor force for the first time, but regardless of whether or not they had worked before, the ethnic group as a whole showed an occupational shift into the employ of non-Japanese corporations. New concentrations developed in skilled and semiskilled occupations as the Nisei moved into the war-related industries that burgeoned during this period.

Speaking in general of the areas of resettlement (not specifically of the West Coast), Spicer et al. (1969:284) state:

> In economic matters, in matters of survival, the Japanese were a relatively undifferentiated segment of the population of the cities in which they settled. True, there were some Japanese stores, restaurants, and professionals that catered to the Japanese. But the income that supported these services to consumers was derived from diversified kinds of activity carried on in many different lines. There was nothing comparable to the well-knit complex of growing, wholesaling, and retailing of produce that the Japanese had built up on the West Coast.

In the rural areas of the Pacific Coast states, returning evacuees suffered a mixed fate economically. For those who had owned farmland outright, as in the Hood River Valley of Oregon, return to prewar proprietorship was possible (Spicer et al., 1969: 288). In most rural areas, though, rental land had been irretrievably lost to others. Owned land, too, had often been sold, and many farmers who returned either moved to the cities or were forced to engage in farm labor. Poli and Engstrand (1945: 363-364) concluded that the obstacles to reestablishing Japanese farms made it doubtful "that the Japanese-American [would] soon regain any prominence in the agriculture of the West Coast."

In urban areas as well, the Japanese Americans engaged in business had generally been dispossessed, and they found it difficult after the war to get reestablished. Miyamoto and O'Brien (1947:153) report that in Seattle there was a "greater dependence [after the war] upon Caucasian employers rather than Japanese-American enterprisers" and a "decline in specialization in certain types of private trade." Before the war, Japanese Americans in Seattle operated 206 hotels, 140 groceries, 94 cleaning establishments, 64 market stands, and 57 wholesale produce houses. After the war only "a handful of these establishments" continued operating, and these functioned on a small scale and catered primarily to Japanese.

The decline in Japanese American business was accompanied

by an increase in employment in the general (nonethnic) economy. Miyamoto and O'Brien (1947:153) describe this shift:

> The decline in Japanese-American enterprises has resulted in a corre-
> sponding decrease in the number of clerical workers employed in such
> business. On the other hand, these workers have been largely absorbed
> into Caucasian agencies and firms, as, for example, in Civil Service
> positions which have become a major occupational outlet, particularly
> for the veterans and girls with office training. Similarly, though there
> has been a decrease of operatives in Japanese-owned small industries,
> such as laundries, there is an increase of pressers and power-machine
> operators in Caucasian-owned textile fabricating industries. The largest
> single group of employees today is the building service workers, most of
> whom are employed by several of the leading Seattle hotels and three
> major hospitals, which hired almost no Japanese-Americans prior to the
> war.

Bloom and Riemer's Los Angeles study revealed that, whereas 72
percent of their sample were in family enterprises before the war,
only 17.5 percent of the same people were so engaged in 1946
(Bloom and Riemer, 1949:43-45).

The complex organization of the produce industry was
destroyed by the war. Many truck farmers, especially tenants, lost
their land. Some reentry into wholesaling occurred but came
nowhere near that of prewar levels, and the small wholesalers were
less able to survive (Bloom and Riemer, 1949:109-110). Retail
operations had also declined and, with them, the link between
wholesaling and retailing. Bloom and Riemer (1949:110-111)
report:

> Very little of the produce handled by the wholesalers in our sample was
> going to Japanese American retailers. For instance, of 250 retailers
> having accounts with one Japanese American commission house early in
> 1948, only 16 percent were Japanese Americans. Wholesalers were
> dealing predominantly with chain stores or shippers. This was far
> different from the prewar situation, when at least 50 percent of the
> volume of most Japanese American wholesalers went to local indepen-
> dent retailers, most of them Japanese Americans.

The vertical integration of the produce industry had been
destroyed.

A fine WRA study, completed about two years after the West Coast was reopened to the Japanese, found the same shift from proprietorship in the ethnic economy to employment in the general economy (U.S. War Agency Liquidation Unit, 1947:82-100). Despite these trends the study noted the seeds of a new business community among the former evacuees. Its examination of postwar business conditions in Los Angeles, however, reveals several telling differences from the prewar situation within the embryonic business community.

First, control shifted to the Nisei. Second, businesses depending primarily on a Japanese clientele generally failed, with the exception of cheap hotels catering to temporarily impoverished returnees and thought to be of little long-term profitability. In Little Tokyo, smarter entrepreneurs were looking to black customers. Another shift, already mentioned, was the breakup of the produce industry, but, surprisingly, the flower industry still showed signs of vitality. Even here, however, the competition from whites was much stiffer than before the war. To the extent that small business was emerging, the particular lines of concentration were changing; new focal businesses were hotels, contract gardening, and restaurants. Finally, immediate postwar enterprise faced an intense internal competition, which, at least in the perceptions of the Japanese Americans themselves, was new. To quote a columnist in a vernacular newspaper:

> Competition, fierce now, threatens to become worse as charges of cut-throating and price-cutting are being bruited about in the best non-union manner. Disgruntled Nisei gardeners, fearing that unfair price slashing and underselling of labor will inevitably force them out of business and deprive them of a livelihood, charge the Issei element with practices inimical to their welfare. Almost indefensible, the Issei can only point to their distinct handicap in language, in rebuttal, and blithely go on working for less—unless something is done to set prices (cited in U.S. War Agency Liquidation Unit, 1947:96).

The Nisei, ironically, sound like prewar white competitors. It is apparent that the social bases of the ethnic economy had, at this point, fallen into disarray.

By way of summary, table 6:1 presents changes in occupations of Japanese Americans from 1940 to 1950 (or from pre- to postwar times), as reported by the census. As can be seen, female

TABLE 6:1

PERCENTAGE CHANGE IN JAPANESE OCCUPATIONS BY TYPE, 1940-1950

	Total	*Males*	*Females*
Professionals	+142%	+171%	+203%
Farmers and farm managers	−14	−15	+6
Proprietors and managers	−29	−32	−12
Clerical and sales workers	+60	+3	+156
Craftsmen and foremen	+189	+193	+133
Operatives	+100	+45	+220
Domestic service workers	−5	−30	+14
Other service workers	+29	+39	+13
Unpaid farm workers	−56	−58	−53
Paid farm workers	−9	−20	+77
Laborers	+28	+28	+43
Total	+16	+3	+55

SOURCES: U.S. Bureau of the Census, 1943:47; Census of Population, 1950, Special Reports, vol. 4, pt. 3 (U.S. Bureau of the Census, 1953), pp. 3B-38.

participation in the labor force increased sharply (perhaps reflecting a shift out of unpaid family labor which had previously gone unreported), so that in most occupations there was a rise. The relative increase across occupations is a better indicator of how ethnic economic behavior altered than is the absolute rise or fall in percentage.

Farm ownership and management declined after the war, and more precipitously, so did their work force, especially unpaid family labor. This shows clearly that the essence of the ethnic economy had disintegrated under the impact of the war. Urban proprietorships took a similar turn downward, while craftsmen/operatives and professionals more than doubled. These latter occupations all had much higher proportions working for employers in the corporate or public sector of the economy.

Altogether, the postwar period marked a major shift in the nature of Japanese American economic adaptation. The ethnic economy had been more or less destroyed, and the returnees moved in large numbers into the employ of non-Japanese corporations, where they were enumerated in 1950.

CAUSES OF OCCUPATIONAL CHANGES

A number of factors probably played a part in this dramatic shift. First, and most obvious, was the loss incurred by the evacuation itself, so that, at least in the short run, it would have been extremely difficult to resurrect the original family firms. Some sense of the magnitude of property loss sustained by the Japanese Americans can be derived from the claims put in by evacuees during the year and a half they were permitted to do so following the passage of the Evacuation Claims Act of 1948. No fewer than 23,000 unique claims (or about one per family) were submitted, with an aggregate face value of $133 million, or a mean of almost $5,800 per family. While some claimants may have exaggerated, many could not document their losses, and there were some losses, such as the goodwill of a clientele built up over the years, which were inestimable. The distribution of claims was as follows: 2,371 asked for $0–$500; 3,305 for $500–$1,000; 8,239 for $1,000–$2,500; 3,909 for $2,500–$5,000; 4,393 for $5,000–$25,000; 662 for $25,000–$100,000; and 66 for $100,000 or more (U.S. Congress, Senate, 1951; U.S. Congress, House, 1956). These figures point to the substantial economic position of the ethnic economy prior to the war, as well as to the blow it suffered as a consequence of the evacuation.

Added to financial loss was the fact that the Issei were aging. In Seattle, the average age of returning Issei was sixty-one (Miyamoto and O'Brien, 1947). Their energetic youth had been spent in establishing their businesses, and it now seemed impossible to start all over again. The rate of dependency on public assistance jumped dramatically (though only temporarily) from its nearly nonexistent level before the war.

Another factor in the shift away from the ethnic economy was the order in which people left the camps. Among the male Nisei, the prewar occupational group with the lowest rate of voluntary emergence from camp by the end of 1944 was agriculturalists, with 54 percent having departed by that date. Next lowest in departure rate were professionals and managers. Among male Issei, the pattern was similar, though the overall departure rate was much lower. Twelve percent of the agriculturalists had emerged by the end of 1944, the lowest rate, while 17 percent for professionals and managers marked the second-lowest Issei rate.

Since six in ten of the Nisei professional/managerial people were entrepreneurs or managers of small businesses, and eight in ten of the Issei group, we can probably conclude that the ones most hesitant to reenter the larger society were those whose economic basis had been most fully destroyed by the evacuation: the classic participants in the ethnic economy (U.S. War Relocation Authority, n.d.:51). Thus the first to resettle or return to the Pacific Coast were those least experienced in running businesses, the segment of the Japanese American community least able to reconstruct an economy they had not controlled. Moreover, they returned to an altered world. The depression had been broken by the war. In Chicago, for example, war industries were booming. The job discrimination against them in the corporate and public economy was much reduced. The Nisei could find jobs as white-collar and skilled blue-collar workers. They no longer need to be "carrot washers." Thus the first to return to the world outside of the relocation camps, who might have laid the foundations for an ethnic-economy revival, were able, instead, to move rapidly in the opposite direction.

Meanwhile, changes in the nature of retailing, already a looming threat to the Issei ethnic economy before the war, had continued to the disadvantage of small business in general. In the food industry, supermarkets proliferated, enabling the corporate economy to cut its labor costs drastically. The expansion of chain operations meant that farm produce could be delivered directly to retail outlets, bypassing the middleman wholesaler. The small independent grocery store was no longer a competitive form, no matter how many hours its owners kept it open or how many family members worked for nothing (U.S. Temporary National Economic Committee, 1941:pt. II). Mechanization in other lines had a similar effect. Capital requirements grew markedly, as new economies of scale were achieved. Small business in the United States in general was on the decline, and Japanese American small business was affected by the same forces.

Job discrimination against the Nisei may have declined for various reasons. Perhaps exogenous factors, such as the wartime defeat of Japan or guilt over the evacuation, played a part. Perhaps the fact that the ethnic economy had been virtually destroyed meant that the surrounding society no longer saw Japanese as threatening and was now willing to open its doors to them. Or perhaps the end of the depression, with more jobs available to all, was the key factor. Regardless, we find a double force impelling the Nisei into the corporate economy: they could not any longer get jobs in their parents' firms, and they could get desirable, nonmenial jobs in the outside world.

It might be suggested that the rapid movement into the nonethnic economy after the war proves that the Nisei as a group had really been eager to escape the ethnic small-business economy before the war and jumped at the chance as soon as it was offered. No such conclusion can be drawn, however. The behavior of the Nisei was less a product of choice than of circumstances and does not by itself reveal motivation. Before the war the Nisei had no choice but to work in their parents' businesses; after the war their only option was to work in the general economy.

The changing employment of the Nisei meant that the potential reestablishment of ethnic small business was dealt another blow. Its inexpensive and reliable work force had disappeared. The paternalistic system of offering jobs in exchange for on-the-job training was no longer in operation. And, like vertical integration, such a delicately balanced system was difficult to reconstruct, especially in view of the uncertainties introduced by postwar changes in retailing techniques, organization, and scale.

Thus, Nisei who were able to establish their own small businesses did so under altered conditions. They could not rely on communal resources for a labor supply, and so they either engaged in self-employed occupations that did not require help, such as gardening, or turned to other sources of cheap labor, such as Mexican farm workers. For those who returned to produce wholesaling, the chief outlet was no longer individual Japanese American retailers, but buyers from large supermarkets (Iwata, 1962:34). Informal mechanisms of capital accumulation, which, according to Light (1972), were so crucial to first-generation entrepreneurs, were no longer adequate to the new scale of postwar enterprise. These and similar changes put Nisei small business on a much more even footing with nonethnic businesses.

SOCIAL CHANGES

Partly as a consequence of these shifts, and partly causing them, were changes in the social position of the Japanese American community. Initially isolated socially from the surrounding society, after the war the Japanese American community became increasingly (although not totally) integrated into it.

First of all, any lingering idea of returning to Japan was totally destroyed by the war. The military defeat of Japan, followed by an American occupation, meant that living there was not a viable alternative. Despite the constitutional and personal horror of the evacuation, only 4½ percent of the evacuated Japanese Americans chose to depart for Japan (U.S. War Relocation Authority, n.d:196).

Second, the war had weakened the organization of the Japanese community. Much has been written describing the loss of leadership of the Issei in the camps and the rise to power of an inexperienced young Nisei leadership. The Nisei had nowhere near the extensive network of mutually interdependent organizations evolved by the Issei and before the war had been too young to take over these organizations from their parents. The organizational basis of the ethnic economy had thus been largely destroyed by the war, a factor that undoubtedly contributed to its failure to reestablish itself immediately after the war.

The fact that the ethnic economy was much weakened meant that there was no longer so strong an interest in retaining exclusive ethnic organizations. Farmers who were now unable to use Japanese farm labor and who, like their non-Japanese neighbors, were relying on Mexican workers had no reason to maintain the institutions that had been appropriate for the prewar situation. The shift toward common interests with other farmers is captured by Iwata (1962:34):

> Since World War II the Japanese farmers have not organized into farm associations limited to their own ethnic group. More and more of them, especially in Los Angeles County, are being accepted by and are joining Caucasian organizations, particularly the Farm Bureau Federation. The Japanese farmers have discovered that nominal annual dues paid to the local County Farm Bureau bring them greater benefits than would membership in organizations limited to their own ethnic group.

The Japanese farmers were no longer in competition with fellow farmers on anything more than an individual basis. They no longer had a separate set of class interests, but had become part of the general class of farmers. The class basis of ethnic solidarity had been weakened, and the effects were seen in new organizational alignments.

As workers, too, the Nisei became more open to joining nonethnic organizations. Again the interest structure had changed. As employees of large corporations rather than of ethnic small businesses, they had every reason to join the unions of fellow workers who shared identical class interests. As Rademaker (1945: 99) notes, the Nisei now tried to avoid being used as scabs and openly welcomed trade-union membership. In the postwar atmosphere, such advances were not rejected.

It can be seen, then, that the postwar period marks a decided change in the position of the Japanese American community. A very marked shift out of the ethnic economy and into an employee status in the nonethnic, corporate world occurred, along with a concomitant shift into a more integrated social relationship with the surrounding society. The peculiar middleman-minority position had been broken up. The complex of interdependent factors depicted in figure 2:1 was now destroyed. As a result, the deadly economic competition with other powerful classes was over. The Japanese American community was no longer seen or treated as an undigested, unassimilable element in the body politic. In a word, the Japanese American community was on the road to becoming integrated, both economically and socially, into the larger American community. These changes help to explain why the prewar Japanese could be hated as a "yellow peril" and the postwar Japanese hailed as one of America's "most successful minorities."

Part II

NISEI DIFFERENTIATION AND ITS CAUSES

7

Current Economic Position of the Nisei

If the prewar ethnic economy of the Japanese Americans was ever going to be reestablished, by 1960 enough time would have passed for it to have made itself visible. For the remainder of this volume we will examine the Nisei in the mid-1960s, mainly using data collected by the JARP survey (see Appendix A) in order to explore what happens to the second generation of a middleman-minority immigrant group under conditions of advanced capitalism.

Table 7:1 shows the shifts in occupation within the minority (according to the United States census) between 1950, when the wartime destruction of Japanese small business still held sway, and 1960, by which time the ethnic economy had had a chance to regenerate. We find that both farming and proprietary/managerial occupations showed an upswing in this decade (after a decline during the war and postwar periods; see table 6:1). We must be cautious in interpreting the proprietary/managerial category, since by 1960 a much higher proportion of Japanese Americans could have been managers in non–Japanese American businesses.

While we cannot tell from these data whether urban proprietorships regained their "cheap" labor force, it is evident that farming continued to lose its Japanese American workers. This suggests that even if ethnic small business was being rebuilt, its structure was modified in the postwar period. While thrift could remain as a characteristic of Japanese American business practice, the familial and community cooperation that had been no less

TABLE 7:1

PERCENTAGE CHANGE IN JAPANESE AMERICAN OCCUPATIONS
BY TYPE, 1950-1960

	Total	*Males*	*Females*
Professionals	+292%	+347%	+195%
Farmers and farm managers	+76	+74	+114
Proprietors and managers	+63	+65	+50
Clerical and sales workers	+121	+103	+133
Craftsmen and foremen	+82	+79	+135
Operatives	+56	+48	+65
Domestic service workers	+5	−45	+28
Other service workers	+21	−14	+97
Farm workers	−31	−32	−28
Laborers	−38	−39	+39
Total	+63	+52	+85

SOURCES: Census of Population, 1950, Special Reports, vol. 4, pt. 3 (U.S. Bureau of the Census, 1953), pp. 3B-38; Census of Population, 1960, Subject Reports, Nonwhite Population by Race, Final Report PC(2)-1C (U.S. Bureau of the Census, 1963), pp. 142, 152.

central was seemingly less in evidence in 1960. As we shall see, extended education among younger Japanese Americans explains much of this decline and is part of a new recruitment pattern that reflects and emphasizes the decreasing attraction of the ethnic economy, although, again, table 7:1 does show signs at least of a partial regeneration.

The prewar ethnic economy was most seriously resuscitated by the oldest Japanese Americans, as table 7:2 indicates. Comparing Japanese American participation in the economy in terms of industrial distribution in 1930, when the ethnic economy was at its height, with 1960, we find an overall shift out of agriculture and service into trade and the professions by the later date (table 7:2). If we compare the data on those sixty-five and older in 1960 to the data for the same cohort in 1930—the thirty-five- to forty-four-year-olds—we see quite remarkable similarities. Indeed, for this group, the proportions both in agriculture and in trade were greater by 1960 than they had been in 1930; yet for the next youngest cohort—those who were forty-five to sixty-four in 1960—the return to agriculture was not fully accomplished. The

TABLE 7:2
INDUSTRIAL DISTRIBUTION OF JAPANESE AMERICAN LABOR FORCE
BY AGE, 1930 AND 1960 (MALE AND FEMALE COMBINED)

	To 25	*25-34*	Age *35-44*	*45-64*	*65+*
1930					
Agriculture, forestry, mining, fishing	40.0%	40.9%	40.8%	54.3%	51.8%
Manufacturing, mechanical, construction	7.5	7.7	6.9	6.9	8.8
Transportation, communication, public service	8.4	7.4	6.4	5.3	4.0
Wholesale and retail trade	19.1	18.1	15.7	10.3	7.1
Domestic and personal service	20.9	21.5	25.5	20.6	24.1
Professional service	4.0	4.4	4.5	2.6	4.2
Total	100.0	100.0	100.0	100.0	100.0
1960					
Agriculture, forestry, mining, fishing	14.7	13.5	22.4	29.6	48.1
Manufacturing, mechanical, construction	16.4	23.8	19.6	16.1	7.4
Transportation, communication, public service	7.9	11.3	9.2	4.3	1.0
Wholesale and retail trade	31.8	27.5	28.3	24.9	18.6
Domestic and personal service	8.5	5.3	8.0	16.7	25.6
Professional service	20.6	18.6	12.4	8.4	5.6
Total	100.0	100.0	100.0	100.0	100.0

SOURCE: For 1930: Fifteenth Census of the United States, 1930, Population, vol. V, General Report on Occupations (U.S. Bureau of the Census, 1933), pp. 210-213. For 1960: Census of Population, 1960, Subject Reports, Nonwhite Population by Race, Final Report PC(2)-1C (U.S. Bureau of the Census, 1963), p. 182.

occupational distribution, too, was distinctly new. Those who were under forty-five in 1960 were principally Nisei, and here is where the industrial shift was most marked.

The JARP survey allows us to look far more closely at the concept of ethnic economy than does the census and, more importantly, allows us to explore the social correlates of economic form. In addition, the survey permits us to isolate the second generation, thereby simplifying the issues under discussion. Unfortunately, the JARP survey focused more than we do here on questions of status rather than of class, and we are not able to explore the topic of Japanese American small business in as much descriptive detail as we would wish. We are forced, as the reader will see, to make certain inferences in order to find out the degree to which ethnic small business has been reestablished and the mechanisms by which this concentration has been maintained.

As chapter 3 has discussed, middleman small business among the Japanese Americans was characterized by self-employment or potential self-employment among current employees, the use of unpaid family or below-market-wage labor, a preference for hiring relatives or family acquaintances and for developing paternalistic labor relations, and the communal accumulation and distribution of resources and control of competition. Our questionnaire offers clear information on only two components of this complex: self-employment and employment by other Japanese Americans. Recognizing that these are imperfect indicators of the larger phenomenon, we will hereinafter employ these two variables as an indicator of a return to something resembling the parental economic form. We do not contend that the indicator is ideal: it probably overstates the degree of return to the ethnic-economic form and thereby weakens the differentials we will discuss in subsequent chapters. Though annoying, the flaw is not disabling, but it is of the order that investigators (both sociological and sociohistorical) ordinarily face in using data to answer questions not anticipated by the creators of those data. We will, then, depend upon the JARP Nisei data to demonstrate, first, the bearing of economic form, or class, upon several aspects of Japanese American ethnicity, and, second, the future of the Japanese Americans as a distinct community in American society.

The proportion of males in the JARP Nisei sample who were self-employed (including the spouses of married sample females) was 40 percent (of 2,083), a proportion more than three times as great as 1970 census figures showed for the general population of males sixteen years old and older. Some of the firms of these self-employed men were probably not part of an ethnic economy in that they did not use unpaid family labor, had unionized work forces that did not have any paternalistic tie with the owners, and so on.

A small majority of the self-employed (eighty-three individuals, or 4 percent of the sample) told us that they primarily served the Japanese American community. This group was unambiguously participating in the ethnic economy; but serving the ethnic community is not an essential feature of the classic middleman minority—quite the contrary; as we have seen, the clientele of the typical prewar Issei firm was not primarily Japanese American. The ethnic economy served the surrounding society, including other minority groups, even in its earliest days, and so do the self-employed Nisei.

Sixty percent of the male Nisei in the mid-1960s were employees. Of these, 10 percent were working in firms that they identified as Japanese American.[1] These employees, together with the self-employed, will be treated as working within the Japanese American ethnic economy. Forty-seven percent of the males (including spouses of married females) in our sample were working in the ethnic economy; the balance were employees in non-Japanese American firms. Although we cannot distinguish whether they worked in public bureaucracies or private firms, we lump these together as workers in the corporate economy, organized in most cases along lines quite different from those of the ethnic economy.

As we earlier showed, the classic ethnic economy maintained its form in part through distinctive recruitment patterns. It stands to reason that among those who reestablished the modified postwar ethnic economy would be an overly high proportion of those whose careers showed signs of these kinds of recruitment. Thus, a small test of the validity of our ethnic-economy indicator is to examine it in connection with a survey question regarding the family economic assistance respondent Nisei had received. The Nisei were presented with the following question:

> Here is a list of some types of aid families can give. For each one, we would like to know whether you received such aid from anyone in your family or your wife's family.
>
> Advice in choosing a career

1. It is possible that some of the Japanese employers of Nisei belonged to the group of firms from Japan which have set up branches in the United States since the war. This group is not part of the pattern we described for the Issei, resembling more the corporate organization of white businesses than the independent small businesses of the immigrants. We do not know what proportion, if any, of Nisei employees in firms with Japanese employers worked for such businesses, but assume it must have been small, given the timing of the survey. Large-scale Japanese investment in the United States is mainly a phenomenon of the middle 1970s.

Work for pay, even part time, in a business or farm owned by
members of the family
Help in acquiring a farm
Help in acquiring a business
Help in getting a job

Since married women responded for themselves, not for their
husbands, we report the results of the male respondents alone. Of
those Nisei men whom we have classified as being part of the
ethnic economy, 62 percent had received some aid other than
advice from their family. In contrast, 43 percent of corporate-
economy Nisei had received such aid. Thirty-six percent of those
in Japanese American businesses at the time of the survey had
worked for pay in a family business, 41 percent had received
family help in acquiring a farm or business, and 21 percent had
been given help by their families in getting a job. These findings
are reminiscent of prewar patterns.

Table 7:3 presents a complete list of the occupations found
among the male Nisei in our sample. The total (column 1) combines persons in the corporate economy and those in ethnic small
business (columns 2 and 3, respectively). The figures in the next
two columns represent a breakdown of the ethnic-small-business
group, which here is divided into the self-employed and employees. The last column, a further subclassification of the self-
employed, gives us the distribution of the special subgroup that
reported serving the Japanese American community.

Setting aside the small-business/corporation distinction for
the moment, let us consider whether the occupational distribution
of the Nisei was unusual in any way. Table 7:4 groups the
occupations into six occupational types. We can generally expect
that those higher on this dimension earned more money and were
especially likely to have received more education. Thus in exploring Nisei economic activity, we shall consider two dimensions that
are related to each other (though not in a linear way): occupational type and type of firm.

In comparing the 1960 and 1970 census findings for the
entire mainland Japanese American population, it is evident that
major shifts have occurred over the last ten years, with a movement out of farming and into the professions and service work/
labor. The JARP sample, collected midway between the two
censuses, would appear to be overrepresented in professional and

DETAILED OCCUPATION AND TYPE OF FIRM FOR MALE NISEI (MALES AND MARRIED FEMALES REPORTING)

	Total	Corporate Economy	Japanese American Small Business	Self-employed	Employee of Japanese American	Self-employed Serving Japanese Americans
All occupations	1998	1049	949	829	107	81
Professional, technical, and kindred workers	640	508	132	117	15	17
Accountants and auditors	47	36	11	8	3	3
Actors	1	1	0	0	0	0
Architects	19	12	7	6	1	1
Artists and art teachers	21	15	6	6	0	0
Authors	2	2	0	0	0	0
Chiropractors	3	0	3	3	0	0
Clergymen	8	2	6	2	4	2
College professors	21	19	2	2	0	0
Dentists	26	0	26	26	0	3
Designers	20	19	1	1	0	0
Dietitians and nutritionists	1	1	0	0	0	0
Draftsmen	21	20	1	0	1	0
Editors and reporters	5	4	1	0	1	0
Engineers	179	166	13	12	1	0

TABLE 7:3 (Continued)

DETAILED OCCUPATION AND TYPE OF FIRM FOR MALE NISEI (MALES AND MARRIED FEMALES REPORTING)

	Total	Corporate Economy	Japanese American Small Business	Self-employed	Employee of Japanese American	Self-employed Serving Japanese Americans
Professional, technical, and kindred workers (continued)						
Foresters and conservationists	1	1	0	0	0	0
Lawyers and judges	11	3	8	8	0	4
Musicians and music teachers	3	1	2	2	0	0
Natural scientists	50	50	0	0	0	0
Optometrists	6	1	5	5	0	0
Pharmacists	13	3	7	6	1	1
Photographers	23	16	7	6	1	0
Physicians and surgeons	29	19	10	10	0	1
Public-relations men and publicity writers	3	2	1	0	1	0
Radio operators	1	1	0	0	0	0
Recreation and group workers	1	1	0	0	0	0
Social and welfare workers except group	7	7	0	0	0	0
Social scientists	4	3	1	1	0	0

Sports instructors and officials	3	0	3	3	0	1
Surveyors	4	4	0	0	0	0
Teachers	36	36	0	0	0	0
Technicians	57	48	9	8	1	1
Therapists and healers	1	1	0	0	0	0
Professional, technical and kindred workers (other)	26	24	2	2	0	0
Managers, officials, and proprietors, excluding farm	405	124	281	252	29	28
Buyers and department heads, store	34	24	10	4	6	0
Buyers and shippers, farm products	4	0	4	2	2	0
Inspectors, public administration	7	6	1	1	0	0
Managers and superintendents, building	8	1	7	7	0	2
Officers, pilots, pursers, and engineers, ship	1	1	0	0	0	0
Officials and administrators, public administration	33	33	0	0	0	0
Officials, lodge, society, union, etc.	1	1	0	0	0	0
Postmasters	1	1	0	0	0	0
Purchasing agents and buyers (other)	45	20	25	17	8	4
Mangers and executives (other)	29	20	9	2	7	0
Managers, officials, and proprietors, manufacturing	6	1	5	5	0	0
Food and dairy-products stores	41	0	41	40	1	3

TABLE 7:3 (Continued)

DETAILED OCCUPATION AND TYPE OF FIRM FOR MALE NISEI (MALES AND MARRIED FEMALES REPORTING)

	Total	Corporate Economy	Japanese American Small Business	Self-employed	Employee of Japanese American	Self-employed Serving Japanese Americans
Managers, officials, and proprietors, excluding farm (continued)						
Eating and drinking establishments	18	3	15	15	0	0
Apparel and accessories stores	32	0	32	32	0	4
Landscape contractors	7	0	7	7	0	0
Export-import business	11	0	11	8	3	1
Dry-cleaning and laundry establishments	17	1	16	16	0	1
Construction and land development	9	1	8	8	0	1
Recreation establishments	3	1	2	2	0	0
Hotels and boardinghouses	9	0	9	9	0	0
Bankers and financiers	8	6	2	0	2	0
Automobile-repair services, garages, and gasoline sales	79	3	76	76	0	12
Managers, officials, and proprietors (other)	2	1	1	1	0	0

Craftsmen, foremen, operatives, and kindred workers	249	205	44	24	20	6
Bakers	1	0	1	1	0	0
Boilermakers	1	1	0	0	0	0
Bookbinders	1	1	0	0	0	0
Brickmasons, stonemasons, and tile setters	1	1	0	0	0	0
Cabinetmakers	2	2	0	0	0	0
Carpenters	8	3	5	5	0	3
Compositors and typesetters	7	6	1	0	1	0
Decorators and window dressers	3	1	2	2	0	0
Electricians	3	2	1	1	0	0
Excavating-, grading-, and road-machinery operators	1	1	0	0	0	0
Foremen	30	29	1	1	0	0
Inspectors	2	2	0	0	0	0
Jewelers, watchmakers, goldsmiths, and silversmiths	9	4	5	5	0	1
Job setters, metal	1	1	0	0	0	0
Linemen and servicemen, telegraph, telephone and power	3	3	0	0	0	0
Machinists	13	13	0	0	0	0
Mechanics and repairmen	88	75	13	5	8	1

DETAILED OCCUPATION AND TYPE OF FIRM FOR MALE NISEI (MALES AND MARRIED FEMALES REPORTING)

	Total	Corporate Economy	Japanese American Small Business	Self-employed	Employee of Japanese American	Self-employed Serving Japanese Americans
Craftsmen, foremen, operatives, and kindred workers (continued)						
Millwrights	1	1	0	0	0	0
Opticians and lens grinders and polishers	1	1	0	0	0	0
Painters, construction and maintenance	1	0	1	0	1	0
Pattern and model makers, except paper	3	3	0	0	0	0
Photoengravers and lithographers	1	1	0	0	0	0
Plumbers and pipe fitters	3	1	2	0	2	0
Pressmen and plate printers, printing	2	1	1	1	0	0
Stationary Engineers	2	2	0	0	0	0
Tailors	1	0	1	1	0	0
Toolmakers and die makers and setters	1	1	0	0	0	0
Upholsterers	2	2	0	0	0	0
Apprentice, metalworking trades	1	1	0	0	0	0
Assemblers	5	5	0	0	0	0
Attendants, auto service and parking	1	0	1	0	1	0

Occupation	1	2	3	4	5
Checkers, examiners, and inspectors, manufacturing	4	0	0	0	0
Deliverymen and routemen	3	2	0	2	0
Filers, grinders and polishers, metal	1	0	0	0	0
Furnace men, smelters, and purers	1	0	0	0	0
Meat cutters, excluding slaughterhouse and packing house	4	1	0	1	0
Painters, excluding construction and maintenance	3	1	0	1	0
Photographic-process workers	1	0	0	0	0
Sailors and deck hands	1	0	0	0	0
Sewers and stitchers, manufacturing	1	0	0	0	0
Taxicab drivers and chauffeurs	1	0	0	0	0
Truck and tractor drivers	7	2	0	2	0
Welders and flame cutters	2	0	0	0	0
Operatives (other)	21	18	2	3	1
Service workers and laborers, excluding farm and mine	211	38	173	168	5
Attendants, recreation and amusement establishments	1	1	0	0	0
Barbers	5	5	5	0	3
Bartenders	3	1	0	1	0
Cooks, excluding private household	3	0	0	0	0

DETAILED OCCUPATION AND TYPE OF FIRM FOR MALE NISEI (MALES AND MARRIED FEMALES REPORTING)

	Total	Corporate Economy	Japanese American Small Business	Self-employed	Employee of Japanese American	Self-employed Serving Japanese Americans
Service workers and laborers, excluding farm and mine (continued)						
Hairdressers and cosmetologists	2	0	2	1	1	0
Janitors and sextons	7	7	0	0	0	0
Firemen, fire-protection workers	1	1	0	0	0	0
Guards, watchmen, and doorkeepers	1	1	0	0	0	0
Policemen and detectives	2	2	0	0	0	0
Service workers (other)	9	1	8	7	1	0
Fishermen and oystermen	1	0	1	1	0	0
Gardeners, excluding farm, and groundskeepers	162	6	156	154	2	2
Warehousemen	10	10	0	0	0	0
Truck loaders, swampers	1	1	0	0	0	0
Laborers (other)	3	3	0	0	0	0

TABLE 7:4

OCCUPATIONAL TYPE OF NISEI SAMPLE, MAINLAND JAPANESE
AMERICAN MALES FOURTEEN AND OLDER IN 1960 CENSUS AND
SIXTEEN AND OLDER IN 1970 CENSUS, AND TOTAL UNITED STATES
MALES FOURTEEN AND OLDER IN 1960 CENSUS AND SIXTEEN AND
OLDER IN 1970 CENSUS

	Nisei Sample	Japanese American		United States	
		1960	*1970*	*1960*	*1970*
Professional, technical, and kindred workers	32%	19%	26%	10%	14%
Managers, officials and proprietors, excluding farm	20	10	11	11	11
Clerical, sales, and kindred workers	11	12	15	14	14
Farmers and farm managers, laborers, and foremen	14	26	7	8	5
Craftsmen, foremen, operatives, and kindred workers	12	21	22	42	41
Service workers, and laborers, excluding farm	11	12	19	14	15
Total	100	100	100	100	100
	(1998)	(62,848)	(88,666)	(43,562,353)	(47,730,661)

SOURCE: For Japanese American 1960: Census of Population, 1960, Subject Reports, Nonwhite Population by Race (U.S. Bureau of the Census, 1963), pp. 108, 110. Calculated by subtracting Hawaiian from total Japanese in the United States. For Japanese American 1970: Census of Population, 1970, Subject Reports, Japanese, Chinese, and Filipinos in the United States (U.S. Bureau of the Census, 1973), pp. 31, 35. For United States 1960: Census of Population, 1960, Subject Reports, Occupational Characteristics (U.S. Bureau of the Census, 1963), table 1. For United States 1970: Census of Population, 1970, Occupation by Industry (U.S. Bureau of the Census, 1973), table 1.

managerial occupations and underrepresented among craftsmen/ operatives and service workers/laborers. The comparison is very crude, however, in that both the foreign born and the third generation are included in the census enumerations. The JARP sample is more likely than not a fairly accurate representation of Nisei concentrations as of the date of the survey.

The occupational distribution for the United States male population in 1960 and 1970 (presented in columns 4 and 5 of table 7:4) reveals some small changes over the decade, particularly a decrease in farming and an increase in the professions. These changes, though, are minor compared to those among the Japanese. The latter showed some marked deviations from the national totals in occupational concentrations. They were overrepresented in the professions, a discrepancy that seemed to be increasing with time, and were highly underrepresented among craftsmen, foremen, and operatives. The traditionally heavy concentration in farming appeared for the most part to have disappeared.

The Nisei economy was a congregated economy, even when the Nisei were working for corporations. We can get some sense of this by comparing the overall distribution of male Nisei occupations (table 7:3) with that of all American males in 1960.[2] Leaving aside farm occupations, which clearly reflect an unusual concentration, we still see a considerably more grouped occupational structure for the Nisei. The most common nonagricultural occupation among the Nisei sample was engineering, accounting for 9 percent of the Nisei, the bulk of whom clearly worked in the corporate economy. Engineering was a common occupation, also, among all males in the United States, but at 2 percent of the work force the concentration is far less than among the Nisei. Among Nisei professionals alone, 28 percent were engineers, while only 19 percent of the nation's professionals were employed in this field.

The fact of Nisei job concentration is visible no matter how one analyzes it, and even though such ethnic concentration is not rare, given the nature of the job market, it is both surprising in its degree and consequential. The tendency to concentrate was not only at the very top, among professionals; it is also evident at the lower occupational levels. Thus, the second most common Nisei job, gardening—which, unlike engineering, was within the ethnic economy—constituted fully 8 percent of all Nisei jobs reported to us, whereas by comparison the second most common job in the population at large, carpentering—self-employed about one-fifth of

---

2. The 1970 census used a slightly different classification system, making a precise comparison more difficult than for 1960, whose classification we used for coding purposes. The 1960 comparison is also rendered imperfect by the inclusion of Hawaii, and of Issei and Sansei age groups in the total United States figures. Still, although the figures may be slightly off, the thrust of the generalizations is probably correct.

the time—employed only 2 percent of all male workers. The Japanese American concentration level declines somewhat as we move down the list, to a bit over 4 percent for the third most common Nisei job, and about half these many in the fourth and fifth most common jobs, concentrated also by comparison with the general population.

Within the category of managers and proprietors, Nisei were more likely than others to be working in produce stores (a concentration that also showed up among clerical and sales workers), dry-cleaning establishments, and the like, and especially to be in automobile servicing and gasoline sales (20 percent of the Nisei in managerial occupations were in this field, compared to 8 percent of United States male workers in the same occupational category). A similar overrepresentation appeared among craftsmen and operatives, where 35 percent of the Nisei were mechanics and repairmen, compared to 12 percent of the general population. Among service workers and laborers, no fewer than 77 percent of the Nisei were gardeners, an occupation that accounts for only 3 percent of the country's total male work force in service and labor.

The fact of job concentration among the Nisei points to the economically meaningful (nonrandom) nature of the ethnic designation. There were very distinct "Nisei careers," both within the small-business economy and in the general economy. These appeared to have followed certain themes: food production and distribution, and work requiring manipulative skills or mechanical aptitude. However, too much should not be made of these particular concentrations. One glance at table 7:3 should remind us that there was also great diversity in the occupations of the Nisei.

Throughout this study we shall use the variable of occupational type as laid out in table 7:4. It is too cumbersome, and the numbers are too small, to continue to refer to particular lines of work. It is nevertheless important to keep in mind the kinds of jobs we are talking about when we speak of occupational types. For example, for the Nisei, the classification of service workers and laborers was almost synonymous with gardeners.

Close scrutiny of table 7:3 shows that there was some clustering in small business of particular occupations within each occupational type. Thus, among professionals, dentists fell exclusively in the small-business mold, while natural scientists and, to a large extent, engineers were found in the corporate economy. There was also a fairly clear division between managers, officials, and proprietors who were in small business (generally the owners or managers of food and dairy-product stores and the like) and those who worked in corporate firms (these were more typically managers and officials rather than proprietors). Clerical and sales workers fell almost entirely in the corporate-economy category, but with a few striking exceptions, notably insurance and real-estate salesmen. Among craftsmen and operatives there were a few occupations that showed a majority in small business, and in those cases the numbers were too small to permit us to draw conclusions, but carpenters, jewelers, and plumbers seemed to lean in this direction. Finally, among service workers and laborers, the preponderance of gardeners went a long way toward explaining why 82 percent of the occupational type were in the small-business economy; yet some of the other service workers, such as barbers, showed a similar propensity.

In looking at the particular occupations that were typical in the ethnic economy, one sees a similarity that overrides the occupational type into which they fall. There is not much difference in operating a barbershop, a real-estate business, and a food store, even though these enterprises fall into service, sales, and managerial categories, respectively. This is the similarity that, as we mentioned in chapter 3, is pointed to by Miyamoto and Bloom and Riemer; it provides some confirmation for the validity of our operational definition of *ethnic economy*.

It might be argued that two of the most common forms of Nisei nonagricultural participation in the ethnic economy, gardening and dentistry, do not conform to the prewar small-shop image. Typical gardeners probably work alone, sometimes employing a helper or two, owning their own tools, and contracting their services in small bits to a limited public who learns of these services by word of mouth. It is not a business that can easily utilize family labor or take advantage of having the family dwelling and the work establishment occupy the same premises. Similarly, dentistry and other independent professions deviate in some respects from the family-business model. People in these occupations, however, can benefit from other features of communal solidarity, such as low-interest loans to get established and the passing around of information on techniques of work or potential clients. (Some, of course, will have been misclassified, especially those independent professionals who did not use community ties for business purposes.)

The distribution of small business by occupational type is summarized in table 7:5. It is evident that the occupations differed substantially on this dimension. Professionals, persons in clerical and sales occupations, and craftsmen and operatives tended to concentrate in the corporate economy, while proprietors, service workers and laborers, and especially farmers clustered in small business. Almost half of the Nisei who were in the corporate economy were professionals, while most of those in small business were proprietors and farmers.

The great majority of those Nisei whom we have assigned to the ethnic economy were self-employed rather than employees of Japanese Americans, a feature that differed from the prewar situation. We cannot compare the distribution of ethnic small business by occupational type for the United States population as a whole because the census does not provide information on ethnicity of employers. We can, however, compare self-employ-

TABLE 7:5

OCCUPATIONAL TYPE AND TYPE OF FIRM FOR NISEI MALES
(MALES AND MARRIED FEMALES REPORTING)

	Japanese American Small Business	*Corporate Economy*	*% of Occupational Type in Japanese American Small Business*
Professional, technical, and kindred workers	14%	48%	21 (640)
Managers, officials, and proprietors	30	12	69 (405)
Clerical, sales, and kindred workers	7	15	29 (218)
Farmers and farm workers	27	2	93 (275)
Craftsmen, foremen, operatives, and kindred workers	5	20	18 (249)
Service workers and laborers	18	4	82 (211)
Total	100 (949)	100 (1049)	

ment in the various occupational types for the Japanese and the total United States population who work in that line. Overall, the Nisei were just a shade on the high side in self-employment, with only two categories showing markedly divergent patterns: service workers and laborers (where the aforementioned concentration of self-employed Nisei gardeners raised the Nisei proportion of self-employment to ten times that of the whole population), and managers, proprietors, and officials. Here, a bit more than one-third of all workers in the general population were self-employed, but among the Nisei the figure was about two-thirds. If these broad occupational categories can be taken as strata, the Nisei tendency to concentrate in the small-business form can be seen to be a combination of emphasis by stratum and specific (and historically understandable) concentrations within strata.

As a functioning system within which distinctive careers were to be achieved, certain occupational types within the ethnic economy were significantly composed of employees of Japanese American firms. Among Nisei clerical and sales workers in the ethnic economy, and among craftsmen and operatives as well, nearly half were employees of Japanese American firms. In many cases, these were probably the future self-employed, working in ethnic small business because they knew that the community could ease the initial problems of capital and custom which plague most newly established small businesses. Future-oriented employees of this sort might or might not stay in the same occupational type; current sales personnel, for example, might be working for persons categorized as proprietors and hope eventually to take over those positions or establish similar firms of their own. In contrast, working as a gardener's assistant does not seem to be a route that was available for future self-employment, judging from the small number of gardeners who worked for other Japanese Americans. It is possible that, like farmers, Nisei gardeners could no longer get Japanese help and had to turn to other ethnic groups, such as Mexican Americans. The routes of mobility may have changed, so that self-employed gardeners moved to other types of self-employment, such as the proprietorship of a nursery, which required more capital accumulated in the course of low-capital gardening.

Again returning to table 7:3 we find that the small segment of self-employed Nisei who served the Japanese American community were concentrated in certain occupations. For example, four out of seven lawyers had a Japanese American clientele, as did six out of twenty insurance agents, three out of eight carpenters, and three out of five barbers. It may be that certain kinds of service were seen as more "personal" and that clients requiring those services felt more comfortable dealing with a fellow ethnic.

INCOME

By the time of the JARP survey, the Nisei were on the whole a fairly prosperous group and looked to the future with considerable confidence. Poverty was far from the majority's current experience: only 1 percent of Nisei respondents told us that their family income was $2,500 or less, and no Nisei expected to be earning so little five years hence. Indeed, only 37 percent reported family incomes below $10,000, although two-thirds of all American families had incomes this low in 1967. Poll data, in fact, indicate that at this time, *no* ethnic group (defined by self-identification, to be sure) had such a high proportion of prosperous families, their nearest tabulated competitor in this regard being the Eastern European Jews, of whom a slight majority had family incomes exceeding $10,000 (Greeley, 1974:56).[3] Of course, these comparisons are not completely fair since the Nisei do not include immigrants, the very young, or the elderly; most Nisei, at the time of the survey, were at or approaching the peak of their earning capacity. Thus only 9 percent expected to remain in the below-$10,000 income bracket within five years.

Thirty-five percent of our respondents had an annual income of $10,000 to $15,000 (the modal income), 14 percent earned $15,000 to $20,000, 9 percent between $20,000 and $30,000, and 5 percent earned more than $30,000 a year. The modal expected income was $15,000 to $20,000, with 53 percent of the sample expecting to earn this much in five years.

Strong connections existed among the Nisei between occupation and family income, as one would expect. Professionals were just slightly more often prosperous than were managers and proprietors, with, respectively, 81 percent and 73 percent earning over $10,000 per annum. Clerical/sales workers and craftsmen/

3. The composite poll Greeley (1974) used indicated 27% of all families earned above $10,000, as compared with 34% shown in the *Current Population Survey* conducted by the Bureau of the Census.

operatives tended to have a similar income distribution: about 47 percent earned less than $10,000, some 48 percent earned $10,000 to $20,000, and the small remainder earned over $20,000. Service workers and laborers, contrary to the myth of the wealthy Japanese gardener, were the poorest among the Nisei, with nearly three-quarters reporting a family income below $10,000. Farmers had the broadest income distribution: 23 percent of them earned over $20,000, the highest proportion for any occupational type. (It was 19 percent for professionals and 17 percent for managers and proprietors.) On the other end, though, 43 percent of the farmers earned less than $10,000.

The ethnic economy offered its own structure of economic rewards, as these data indicate. Forty-two percent of those in Japanese American small businesses earned $10,000 or less annually, compared to 33 percent of those working in the corporate economy. In other words, one found more relatively poor people in the ethnic economy. At the same time, though, 20 percent of those in ethnic small businesses earned $20,000 or more, as compared with only 8 percent of the Nisei working in the general economy. That this distinctive structure was recognized or at least perceived by the Nisei is indicated by the fact that for those in small business, the pattern of expected incomes was also different, and in the same way, from the expected-income pattern for those working in the corporate economy. More Nisei in the ethnic economy expected to be earning either under $10,000 or over $20,000 than was the case for those who had left the ethnic economy (27 percent versus 16 percent for under $10,000, and 31 versus 23 percent for $20,000 and over).

These different income distributions suggest that the two economies—corporate and ethnic—had different meanings in terms of income, as in terms of other things, as we shall see in the body of this book. The corporate economy seemed to promise security—a good income without too much risk—whereas the ethnic economy appeared to offer more of a gamble. One might achieve greater monetary rewards than one could ever hope to attain in the employ of a large corporation or public bureaucracy; but one might also have to struggle. This is the fate of small business in America in general, and Japanese American small business is no exception.

Within small business, there were naturally differences between the incomes of the self-employed and those of employees. The latter tended to earn a bit less than employees in the corporate economy; 40 percent of them earned less than $10,000, compared to 33 percent in the general economy. On the other hand, the minority of the self-employed who served the Japanese American community were somewhat wealthier than the rest of the self-employed. For example, only 19 percent of them expected to be earning less than $10,000 in five years, compared to 28 percent of all self-employed. On the whole, however, the difference was not large.

Within each occupational type, the relationship between type of firm and income varied a good deal. Among professionals, for example, those working in ethnic small businesses did considerably better than employees in corporations. Managers and proprietors, on the other hand, balanced out so that neither type of firm had an advantage, although the small-business type of organization had a wider income distribution. Among service workers and laborers, those working in ethnic small businesses averaged lower incomes than corporate employees.

Within the ethnic economy, the self-employed of all occupational types except managers and proprietors displayed an advantage in income over employees. The exception suggests that ethnic businesses that could employ a manager were probably not in the same economic echelon that most small stores were in. Apart from this exception, the economic differentiation within the ethnic economy was quite large, with employees earning much less than owners. For example, among clerical and sales workers, 30 percent of the self-employed earned over $20,000 per annum, while for employees the corresponding figure was 4 percent. In addition, within each occupational type, employees of ethnic small businesses generally had lower incomes than employees in the corporate economy. Thus among craftsmen and operatives, 63 percent of employees in the ethnic economy earned under $10,000, compared to 47 percent of corporate-economy employees. This serves to reinforce our operational definition: ethnic-economy firms appeared, still, to use cheaper Nisei labor than did the economy at large.

On the whole, it appears that the Nisei faced a choice on entering the job market, in part analogous to the one their parents faced before the war. They could either integrate into the general economy and accept financial security with a ceiling on potential income, or they could take their chances striving for self-employment in an ethnic economy, where there was the possibility of achieving a fair degree of wealth but where some degree of social isolation from the majority society would have to be accepted as well.

POLITICS

It seems reasonable to expect that choice of the small-business or of the corporate economy would be associated with different sets of interests and that these would in turn be associated with different political leanings. Thus, *ceteris paribus*, persons in the ethnic economy might well be expected to oppose strong labor unions, to favor regulatory legislation only where benefit to small operators is visible, and the like.

We have generally equated being outside of the ethnic economy with working for large organizations (some, but not all, profit oriented), although undoubtedly there were Japanese Americans who were employees of non-Japanese-owned small businesses. This is less of a distortion than it might seem, for without an ethnic or family tie with the owner of the firm, it is less likely that the employee identifies with the owner and plans to establish his or her own small business. In any case, people in the corporate economy tend to be more divided in their interests; owners and managers in the corporate economy have interests clearly distinct from those of their employees, much more so than in Japanese American small businesses (Modell, 1977:127-153). Since all the Nisei we have defined as being in the corporate economy were employees, we can predict, for instance, that they would reveal distinctive political attitudes with respect to unions.

Unfortunately, on this score the JARP survey revealed only whether the respondent had ever belonged to a labor union. Even so, responses did show a relationship to type of firm. Union experience was very low among the self-employed, with only 22 percent ever having been members. While 48 percent of employees in the corporate economy had at some time been union members, a lower figure characterized employees in the ethnic economy—36 percent. With many exceptions, to be sure, their careers have been consistent in this politically relevant regard with their 1966-1967 position within or outside of the ethnic economy.

The political parties in the United States do not, of course, closely represent economic class interests, but they do reflect such interests to a degree. Party affiliation thus offers another indicator of class-based behavior among the Nisei, if only a blunt one. The Nisei, we found, did not have a united party stance. About 53 percent were Democrats, 37 percent Republicans, and 10 percent without party affiliation. Obviously, ethnicity per se did not determine Nisei party affiliation. If they did not engage in bloc voting, then how are we to explain their choices? While almost no simple variable such as religion, education, or occupational type correlated significantly with political-party affiliation among the Nisei, participation in the ethnic economy did. Generally, those in ethnic small businesses were more likely to be Republicans. Forty-seven percent of the self-employed were Republicans, compared to 32 percent of those working in the corporate economy. The employees in ethnic small businesses fell in between, with 40 percent of them Republicans, like many of their employers, a finding which strengthens our sense that many of these employees anticipated continuing in the ethnic economy as proprietors and shared the political consciousness of the petite bourgeoisie.

The relationship between political-party affiliation and ethnic-economy participation is made clearer when we look at income (table 7:6). Generally, in the ethnic economy, the higher the income, the more likely were the Nisei to be Republicans. For those working in the corporate economy, though, higher income did not seem conducive to Republican partisanship. This becomes even clearer when we control for occupational type. Of the thirty-

TABLE 7:6

TYPE OF FIRM BY POLITICAL PARTY, CONTROLLING FOR FAMILY INCOME

| | Percent Republican | | |
Income	*Self-employed*	*JA Employer*	*Corporate Employer*
To $10,000	37% (153)	38% (21)	31% (194)
$10,000 – $20,000	46 (138)	46 (37)	33 (355)
$20,000 +	62 (107)	(6)	38 (37)

four Nisei who were managers and proprietors in Japanese small businesses and earned $20,000 a year or more, 71 percent were Republicans, while the poorer self-employed Nisei, who were receiving fewer of the monetary rewards of their calling, were far less strong in their support of the Republican party, the policies of which would seem to favor successful small business. Thus, the modified Japanese American ethnic economy of the postwar period, though a pale reflection of the economy destroyed by the evacuation, nevertheless reflected a distinct class orientation and set of interests.

We have found, then, that a middleman-minority economic form was recreated by a substantial segment of the Nisei by the mid-1960s. An even larger segment, however, had moved out of this form and into the surrounding economy. We will examine some of the factors that contributed to this differentiation of the Nisei in the remainder of part II. This should help us understand some of the forces that perpetuate or undermine the persistence of middleman minorities into the second generation within advanced capitalist societies.

8

Year of Birth

In the mid-1960s, the Nisei were anything but a homogeneous group with regard to their economic activity: they were in fact divided into two large classes, which we have designated as small-business entrepreneurs and corporate employees. In addition, as the previous chapter has also shown, they were divided by occupational type, to some extent overlapping the type of firm. Although we cannot explicate the nature of this two-class arrangement much further with our survey data, we can make with them at least some assessments of the causes of this differentiation. In this chapter we look at one of the most important differentiators: age. Subsequent chapters in part II examine the impact of those background factors that have led, historically, to this intragenerational division in economic form.

Five percent of the sampled Nisei men were born before 1915, 41 percent between 1915 and 1924, 36 between 1925 and 1934, and 18 percent after 1934. These cutting points were chosen for historical reasons that will be made clear shortly. The smallness of the oldest cohort, and, to a lesser extent, of the youngest, has forced us to combine them with their neighbors on occasion.[1]

1. Because women were not asked the age of their husbands, this chapter and any subsequent chapters that introduce age must be based on the responses of only half of the sample, the males. This affects some distributions a bit since the male respondents and female reports of their husbands do not always reveal identical distributions of characteristics. One obvious difference is that male respondents include unmarried people, while females could only report on married men. Other differences may stem from possibly different response propensities by subgroups of male and female sample members. However, the overall differences are quite minor, and we have chosen to ignore them.

YEAR OF BIRTH, TYPE OF FIRM, AND OCCUPATIONAL TYPE

The type of firm in which the Nisei worked in the mid-1960s was very much a product of factors indexed by age. The youngest group was in fact twice as likely as the oldest to work in the corporate economy—73 percent versus 38 percent. In between these extremes, 61 percent of those born between 1925 and 1934 and 44 percent of the 1915-1924 birth cohort worked outside of small business. Three aspects of this breakdown deserve notice. The first is, of course, the steepness of the age gradient out of the ethnic economy, intragenerational differences of a magnitude that would be striking even between generations. The second remarkable fact is the extent of involvement in the ethnic economy among the older Nisei: almost two out of three who were over fifty years of age at the time of the survey were, even in the mid-1960s, working in the ethnic economy. Finally, we should recall that even for the youngest Nisei, roughly those under the age of thirty, the proportion in small business was about double that for all American men of all ages. We are, again, dealing with a characteristic Japanese American economic form, but one sustained quite unequally by different subgroups within the ascriptive category of Nisei.

Interpreting the findings in this chapter is complicated by the fact that age has a peculiar double meaning at any given moment in historical time. On the one hand, age can mean stage in the life cycle through which everyone passes. One would expect older people to be wealthier and to have had more experience than younger people in the ordinary course of events. Aging itself is the prime consideration. On the other hand, though, age can also signify *cohort*, with all those individuals born during a certain period experiencing certain historical events in common as they progress through life, their reactions to these events affected by common life-cycle stage (Ryder, 1965). How we interpret age is important for our predictions of the future. If we assume that life-cycle stage is the primary explanation for a table in which the young are different from the old, one would expect that in twenty years' time a similar study would produce a similar table. If we accept a cohort view, however, the characteristics of the young could be used to predict directions of change in the future.

For the Nisei, year of birth suggests the following cohort-related interpretations: those born prior to 1915, who were fifty-four years of age or older at the time of study, entered school before 1920 and were adults before World War II. Those born between 1915 and 1924 were between sixteen and twenty-five years old when the war started. The Nisei born in the 1925-1934 period were still children at the outbreak of the war, though typically they had attended school before the war. In most cases they entered the labor market after the war. Those born from 1935 on were at most ten years old at the conclusion of the relocation period; they were educated in the postwar world for the postwar job market. Even this cohort interpretation can sustain either a strong or a weak historical meaning. Where substantial discontinuities show up, we prefer a strong interpretation, suggesting a cleavage between groups maturing earlier from those following. In the weak historical interpretation, year of birth would appear as a continuous variable, reflecting, perhaps, a quantitative phenomenon such as "years of exposure to the Issei-dominated prewar ethnic economy."

Among those Nisei who were in small business, life-cycle effects are evident. The younger Nisei were more likely to be employees, while the older people were more likely to be self-employed. Thus 29 percent of those in the small-business economy who were born after 1934 were employees, but only 18 percent of the 1925-1934 group, 11 percent of those born in 1915-1924, and 6 percent of the pre-1915 cohort were. It takes time to acquire the capital necessary for self-employment, and we can expect many of the young employees of Japanese American small businesses today to be the self-employed of tomorrow. At the same time, however, the proportion of young employees in small business was hardly large—only 8 percent of the entire group born after 1934 and 7 percent of the 1925-1934 cohort, which suggests that cohort-based change may also be occurring. If the younger Nisei were collecting capital to get established on their own when they are a bit older, it is likely that more of them would have been employees of the types of firms they aspire to run, since experience and contacts are important factors in the success of a small business.

Further support for a cohort interpretation comes from a discontinuity in the relationship between age and small-business concentration. The difference in small-business concentration between those born before 1915 and those born in 1915-1924 (all of whom matured in the prewar period) is a small 6 percent. The difference between the 1915-1924 group and the next younger cohort (which matured in the immediate postwar period), however, jumps to 17 percent. Since most prewar capital accumulation was wiped out by the evacuation, the first cohort maturing in the postwar period need not, for reasons of capital accumulation, be so much higher than the previous cohorts in propensity to involvement in small business. This pattern suggests a strong historical interpretation: the Nisei who had, as adults, experienced the Issei ethnic economy (and indeed had often participated in it) are appreciably the most likely to have worked to reestablish it, in modified form, after the war.

Aspects of both interpretations are suggested by table 8:1, which shows the relationship of Nisei year of birth to occupational type, with comparative data from the 1970 census for all United States males. Here the discontinuity in ethnic-economy orientation is seen to be largely a product of a massive decline in farming. The farming component, once the primary production base on which the ethnic economy rested, remains an important commitment to that group of Nisei who had reached economic maturity before the war, but virtually for them alone. Presumably those who had or could acquire training for other occupations avoided the option of agriculture, given that new food-distribution patterns and the absence of unpaid family labor made lucrative farming a virtually unattainable goal.

Managers and proprietors, in contrast, suggest no historical decline from the prewar to the postwar period (although of course there is a shift into managerial positions in the corporate economy and out of ethnic small business). Even more striking is the great rise among the young in the professions. Almost certainly this is a cohort phenomenon, a product of real changes within the generation. It is hard to imagine that younger Nisei are entering the professions with the intention of using them as a stepping stone to other occupations. The figures, however, reveal this to be a regular trend and not a product of historical discontinuities. The finding is consistent with Nisei perceptions, both pre- and postwar, of increasing preparation for the professions through higher education, and even in the period during which discrimination in the job market postponed attainment of such occupational goals. We should note, too, that the rise in the professions and the decline in

TABLE 8:1
OCCUPATIONAL TYPE BY YEAR OF BIRTH FOR MALE NISEI
AND U.S. MALES TWENTY FIVE AND OLDER, 1970

	Year of Birth			
	Before 1915	*1915-1924*	*1925-1934*	*After 1934*
Male Nisei				
Professionals	14%	24%	39%	54%
Managers and proprietors	25	19	21	6
Clerical and sales workers	8	13	10	16
Farmers	29	16	11	7
Craftsmen and operatives	8	15	11	11
Service workers and laborers	15	13	7	6
Total	100	100	100	100
	(59)	(485)	(433)	(183)
Total U.S. males				
Professionals	10	13	17	20
Managers and proprietors	13	14	14	10
Ckerical and sales workers	15	14	13	14
Farmers	8	5	4	3
Craftsmen and operatives	37	42	42	42
Service workers and laborers	17	12	11	11
Total	100	100	100	100
	(8,877,346)	(10,002,606)	(10,170,637)	(10,644,176)

SOURCE: For U.S. males: Census of Population, 1970, Detailed Characteristics,
PC(1)-D1 (U.S. Bureau of the Census, 1973), table 226.

farming among Nisei parallel trends in the population at large, but they are much stronger among Japanese Americans.

Among professionals there was a shift across cohorts from working in small business to working in the corporate economy. Among those born after 1934, only 8 percent were in small business. The proportion was 15 percent for the 1925-1934 cohort and 31 percent for those born before 1925. This probably reflects a difference in choice of professions: the older Nisei were more highly concentrated in the independent professions (doctors, dentists), while more of the younger Nisei have selected professions that are under corporate control, such as engineering. If so, this is a cohort phenomenon that should survive over time. (Some of the younger professionals may intend to go into private practice later on and perhaps see corporate or public employment as a temporary phase en route to self-employment. For example, a doctor might work temporarily for a health-maintenance organization while intending to move into private practice as he or she gains experience, contacts, and capital).

If year of birth is interpreted in cohort fashion, it is possible to get a glimpse of the changing structure of the two economies by looking at the occupational distribution within each according to age group. Table 8:2 presents the data in this way, revealing that the Japanese American small-business economy did not appear to be "changing" very much in character, although it had experienced overall decline. A feeder relationship undoubtedly existed between clerical/sales and proprietorship. There was some drop in farming and a very small shift into the professions, but neither was as dramatic as the "shifts" out of the small-business economy.

In contrast, the character of Nisei participation in the corporate economy "changed" a great deal from cohort to cohort. While almost one-third of those belonging to the oldest cohort occupied blue-collar positions (crafts/operatives and service/labor), this figure dropped to 15 percent for the youngest group. Although there was some apparent decline in managerial occupations, it probably reflects life-cycle factors. The biggest change was the increase in professionals: over two-thirds of the youngest Nisei working for corporations or the public had this kind of occupation, which suggests that Nisei recently entering the corporate economy played a very specialized role. Indeed, of all twelve occupation/firm-type categories together, only the corporate professionals category was unequivocally "growing," from 16 percent among the pre-1925 birth cohort to 50 percent in the post-1934 group.

BIRTH ORDER

We have so far stressed cohort explanations for the shift in economic form, but other tendencies revealed by the JARP survey

TABLE 8:2
MALE NISEI OCCUPATIONAL TYPE BY YEAR OF BIRTH,
CONTROLLING FOR TYPE OF FIRM

	Year of Birth		
	Before 1925	*1925-1934*	*After 1934*
Small Business			
Professionals	13%	15%	19%
Managers and proprietors	27	32	19
Clerical and sales workers	7	7	16
Farmers	30	27	21
Craftsmen and operatives	5	4	7
Service workers and laborers	18	14	19
Total	100	100	100
	(304)	(168)	(43)
Corporate economy			
Professionals	37	55	66
Managers and proprietors	11	14	2
Clerical and sales workers	19	12	15
Farmers	2	1	1
Craftsmen and operatives	27	16	13
Service workers and laborers	5	2	2
Total	100	100	100
	(232)	(257)	(134)

suggest that complementary factors were also at work in the differentiation of the Nisei. By examining variation by birth order, we find that beyond indicating a Nisei's historical placement, age also points to a distinctive placement within the family in which he or she grew up. First sons among the Nisei were considerably more likely than younger brothers to have entered small business, presumably a function of their having been more likely to take over the family business. Fifty-two percent of first sons, as compared to 39 percent of later-born sons, were in small business in the mid-1960s (although birth order had little effect on occupational type, apart from a slight tendency for oldest sons to be farmers). Birth order was related to type of firm entered within each occupational category: in each occupational type (with the exception of craftsmen and operatives), firstborn sons were more likely to enter small-business-type firms. This was most marked in the case of proprietors and managers, of whom 80 percent of oldest sons were in small business, and only 56 percent of younger sons.

At the same time, cohort placement also had an effect, as table 8:3 shows. While year of birth had the more powerful impact on small-business participation, birth order indicated selectivity within each cohort, especially within the youngest. This suggests a specification of the cohort interpretation offered earlier. The structure of opportunities outside and within the ethnic economy changed historically, and perceptions of these changes affected choices made by Nisei preparing to enter the labor market. One's relationship to historical change was not solely a function of age, however, and in cohort after cohort the small-business opportunities open specifically to firstborn sons continued to attract these into the ethnic economy.

The basic finding of this chapter has been that age and small business are positively correlated: the older the Nisei male, the more likely he is to be working in the type of firm the Issei had developed so effectively. This can be interpreted in terms of life cycle: younger Nisei are not in small business now but will enter it when they are older. This was the interpretation of Bloom and Riemer's findings that age correlated with self-employment for the

TABLE 8:3
PROPORTION OF MALE NISEI IN SMALL BUSINESS
BY YEAR OF BIRTH AND BIRTH ORDER

| | Year of Birth | | |
	Before 1925	1925-1934	After 1934
Older Son	59%	45%	36%
	(333)	(165)	(72)
Younger Son	52	36	22
	(207)	(261)	(125)

Issei which we made in chapter 3. For the Nisei, however, the small proportion who are employees of small businesses and the high proportion of professionals among the later born point to a fundamental change in the economic activity of this group: a gradual movement away from small business, with its communal supports and obligations, and into the employ of the corporate economy. If we accept a cohort interpretation, then, the middle-man-minority position of the Japanese Americans would appear to be disappearing over time. In the next few chapters we consider some of the factors that might be contributing to this dissolution, as well as those that bind the remainder to the ethnic economy.

9

Education

As a group, the Japanese Americans are one of the most highly educated ethnic elements in the United States population (Kitano, 1976b:1-2), both sexes enjoying a longer median period of education than blacks, whites, Chinese, Filipinos, and Native Americans (Schmid and Nobbe, 1965). Their educational excellence has been demonstrated qualitatively as well as quantitatively. Schwartz (1971), for instance, found that Japanese American pupils in Los Angeles scored much higher on performance than any other minority group and somewhat higher than native whites as well. This general pattern, visible now among the Sansei, was one of the conditions of prewar Nisei life that they and their supporters felt to be in ironic contrast with the general failure of Japanese Americans to break into the corporate economy and out of near-exclusive reliance on the small-business mode.

Although our Nisei survey oversampled the more educated, there is nevertheless considerable variation in educational attainment within the sample. Thus, 136 sample Nisei men (including those reported on by their wives) did not complete high school, and an additional 691 were only high-school graduates. This leaves 58 percent who continued past high school. Of these, well over half completed four years of college, and no less than 16 percent of the entire group received some postgraduate education.

Generally, the less education a person received, the more likely he was to be involved in the ethnic economy. The correlation is strong: 60 percent of those with up to twelve years of schooling were in small business, compared to 47 percent of those with thirteen to fifteen years, 31 percent of the college graduates, and 29 percent of those with some postgraduate education. We cannot, of course, do more than speculate about whether

. education has permitted or encouraged the Nisei to leave
ısiness, or whether the lack of such an education has
the Nisei to follow in the economic footsteps of their
, (or if it reflects a prior decision to do so).

Education is an important determinant of occupational type
ımerican society in general. Among the Nisei, as table 9:1
ıws, education has had an overwhelming effect on the propen-
.ty to enter the professions, with a range of 73 percent between
those with a high-school education or less and those who have
some graduate-level training. The range for all Americans was
large, too, but not quite this large, because of the extreme propensity of the best-educated Nisei men to enter the professions. Nisei
education was related to current occupation in the same direction
as for American men in general, with a single exception. That
exception was among managers and proprietors, and it is diagnos-
tically interesting, for whereas managers and proprietors were
numerous among the better-educated males in the general community, among the Nisei these occupations were most common
among those with middle levels of education. The single highest
proportion of managers and proprietors seen anywhere in table
9:1 is among Nisei with some college education but no diploma, to
whom occupations in this category were seemingly very attractive.
The more educated Nisei were led elsewhere, so that among all
college graduates a lower proportion of Nisei than of all American
men were so occupied.

The more educated Nisei moved into the professions, as
noted. Since the professions were generally less likely, for the
Nisei at least, to be organized along small-business lines, a strong
relationship obtained between education and ethnic-economic
form. Thus, the relationship between small business and education
is mainly accounted for indirectly: with the exception of managers
and proprietors, within each occupational type there was a small
tendency for the *more educated* to enter ethnic firms. This suggests that the tie between education and participation in the
corporate economy was less a function of the Nisei being socialized into more "American" economic behavior than of opportunities being created to enter certain occupational types.

Managers and proprietors, however, were an important exception to the general trend, since for them the impact of education
on leaving small business was even stronger than for the sample as

TABLE 9:1

OCCUPATIONAL TYPE BY YEARS OF EDUCATION FOR MALE NISEI
(MALES AND MARRIED FEMALES REPORTING) AND U.S. MALES
SIXTEEN AND OLDER IN 1970

	Years of Education			
	0-12	*13-15*	*16*	*17+*
Male Nisei				
Professionals	8%	24%	60%	81%
Managers and proprietors	20	26	20	11
Clerical and sales workers	10	18	9	4
Farmers	21	14	5	2
Craftsmen and operatives	20	13	2	2
Service workers and laborers	21	5	4	0
Total	100	100	100	100
	(809)	(480)	(304)	(310)
Total U.S. males				
Professionals	4	8	59*	
Managers and proprietors	8	7	20	
Clerical and sales workers	13	9	14	
Farmers	6	1	1	
Craftsmen and operatives	51	71	5	
Service workers and laborers	18	4	2	
Total	100	100	100	
	(34,774,626)	(16,192,824)	(6,656,304)	

SOURCE: For U.S. males: Census of Population, 1970, Detailed Characteristics, PC(1)-D1 (U.S. Bureau of the Census, 1973), p. 785.

*For U.S. males, figures in this column represent sixteen or more years of education.

a whole. Eighty-one percent of those with up to twelve years of education were in small business, compared to 55 percent of those who had completed college and 34 percent of the postgraduates. The occupational category, of course, contains both managers and proprietors: we suspect that the latter concentrated more in the ranks of the less educated.

The occupational rewards of education were substantially different for Nisei in the two economies, as table 9:2 shows. Within the small-business economy a postgraduate education pretty much guaranteed entrance into the independent professions, but only for this group. For the college educated (thirteen to sixteen years of education) the modal occupation in the ethnic economy was proprietorship, with well over one-third entering this type of work. The less educated clustered in farming and gardening, but even here a fairly large proportion were proprietors. In the corporate economy, on the other hand, lack of education directed Nisei toward blue-collar work, especially as craftsmen and operatives, and, to a lesser extent, into the white-collar occupations of clerical and sales work; but for all educational levels past high school the professions were dominant.

In general, then, there existed two different mobility systems served by differential education. In the ethnic economy the bottom rung was filled primarily by gardeners. With somewhat higher education a person could expect to become a farmer; with more, a proprietor; and finally, with postgraduate training, an independent professional. In the corporate system, the bottom rung was filled by craftsmen and operatives. From there one moved up to clerical and sales work, then some managerial positions, and finally, at the top, the nonindependent professions.

YEAR OF BIRTH AND EDUCATION

As indicated in the previous chapter, educational achievement among the Nisei was closely tied with year of birth. Almost 60 percent of those born before 1915 did not proceed beyond a high-school education. Only one-fifth of this number (12 percent) had so little education among those born after 1934. Considerably more of this youngest cohort, in fact, has had postgraduate training. Each successive cohort received more higher education, with the youngest group in particular taking a large step in that direc-

TABLE 9:2
MALE NISEI OCCUPATIONAL TYPE BY YEARS OF EDUCATION,
CONTROLLING FOR TYPE OF FIRM (MALES AND
MARRIED FEMALES REPORTING)

	Years of Education			
	0-12	*13-15*	*16*	*17+*
Small business				
Professionals	2%	8%	29%	75%
Managers and proprietors	27	39	35	12
Clerical and sales workers	3	14	8	7
Farmers	34	26	17	4
Craftsmen and operatives	6	4	0	1
Service workers and laborers′	28	9	11	0
Total	100	100	100	100
	(477)	(226)	(93)	(89)
Corporate economy				
Professionals	18	37	74	84
Managers and proprietors	10	15	13	10
Clerical and sales workers	20	22	9	3
Farmers	3	2	0	1
Craftsmen and operatives	41	21	3	2
Service workers and laborers	9	2	0	0
Total	100	100	100	100
	(314)	(246)	(206)	(214)

tion. A cohort interpretation is the only one that makes sense in regard to education. Part of this cohort effect may be explained in terms of the general advance of extended education in twentieth-century America. Thus, children of all ethnicities have been attending school for increasing lengths of time since about the turn of the century. In the 1960 census, 31 percent of the 1926-1935 birth cohort of all second-generation Americans had gone beyond high school, as compared with 14 percent of second-generation Americans born before 1915. (To take a migrant stream roughly contemporary with the Japanese, among Polish people in the United States, the proportion going beyond high school increased from 10 percent among second-generation members born before 1915 to 31 percent of those born in 1926-1935 [U.S. Bureau of the Census, 1963:14, 51-67].)

At the same time, a part of the relationship between age and education among the Nisei may be explained by a decline in the discrimination they experienced; they thus would have found school increasingly less distasteful as well as more valuable in the job market after graduation. (This would be another way in which opportunities in the environment were expanding.) Before the war, segregation of Japanese children in public schools was legally permitted in some states (Bell, 1934:7). The most dramatic instance was the well-known school-segregation order of 1906 in San Francisco which precipitated the Gentlemen's Agreement. No Japanese child ever attended the oriental school there, however, and at the time of his research Bell (1935:14) found only four small schools in California which officially segregated Nisei. Contemporary studies (Corbally, 1931) uncovered few signs of racial friction involving Japanese American schoolchildren. By the evacuation, only one segregated school remained, in Courtland, California, and, pressed by successful legal challenges, California repealed its local option of segregation in 1946 (Melendy, 1972:107).

We would not, therefore, expect the decline in discrimination against Japanese Americans to hold great explanatory power in interpreting the increase in Nisei educational attainment after the war. After all, in 1930 in California, 64 percent of the total population between the ages of fourteen and twenty was in school, while among the Japanese the figure was 80 percent (U.S. Bureau of the Census, 1933:1121, 1132; see also Thomas, 1952: 71-78). Explanations of the heavy Japanese American commitment to education which are based upon cultural preferences run up against negative correlations with the JARP data concerning immersion—Nisei or parental—in identifiably Japanese cultural affairs (Buddhism is the clearest example) and extended education. Rather, it was urban Nisei who were most often college bound, and it was they who pressed most intently in the prewar period against the constricting boundaries of the ethnic economy and ethnic community. From these efforts, Issei parents rarely discouraged them, for it was only thus that the expertise could be amassed and the connections made which would permit the ethnic economy to expand enough to accommodate the Nisei (Modell, 1977:94-126).

We have seen that older Nisei were more often involved in small business and typically had less schooling than the younger ones. Since education and small business were negatively related to each other, the cycle is complete and balanced. A question remains, however: Does education entirely explain the relationship between year of birth and small-business participation? Or are there some other aspects of the cohort pattern which remain unexplained?

Table 9:3 answers this question. Just as attained education weakens but does not altogether eliminate the effect of age on small-business involvement, especially in the least-educated category, likewise, the effect of education on small business remains strong indeed, even within age cohorts. For all cohorts, college education was a stepping stone to leaving the ethnic economy by the mid-1960s, though the proportion of college educated who could or did avail themselves of this opportunity was substantially greater among the later born.

Although education is an important differentiator for all age cohorts, its impact is most marked on the youngest. For them higher education virtually ensured a job in the corporate economy.

TABLE 9:3
MALE NISEI IN SMALL BUSINESS BY YEAR OF BIRTH,
CONTROLLING FOR YEARS OF EDUCATION

| | Year of Birth | | |
Years of Education	Before 1925	1925-1934	After 1934
0-12	66%	52%	57%
	(264)	(160)	(23)
13-15	61	40	31
	(135)	(99)	(76)
16	36	26	18
	(72)	(81)	(49)
17+	33	27	13
	(70)	(85)	(44)

On the other hand, those with only high-school education or less were more likely than not to find themselves in small business, almost as likely as Nisei born much earlier. The role of education as a differentiator among Nisei growing up after the war, in terms of type of firm, cannot be overstated.

Similarly, the pattern (discussed in the previous chapter) for firstborn sons to be more likely to enter small business than their younger male siblings was not a function of differential education. Birth order, suggestively, was completely unrelated to years of education, with oldest sons more likely to enter small business regardless of the extent of their education. Eldest sons were not particularly likely to be whisked out of school to keep the family business going (nor the opposite), but they still respected an obligation or parental preference that counteracted the tendencies encouraged by advanced education. Among those with no more than high-school education, 65 percent of oldest sons were in small business, compared to 56 percent of younger sons; for those with thirteen to fifteen years of schooling, the respective percentages in small business were 55 and 39; for college graduates, they were 35 and 21 percent; and for postgraduates, they were 32 and 21 percent. These differences reinforce our finding that more than one channel of occupational recruitment operated at once.

THE MATERIAL REWARDS OF EDUCATION

One of the motives for pursuing education is economic. Education is an investment in human capital: one puts in time and money in hopes of gaining the advantages later on of more interesting and profitable jobs. For the Nisei, education generally brought higher income. Fifty-one percent of those with up to twelve years of education earned $10,000 or less, while 63, 78, and 83 percent, respectively, of those with thirteen to fifteen, sixteen, and seventeen or more years of education earned over $10,000 a year. Expected income in five years was even more strongly related to prior education, so that while only 18 percent of those who did not go to college expected to be earning over $20,000, fully half of the postgraduates did.

In spite of this, however, education is sometimes said not to pay off for the Nisei as it should. At about the time of the JARP survey, for instance, Daniels (1966*b*:381-82) wrote: "Statistics demonstrate conclusively that Chinese and Japanese are still discriminated against . . . . Although California's Chinese and Japanese are better educated than California's white population, they don't get the money which traditionally goes with the skeepskin. Although college graduates are 11 percent more likely to be found among Japanese males than among white males, . . . white men make considerably more money. For every $51.00 received by a white Californian, Japanese get $43.00." The same point has also been made by other authors.

This generalization unfortunately ignores the complexities introduced by the intervening variable of occupation. Between education and income lie a variety of occupational types that were somewhat different for the Nisei than for the general population, as we saw in table 9:1. Also, for the Nisei, there were two types of firm organization which constituted somewhat different reward systems. Perhaps within corporate firms, Nisei who had the same education and particular occupation as non-Nisei received the same pay and chances for promotion. Unfortunately, our data concern family income rather than the earnings of the individual worker and are thus not comparable with census data on this dimension.

For all occupational types, education seems to have enhanced income levels, but in a far from uniform way. In proprietorship and in farming, the absence of post-high-school education did not prevent sizable proportions from making relatively high incomes. Among farmers with a high-school education or less, 21 percent had family incomes of $20,000 or more in the mid-1960s, a figure higher than that for professionals with a college education. On the other hand, though, there were service workers and laborers with college educations, none of whom earned over $20,000. Daniels is correct insofar as opportunities for the Nisei have pushed them into lines where their education could not be used (or, as in farming, where other qualities are rewarded as generously as is education); yet his remarks cannot be understood to imply that in many occupations the educational investments of the Nisei were not rewarded or that there was not a degree of stratification of the Nisei, initiated (or perpetuated) by education and reflected in income. In part, the discrepancies he cites are a function of the continuing ethnic economy.

Table 9:4 allows us to examine the effect of type of firm upon returns to education. In both economies education increased

TABLE 9:4

MALE NISEI INCOME BY EDUCATION, CONTROLLING FOR TYPE OF FIRM
(MALES AND MARRIED FEMALES REPORTING)

| | *Years of Education* | | | |
	0–12	*13–15*	*16*	*17+*
Small business				
To $10,000	53%	35%	24%	11%
$10,000–$20,000	34	42	49	37
$20,000+	13	23	27	52
Total	100	100	100	100
	(460)	(219)	(93)	(89)
Corporate economy				
To $10,000	44	32	19	16
$10,000–$20,000	54	64	73	67
$20,000+	2	4	8	16
Total	100	100	100	100
	(406)	(328)	(217)	(184)

income, but, surprisingly, it did so more within the ethnic economy than outside of it. The high incomes of postgraduates in small business probably reflected the opportunities open to independent professionals; in the corporate economy there was a ceiling on such earnings. The finding reveals a nice paradox. Education tended to drive the Nisei out of small business, but for those with higher education (particularly postgraduate training) who remained, monetary rewards were greater. This suggests that the attraction of the corporate economy to the educated was not entirely a material one.

CONCLUSION

It has been frequently observed that members of middleman minorities tend to provide much education for their children. There are probably many reasons for this, including the solidarity of the ethnic community, which encourages a focus upon family honor and achievement. Working as unpaid family labor in the family business may also serve to keep the children away from distracting peer influences, while familiarity with business practices may facilitate interest in practical school subjects. Generally, we believe, higher education is encouraged by middleman-minority parents, not so that their children can escape from the form, but rather so that they can operate within it skillfully enough that it remains a generally attractive option for them. Children should receive a good education in order to be able to enter the independent professions, the pinnacle of the petit bourgeois world, or to take over the family business or farm and run it more efficiently.

Providing their children with a higher education, however, has an unintended consequence: it enables them to leave the ethnic economy altogether. This is what happened to many of the sons of the Issei (and, we suspect, to the second generation of other middleman minorities in the postwar United States, such as the Jews). Instead of using their education to strengthen the ethnic economy, they departed from it and took jobs in the corporate and public sectors. For those who did remain, as we have seen, the education paid off in the form of higher income, implying more successful businesses. For most, though, higher education was a means of escaping from the middleman-minority position.

This exodus of many of the educated second generation may reflect conditions in the surrounding society. The absence of marked societal hostility toward Nisei taking jobs in the corporate economy eased their path in this direction. In other words, the plans of the first generation in terms of preparing sons for a middleman economic form were predicated on a continuation of the reason for that form: a hostile, tenuous relationship of the minority with the surrounding society. Once this no longer obtained, those Nisei with higher education could utilize it in a manner unintended by their parents—to escape from the ethnic economy. The result of this process has been to leave the ethnic economy increasingly in the hands of the less educated Nisei. In the next chapter we shall get a better picture of how this came about.

10

Work History

In the previous chapter we saw that education was an important determinant of who continued or discarded the middle-man-minority form. We also saw that both education and leaving the ethnic economy were associated with youth. This leads us to examine the careers of Nisei over time, to see whether education had a differential impact on the different cohorts (or age groups) of Nisei in terms of their initial position in the job market and also how their early jobs affected subsequent opportunities. In other words, we want to trace patterns of recruitment to the middleman position over time, given different levels of education and time of entry into the labor market. In the last section of this chapter we consider which Nisei received higher education, given different family backgrounds. The unique, intergenerational design of the JARP survey permits us to trace the effects of Issei characteristics on the probability of their sons retaining the middleman form.

JARP sample members were asked for a brief description of every full-time job they had ever held and when they had held them. (Unfortunately, except in the case of respondents' current jobs, we did not ascertain self-employment or ethnicity of the employer.) For present purposes, we examine their current occupational types and those of the primary (longest-held) jobs in three major historical eras: the prewar period (1932-1941), the immediate postwar period (1946-1952), and the period between 1952 and the time of the survey. By looking at the dominant jobs in each of these eras, we can trace the source and evolution of current economic differentiation.

The Nisei occupational distribution has changed radically over time. In the 1932-1941 period (with a total of 521 males from our sample in the labor force), 43 percent were in farming, while only 6 percent were professionals. The second most common occupational type was clerical and sales work, with 18 percent, followed by craftsmen and operatives with 12 percent and managers and proprietors with 11 percent. Service workers and laborers came close to professionals in bringing up the rear, with only 9 percent.

By the postwar era, the number of our sample in the labor force had doubled (to 1,327), and the occupational distribution had altered considerably. Farmers declined to 23 percent of the labor force, though the field still held a narrow lead over the second most common occupational type, which was now craftsmen and operatives (21 percent). The professions had climbed by 13 points to 19 percent and were now in third instead of last place. Clerical and sales workers declined 6 percent, while the proportion of managers/proprietors and service workers/laborers grew slightly.

By the current time, as we saw in chapter 7, the labor force had expanded again (to 1,998 sample males), and the professions had taken a commmanding 32 percent lead. Farming declined again to a mere 14 percent. The postwar rise in skilled and semi-skilled laborers (craftsmen and operatives) had dropped back to its prewar level of 12 percent. Clerical/sales workers and service workers/unskilled laborers remained about the same, each with 11 percent. Managers and proprietors continued to grow steadily to 20 percent.

Generally, then, a steep decline in farming and a sharp rise in the professions occurred over the three periods. More muted has been a steady growth in non-farm managers and proprietors. And the postwar rise in higher-level blue-collar work did not last.

WORK HISTORY AND YEAR OF BIRTH

One way to look at the changes in Nisei occupational structure is to trace age cohorts over time. Such an analysis is presented in table 10:1. It will be noticed from the totals that only the cohort born before 1915 was substantially established in the labor market before the war. The 1915-1924 group had about half its members working by the war but was only clearly established in the postwar period. The 1925-1934 group were generally postwar

TABLE 10:1
MALE NISEI YEAR OF BIRTH BY OCCUPATIONAL TYPE
IN THREE TIME PERIODS (MALES REPORTING)

| | *Year of Birth* | | | |
	Before 1915	*1915-1924*	*1925-1934*	*After 1934*
1932-1941 Labor force				
Professional	9%	5%	0%	
Proprietary	26	9	0	
Clerical	12	16	0	
Farm	35	51	86	
Crafts	9	11	7	
Service	9	8	8	
Total	100	100	100	
	(43)	(237)	(14)	(0)
1946-1952 Labor force				
Professional	15	21	20	
Proprietary	23	15	8	
Clerical	2	9	12	
Farm	40	25	23	
Crafts	8	18	26	
Service	13	12	12	
Total	100	100	100	
	(48)	(408)	(286)	(9)
Current labor force				
Professional	14	24	39	54%
Proprietary	25	19	21	6
Clerical	8	13	10	16
Farm	29	16	11	7
Crafts	8	15	11	11
Service	15	13	7	6
Total	100	100	100	100
	(59)	(485)	(433)	(183)

labor-force entrants, and those born after 1934 all started working well after the war. The table does not follow individual shifts over time, since it does not distinguish between job changers and new entrants to the labor force; this we will look at in the next section. Here we are concerned with the gross relationship of year of birth to occupational structure over time.

In the 1932-1941 period, the picture was very different from the current one. The eldest Nisei commanded the occupational structure, with a greater likelihood of being professionals and urban proprietors. The younger the Nisei male, the more likely he was to be confined to farming (probably in the role of employee or unpaid family laborer), so that among the youngest Nisei this was almost the only line of work found.

If we trace the oldest cohort over time, we find that their occupational distribution has not changed much. There has been a small decline in clerical and sales work and a slight increase in gardening, but these are minor shifts. The occupational characteristics of this "subgeneration" were fixed before the war and continued right through it.

Their relative position in the occupational structure of the Nisei generation as a whole, however, changed dramatically with time. By the postwar period they had lost their dominance among Nisei professionals, and a growing proportion of younger Nisei were entering the proprietary field, which their elders had once dominated. In addition, the younger Nisei had left farming in large proportions, to become overrepresented as craftsmen/operatives and clerical/sales workers. Thus, by 1946-1952, being older meant being in proprietorships and, especially, in farming. Youth was associated with lower-white-collar and upper-blue-collar jobs, and the professions were more or less evenly distributed over age groups.

The emergence of the youngest cohort straight into the professions in the current period, combined with a doubling in the proportion who were professional in the second-youngest cohort, swung that relationship of age to professional status completely around from the prewar situation. The middle age ranges showed another steep decline in farming and advance into managerial and proprietorial positions. The oldest cohort was left in control of farming, and, to a lesser extent, gardening. Unlike in the prewar period, they now had to share management and proprietorships with younger cohorts.

These trends show that the relationship of year of birth to occupational distribution was hardly something that was fixed early in the history of the generation. What did occur, instead, was a kind of wheeling movement, with the oldest group the most fixed, and the younger elements shifting around it.

OCCUPATIONAL MOBILITY

So far we have looked at the changing structure of the entire occupational distribution. Now we turn to individual movements to see whether there were patterns of mobility which characterized the Nisei. For example, are professionals today people who were always professionals, or have there been well-traveled routes from other occupations into the professions? We want to see the role early job history played in the individuals' current economic positions.

Let us start with the question of "outflow" from each occupational category. What proportion in each occupation remained in the same general line of work, and what proportion left? Of those who left, what occupations did they move to? Table 10:2 examines mobility from the point of view of outflow, for the prewar-to-postwar period and the postwar period to the present.

The major finding is that the persistence of a concentration in small business from prewar times to the present cannot be attributed to a tendency for the Nisei to remain fixed in an occupational type once they became established there. The top half of the table, relating the prewar-to-postwar period, clearly shows that only the professionals can be said to have remained stable in their occupational type through the war. For the other occupational types, 45 percent of the proprietors and managers, 74 percent of the clerical and sales workers, 40 percent of the farmers, 51 percent of the craftsmen and operatives, and 59 percent of the service workers and laborers left their prewar lines and shifted to some other field of endeavor.

One might be tempted to explain this mobility by the disruptions of the war, but an almost equal degree of outflow was evinced between the postwar period and the present (lower half of table 10:2). Moreover, the same basic patterns of outflow tended to remain. Professionals continued as professionals, while over half of clerical and sales workers, farmers, craftsmen and operatives,

TABLE 10:2
MALE NISEI OUTFLOW FROM OCCUPATIONAL TYPES, PREWAR
TO POSTWAR AND POSTWAR TO CURRENT (MALES AND
MARRIED FEMALES REPORTING)

	Job Held 1932-1941					
	Professional	Proprietary	Clerical	Farm	Crafts	Service
Job held 1946-1952						
Professional	86%	9%	14%	6%	5%	9%
Proprietary	0	55	22	10	23	14
Clerical	4	9	26	3	7	7
Farm	4	9	4	60	5	5
Crafts	4	14	22	12	49	25
Service	4	5	13	9	11	41
Total	100	100	100	100	100	100
	(28)	(58)	(93)	(210)	(57)	(44)
	Job Held 1946-1952					
Current job						
Professional	82	8	22	8	16	8
Proprietary	11	71	24	10	23	14
Clerical	2	10	38	9	8	10
Farm	1	2	6	49	3	8
Crafts	2	3	6	11	41	11
Service	2	5	5	14	9	49
Total	100	100	100	100	100	100
	(253)	(182)	(157)	(305)	(283)	(142)

and service workers and laborers changed their line of work. The one exception to this continuity of pattern is the proprietors and managers. Those Nisei who were in this line of work immediately after the war tended still to be there at the time of the survey.

Over the entire period from 1932 to the present, only the professionals retained more than half of their prewar incumbents. Fifty-four percent of prewar proprietors and managers were no longer in this line of work. As for the other four occupational types, two-thirds or more moved out of their prewar lines. It seems safe to conclude that the Nisei who entered the labor force before the war were not locked into a particular type of work from which they could not escape. The current version of the ethnic economy is not merely a remnant from prewar days—if anything, the relatively greater job stability of postwar proprietorships suggests it is primarily a postwar construction (or that, at any rate, the relocation in fact succeeded in dislodging much of the prewar structure for good). As we shall see, however, neither is this current economy entirely unrelated to its previous forms.

To which occupational types were the Nisei moving? From the period before to immediately following the war, all occupations other than professionals flowed toward skilled and semiskilled blue-collar work. This fits with historical writings on the effects of the evacuation. Other movements also occurred, however. In particular, both clerical/sales workers and craftsmen/operatives moved into management/proprietorship in significant proportions. If we assume that the majority of these became proprietors rather than managers, we see a feeder relationship within the small-business economy. To a lesser extent, prewar gardeners went into proprietorships after the war, as did even some of the farmers. On the other hand, hardly any of the nonprofessionals became professionals after the war.

The move into skilled and semiskilled blue-collar jobs tapered off considerably in the later time interval; and even those already in such jobs were leaving. There was, however, an increase of movement into the professions, especially by clerical/sales workers and craftsmen/operatives, while, as usual, few professionals left their lines of work. The mobility channels from clerical/sales and craftsmen/operatives into proprietorships remained strong. None of the other occupations fed into farming (providing one reason for why this field has been declining), while farming itself lost half its incumbents, the largest segment moving into gardening.

Over the whole time span, the movement into proprietorships from clerical and sales and from upper-blue-collar jobs became marked indeed. About one-third of each of these groups made the transition, and they were joined by a substantial proportion of the prewar service workers and laborers. The exodus of farmers was sustained, their ranks having been depleted by two-thirds. Unlike the three urban "lower" occupational types, however, farmers did not move into urban proprietorships but shifted, rather, into gardening, although perhaps a three-step process here—from farming to gardening to urban proprietorship—often obtained. There also appears to have been a three-stage flow from service work and labor before the war to upper-blue-collar jobs immediately thereafter and thence into urban proprietorships. Over the whole period, the professions remained in splendid isolation, losing few from their ranks and recruiting fairly few from other fields. We should note, in conclusion, that movement was not entirely upward. Many proprietors slipped down the occupational ladder, notably into clerical and sales work.

When we turn the subject around and look at mobility from the point of view of recruitment, quite different patterns emerge for the different occupational types. In the prewar-to-postwar interval (top half of table 10:3), the professions depended most heavily on new entrants to the labor force, followed by clerical and sales workers and skilled and semiskilled labor. The occupations more heavily oriented toward small business—proprietorships, farming, and gardening—were, on the other hand, less dependent on (or held less appeal for) newcomers. (The most popular occupations among new entrants were the professions and skilled and semiskilled labor, each attracting 23 percent of the

TABLE 10:3
SUMMARY OF MALE NISEI RECRUITMENT TO OCCUPATIONAL
TYPES (MALES AND MARRIED FEMALES REPORTING)

	Professional	Proprietary	Clerical	Farm	Crafts	Service
Prewar to postwar						
Stable from previous period	9%	18%	15%	41%	10%	13%
Mobile from other occupation	15	33	13	5	23	28
New to labor force	76	49	73	54	67	59
Total	100	100	100	100	100	100
	(254)	(182)	(158)	(305)	(285)	(143)
Postwar to current						
Stable from previous period	32	32	26	53	45	32
Mobile from other occupation	20	44	38	13	26	43
New to labor force	49	24	35	33	29	26
Total	100	100	100	100	100	100
	(655)	(409)	(227)	(279)	(258)	(218)

newcomers. The next most attractive was farming, commanding 20 percent. Clerical and sales work came next with 14 percent, followed by proprietorships with 11 percent and service work and labor with 10 percent.) In two out of three of the chief small-business categories, proprietorships and gardening, recruitment from other occupations was common. Proprietors tended to come from clerical and sales workers (11 percent) and farmers (12 percent), while gardeners were recruited more often from farmers (13 percent) than from any other occupational type. In contrast, farmers showed a high dependence, much higher than any other occupational type, on people who were already in that line before the war.

Recruitment patterns change when we look at the interval between the immediate postwar period and the present. There was greater overall stability during this period, reflecting, in part, a lower rate of new Nisei entry to the labor force. The professions still were most dependent upon new entrants to the labor force, but now craftsmen and operatives had lost their drawing power. (Thus, 44 percent of the new entrants to the labor market between the postwar period and the present entered the professions, a rise of 21 percent over the figure for the previous period. In contrast, only 10 percent of newcomers now entered skilled- and semiskilled-labor occupations, a decline of 13 percent.) As in the previous period, proprietorships and gardening depended heavily upon mobility from other occupations, but, surprisingly, clerical and sales workers showed a rise in recruitment from other occupational types. Of these mobiles, 12 percent came from farming, 10 from crafts, and 8 from proprietorships.

Over the entire time span, although farming drew almost no Nisei men from other occupations, there appears to have been a continual, if small, stream of fresh recruits which prevented the occupation from becoming even less prominent among current Nisei occupations. Thirteen percent of all new male Nisei labor-force members since the war entered farming. Gardening was the occupation most likely to draw people from other occupational types over the entire period. And of the 34 percent who were mobile into this occupation, 22 percent came from farming. By contrast, the professions drew only 8 percent from other occupations, while fully 89 percent were postwar labor-force entrants.

It appears that the professions were a special growth area for the Nisei. This primarily non-small-business occupational type is quite separable from the others. Among the five other occupational types there has been considerable movement. The chief end point of this movement has tended to be urban proprietorships. Clerical/sales workers and craftsmen/operatives have moved directly there. In contrast, farmers have moved into other urban occupations, notably gardening, perhaps en route to other types of proprietorships. At least gardeners themselves have tended to make this shift. Farming has lost many of its incumbents over time and has failed to recruit sufficient replacements, either from new entrants to the labor force or from other occupations, to maintain its proportion of the work force.

The fact that clerical/sales workers and craftsmen/operatives moved into proprietorships suggests that the line between the ethnic and nonethnic economies was not always sharply drawn. People might shift from one to the other, particularly in the direction of corporate to ethnic economy. We see here part of the basis for the continued vitality of small business among the Nisei. The process may involve accumulating enough capital while working in the corporate economy to establish, eventually, an independent small business. The one impermeable boundary is situated between the professions and the rest. Herein lies the strength of the corporate economy among the Nisei. The professions, working within it, are able to attract the young.

WORK HISTORY AND EDUCATION

As we noted in the last chapter, educational attainment increased dramatically among the younger Nisei. We also found that years of education had a sharp impact on occupational type, which suggests that at least some of the changes we have been observing in Nisei occupational structure were due to expanding educational opportunity. In this section we address two questions. First, has education always been a differentiator of the Nisei, or has this pattern only recently emerged? And second, have those Nisei with a particular level of education achieved a similar job distribution, regardless of when they entered the labor market? The two questions are related and together raise the issue of whether it was only an increase in education which accounted for the change in Nisei occupational structure over time, or whether education produced different payoffs in different time periods.

Table 10:4 examines the contribution of formal education to the occupational stratification of the Nisei over time. Looking down the table enables us to explore the effects of educational differences within a time period, while looking across it shows us how people of the same educational level fared in different time periods. It should be noted that we are not tracing the fate of the same cohort of people as we look across the table. Rather, we are looking at the overall shape of the relationship of education to occupational type over time.

Looking within eras first, we see that education has always been an important determinant of occupational type. In the prewar period, almost half of the postgraduates were professionals, while less education than this virtually eliminated the possibility of a professional occupation. Conversely, farming was the chief occupation of the less educated, and it declined with increasing years of education. Some college or a four-year degree led to concentration in clerical and sales work and, to a lesser extent, in proprietorships. The depression job market, thus, was not totally chaotic for the male Nisei: people tended to fall into occupational categories according to their training. This is only a tendency, to be sure. The 69 percent of college graduates who were employed as farmers or clerical and sales workers is a mark of hard times. Only postgraduate training provided a substantial chance of securing a professional job.

While the basic pattern remains in the postwar period, major changes occurred in the effects of education on job opportunities. At every level, education paid off much more handsomely than formerly in the form of professional work. Meanwhile, the less educated tended to concentrate less in farming and more in upper-blue-collar jobs. To a lesser extent, they were also more frequently involved in service work and unskilled labor after the war.

Finally, in recent times, the tie between higher education and the professions became dominant: there was a 73 percent difference between highest and lowest educational categories. With the exception of the professions and clerical and sales work, the less educated, especially those who did not attend college at all, were distributed over the rest of the occupational spectrum. Farming was more common, as was upper- and lower-blue-collar work, among those with less education. In every era, education has been a differentiator of the Nisei.

TABLE 10:4

MALE NISEI YEARS OF EDUCATION BY OCCUPATIONAL TYPE,
PREWAR, POSTWAR, AND CURRENT (MALES AND
MARRIED FEMALES REPORTING)

Years of Education	Occupational Type	1932-1941	1946-1952	Current
0-12	Professional	2%	4%	8%
	Proprietary	8	12	20
	Clerical	13	10	10
	Farm	53	33	21
	Crafts	13	26	20
	Service	12	16	21
	Total	100 (301)	100 (614)	100 (809)
13-15	Professional	1	12	24
	Proprietary	18	18	26
	Clerical	28	16	18
	Farm	34	21	14
	Crafts	14	24	13
	Service	5	8	5
	Total	100 (111)	100 (312)	100 (480)
16	Professional	15	42	61
	Proprietary	12	13	20
	Clerical	37	14	9
	Farm	32	13	5
	Crafts	2	10	2
	Service	2	7	4
	Total	100 (41)	100 (161)	100 (304)
17+	Professional	42	68	81
	Proprietary	9	10	11
	Clerical	15	8	4
	Farm	24	7	2
	Crafts	6	5	2
	Service	3	1	0
	Total	100 (33)	100 (158)	100 (310)

Looking across the table now, we see that every educational group participated—but not to the same degree—in the major changes in the Nisei occupational structure: the enlargement of the professional category and the decline of the agricultural sector. The enlargement of professional opportunities among college graduates (sixteen years of education) and postgraduates (seventeen years or more) in the postwar and current periods has been so great that the professions dominate the occupational distribution in these more-educated categories. By the more recent era, more than seven in ten male Nisei who had completed college, whether or not they had continued their education after college, went into the professions.

At the other end of the educational spectrum, the increase in professional opportunities was relatively slight, though it was surprisingly large for those with some college training but lacking the baccalaureate. There was a sharp decline in farming, even among those with a high-school education or less. Two occupations showed growth for this stratum: proprietorships and gardening. It is evident that education per se has not determined or restricted the occupational choices of the Nisei completely. In different time periods, lack of higher education led to different occupational types. Despite the era, it is likely that most of the jobs available to the least educated lay within the ethnic economy. The nature of these jobs has shifted with time, from farming to gardening and proprietorships.

We have seen, then, that education has always played a part in securing the Nisei better jobs, even during the prewar period of extremely constricted opportunities. However, the changing times (comprising a complex of factors, including changing job market, decline in racism, opportunity to recoup from wartime losses, and maturation of the generation) have also had an effect independent of education. By and large, the passing of time has worked to the benefit (if we assume the professions are a desirable line of work) of the Nisei. Meanwhile, the ethnic economy has come to be increasingly concentrated in the hands of the less educated.

It seems evident that, to the degree that Japanese Americans continue to pursue higher education in increasing numbers, the professions will grow. If the younger Nisei professionals continue to work for the corporate economy and shun self-employment (a big "if"), we should witness the continuing overall decline of Japanese American small business. On the other hand, the findings in this chapter indicate that, at least in the past, clerical/sales workers and craftsmen/operatives were not locked into the corporate economy. If this is still true today, we may see a continuing movement back into the ethnic economy among some of the younger Nisei.

Despite its overall decline, the small-business economy has been far from static. Heavily dominated by farming in the prewar days, there has been considerable movement into gardening and proprietorships. In addition, Nisei small business has apparently been able to draw on people working in the lower echelons of the corporate economy—clerical and sales workers and craftsmen and operatives. The immediate postwar integration of the Nisei, especially as craftsmen and operatives, was short-lived. Upper-blue-collar workers have gradually moved into small business for themselves, returning to prewar levels in this occupational type.

EFFECTS OF ISSEI OCCUPATION AND EDUCATION

In view of the substantial degree of shuffling of Nisei occupations between the prewar period and more recent times, we might well anticipate that characteristics of the immigrant generation explain but little of current Nisei economic patterns. In the following section we examine the degree to which this supposition is correct.[1] We begin by looking at the effects of Issei occupation on the Nisei, moving from there to an exploration of the consequences of Issei education.

The direct impact of Issei occupational type on Nisei occupational type is shown in table 10:5. The most striking feature of this table is the weakness of occupational transmission. Among the sons of Issei fathers whose primary occupation in the prewar period was farming, only one in four was in farming in the mid-1960s. Fewer than one-quarter of the surveyed sons of Issei proprietors were themselves proprietors. Only professionals among the Issei—and these were very rare—were able to hand down their occupational grouping to as many as half of their sons. The sons of

---

1. About one-third of the Issei in our sample were women, widows in every case, and generally surviving Issei older than the living fathers of other Nisei respondents. Because of this difference, and because of the possibility of misremembering the educational histories of deceased spouses, we will focus here on Nisei whose fathers lived long enough to be respondents to the JARP questionnaire.

TABLE 10:5
MALE NISEI CURRENT OCCUPATIONAL TYPE BY FATHER'S
OCCUPATIONAL TYPE, 1932-1941

Nisei Occupational Type	Issei Occupational Type					
	Professional	Proprietary	Clerical	Farm	Crafts	Service
Professional	61%	44%	43%	29%	42%	38%
Proprietary	11	23	14	14	16	18
Clerical	11	15	18	7	16	8
Farm	4	2	4	24	2	3
Crafts	7	9	11	14	16	14
Service	7	7	11	11	7	18
Total	100	100	100	100	100	100
	(28)	(198)	(28)	(360)	(43)	(71)

other Issei drifted toward the professions. This dominant tendency was remarkably equal for all but the sons of farmers, the distribution of whose careers seems to reflect the usual tendencies of sons of the soil who have moved into more urban settings.

Self-employment of the Issei was not closely reflected in Nisei patterns of self-employment: self-employed Nisei were only slightly more often sons of self-employed immigrants than were other Nisei. Moreover, the sons of the self-employed were not more likely to work as employees in Japanese-owned businesses. Participation in the ethnic economy was not directly transmitted from the first generation to the second.

Although only weak effects upon their sons' current occupations flowed from the self-employment of Issei, their occupational type seems to have been an important factor in Nisei propensity to enter the small-business world. Children of proprietors generally left the ethnic economy, while children of farmers were more likely to remain in it. More than half of the surveyed sons of farmers were in small business in the mid-1960s, as compared to about a third of sons of Issei proprietors. The effect persists within certain occupational types among the Nisei. Thus, even within the professions, Nisei whose fathers were farmers were somewhat more likely to follow the small-business form of self-employment. Many more Nisei proprietors, managers, and officials, of course, did so, but among them, it was similarly the sons of farmers who most often were in the ethnic economy. The effect was even stronger among service workers and laborers, where gardeners were more likely to be farmers' sons. Generally, then, farmers seem to have prepared their sons for perpetuation of the ethnic-economy mode, while urban businessmen did not.

To what extent are these findings the reflection of different formal educational careers afforded to Nisei from different backgrounds? Table 10:6 shows the impact of Issei occupation and self-employment on Nisei education, asking how much education sons of Issei with different prewar occupations attained. Apart from the expected discovery that Issei professionals produced more-educated Nisei offspring, a strong finding emerges from the table. The children of urban proprietors often received higher education, while the children of farmers rarely did. The two categories of self-employed Issei had sons many of whose educational (and thereafter occupational) careers differed markedly. This is important because it suggests that while farmers were preparing their sons to continue in their own line of work by not sending them to college, urban proprietors were in effect paving the way for the decline of their own economic form. This was not necessarily the intention of Issei store owners, who, as we have suggested, probably sent their children to college partly hoping it would help make them better business operators. As we have seen in chapter 9, however, higher education had the effect of enabling Nisei to leave their parents' businesses.

These differences may be a product of many factors, including exposure to opportunities in the cities, the educational requirements of farming versus those of proprietorships, more wealth in the hands of proprietors, and a greater conservatism among farmers; but whatever the reasons, the occupations of the fathers of the Nisei had important effects on Nisei educational attainment—and this in turn was closely tied to Nisei occupational differentation.

Was it because urban proprietors gave their children more education than farmers that these Nisei left the ethnic economy? Or was there a direct relationship between Issei occupation and Nisei small-business concentration, even if we control for Nisei education? We find that Nisei education cannot entirely explain the effects of Issei occupational type, though it does to some extent. If a male Nisei only received high-school education or less, the occupational type of his father was an important factor in determining whether he participated in the ethnic economy. Thus, even if a proprietor did not send his son to college, that son was

TABLE 10:6

MALE NISEI YEARS OF EDUCATION BY FATHER'S OCCUPATIONAL TYPE AND SELF-EMPLOYMENT

Nisei Years of Education	Issei Occupational Type						Issei Type of Employment	
	Professional	Proprietary	Clerical	Farm	Crafts	Service	Self-employment	Non-self employment
0–12	14%	23%	14%	49%	13%	36%	39%	25%
13–15	28%	27	41	24	47	36	26	34
16	14	24	17	14	24	14	17	19
17+	45	26	28	13	16	14	18	21
Total	100	100	100	100	100	100	100	100
	(29)	(209)	(29)	(374)	(45)	(74)	(568)	(182)

more likely than a farmer's high-school-graduate son was to work in the corporate economy. On the other hand, among the college-educated Nisei, father's occupation was less important. College-educated Nisei were likely to be found in the corporate economy regardless of their fathers' occupations. The two effects, father's occupation and Nisei's education, were additive.

The data show, then, that Issei occupation did have an impact on whether the Nisei continued in small business, and this impact was mediated, in part, by the educational opportunities Issei with different occupations could afford their sons. Generally, urban proprietors paved the way for their children's departure from the ethnic economy, while the sons of Issei farmers became the stronghold of Japanese American small business.

The education of the Issei also affected their sons' careers. Interestingly, this was true regardless of whether the Issei had received their education in Japan or in the United States. There was a strong tendency, on the one hand, for the sons of Issei fathers who had had little formal education in Japan and none in the United States to go no further than high school. On the other hand, if the immigrant had received a fairly high level of education in Japan and/or some education in this country, his sons were more likely to attend college and to graduate.[2]

The effect of fathers' educational levels on the occupations of the Nisei is presented in table 10:7. As can be seen, a combination of a low level of education in Japan and no United States schooling for the Issei was more likely to lead, among the Nisei, to small business and a lower concentration in the professions. Surprisingly, whether the Issei received high education in Japan or some education in the United States, consequences were more or less the same for Nisei occupational patterns. In combination, however, the two types of Issei education led to a second generation especially unlikely to participate in the ethnic economy and severely underrepresented as farmers. This suggests that education, whether here or in Japan, had a modernizing influence on the immigrants and their economic orientations, an influence that was transmitted through to the second generation.

2. High education in Japan refers to nine or more years of schooling there. Given the relatively small numbers of Issei with any schooling in the United States, we decided to dichotomize this variable into "none" and "any," a decision that makes some sense in light of the fact that any United States schooling probably had a major impact on language facility.

TABLE 10:7
MALE NISEI OCCUPATIONAL TYPE AND TYPE OF FIRM BY FATHER'S
EDUCATION IN JAPAN AND THE UNITED STATES

	Issei Education			
Nisei Occupational Type	Low Japan None U.S.	High Japan None U.S.	Low Japan Some U.S.	High Japan Some U.S.
Professional	28%	46%	44%	47%
Proprietary	18	15	18	18
Clerical	10	11	11	14
Farm	19	9	8	2
Crafts	13	11	13	13
Service	13	9	6	6
Total	100	100	100	100
	(361)	(139)	(120)	(85)
Nisei in small business	52	37	42	31
	(358)	(137)	(122)	(91)

We must ask whether the link between Issei education and Nisei economic activity was not strictly a function of related Nisei educational differences. Issei education might have affected the probability of Nisei pursuing an education, and this in turn might have affected their economic choices and opportunities. While a substantial part of the impact of fathers' education on Nisei economic form was a product of Nisei education as an intervening choice, not all of it was so accounted for. When we controlled for Nisei education, Issei education still had an effect on Nisei economic participation. In particular, apart from their own educational attainment, sons of the less educated Issei were more likely to be farmers. Educated Issei, conversely, especially often had sons who became professionals, even in those rare instances when the sons themselves did not complete college.

Thus, part of the differentiation among the Nisei is accounted for by differences among their parents. If their parents received a certain amount of education in Japan or in the United States or if they became urban proprietors, the Nisei were more likely to receive college education and leave the ethnic economy. Those who remained in the small-business mold, on the other hand, were more likely to have had less-educated fathers who had become farmers.

CONCLUSION

This chapter has traced the historical processes that have encouraged differentiation among the Nisei. We found that Nisei who have perpetuated the middleman-minority form are more likely to be the sons of less-educated Issei and of farmers. In contrast, Issei urban proprietors were more likely to have provided their sons with education, enabling them to leave the middleman form. Parental effects were muted, however, by the timing of Nisei entrance into the job market. While education always increased the likelihood of leaving the ethnic economy, its impact was less for those Nisei entering the labor force before the war. The ethnic economy has become increasingly the province of educationally distinctive Nisei.

Once the Nisei came into the job market, certain mobility tracks were available to them, while others were closed. In particular, the professions depended on people with higher education and tended to attract fresh labor-market entrants rather than recruits from other occupations. The other occupational types experienced considerable movement. The ethnic economy sat upon a shifting structure, with the sons of farmers moving into gardening and urban proprietorships. Since the Nisei seem to have followed the pattern of their parents in providing considerable education for their children, we would anticipate that few third-generation Japanese Americans will operate ethnic small businesses for long. Their careers will most likely resemble those of the youngest Nisei, although they will have even less reason to develop a niche in an ethnic economy than did the youngest of their parents' generation.

11

Residence

The Japanese American community differs markedly from place to place, as do Nisei occupational concentrations. In this chapter we ask whether the ethnic economy is more prevalent in certain localities, and if so, why.

From the start, the few Japanese who settled in eastern states had quite different experiences from those living on the West Coast. In the East, according to Conroy and Miyakawa (1972: 153), "Issei did not face organized anti-Japanese movements. . . . They were occupationally and residentially more urban than the West Coast Issei. . . . They lived in various parts of the cities and did not develop the organized community life found in a number of West Coast cities." Some of the eastern Issei were representatives of Japanese corporations, some were international artists and intellectuals, and some were not, rightly speaking, immigrants at all but rather men and women of the world. These eastern Issei were not traditional agriculturalist or fishers seeking economic opportunities, but an adventuresome arm of the most advanced part of Japanese society. On the East Coast, a region certainly not free from racism, nativism, and anti-immigrant movements, there never developed an anti-Japanese movement. Neither was there the type of small-business ethnic economy that put the Pacific Coast Japanese on such a collision course with the surrounding society. In other words, the East Coast Japanese did not become a middle-man minority.

Even in the more homogeneous western region there was some differentiation by residence. Thomas (1952:26) describes how it was harder to get a foothold in agriculture in Washington than in California because in the former state, "there was no ready-made labor demand of the sort existing in California, where the withdrawal of the Chinese coincided with a tremendous expansion of intensive agriculture at the height of the Japanese immigration."

Differences between rural and urban areas existed. Broom and Kitsuse (1956:9-11) point out that rural families maintained much tighter parental control over the second generation, in part because the Nisei were tied into the family farm as unpaid family labor. In urban areas, Nisei were more likely to be paid workers, which made their economic contribution more apparent and gave them a measure of independence. City living also fostered more social emancipation from parental authority by permitting Nisei peer groups to develop, in which they might voice common complaints against their parents. Even among urban areas there were important differences. San Francisco, with its powerful labor unions, proved to be an unfavorable environment for Japanese small business, while Seattle and open-shop Los Angeles were centers of rapid ethnic-economy development (Thomas, 1952:31-33).

The war and the forced relocation of all Pacific state Japanese Americans created some new centers of Japanese American residence—notably Chicago—and of course disrupted all varieties of Japanese American community life but failed to prevent a gradual return by the majority to the Pacific. The return to the West Coast, however, did not mean that the same areas of concentration were being established there. Most notable was a marked residential shift from rural to urban areas.

Regional differentiation developed after the war, too, in part because different areas of the country attracted different types of people. Using census materials to compare the occupations of Japanese American male urban dwellers who were twenty-five to forty-four years old in 1950, in the western, northern, central, and eastern areas, Thomas (1956:102-105; see also Varon, 1967, for a somewhat similar set of relationships, by 1960 overlaid by a general high rate of recruitment into the professions) found that the northeasterners had a very high concentration in the professions (34 percent) and a low concentration in laboring and service (18 percent). In contrast, only 10 percent of western city dwellers were professionals, while 32 percent were in service and labor. The north central region fell between these extremes and also stood out for a concentration in skilled blue-collar occupations: 49 percent of the male Nisei living there (predominately in Chicago) were craftsmen and operatives, almost double the proportions of northeastern and of western city dwellers found in this occupational type. The JARP data enable us to analyze regional and local variations in economic activity in more detail than does the census and, more importantly, to examine variations in the degree to which an ethnic economy has been retained or reestablished.

REGIONS

Table 11:1 reveals how general was the tendency for Nisei outside of the traditional Japanese American enclaves also to be outside the small-business economy in the mid-1960s and how widespread was the reestablishment of small business in the resettled areas in the Pacific region (as well as in the nonrelocated communities in the intermountain region, though to a lesser degree). Summarizing the detailed information in terms of regions, we find that from west to east the concentration in small business dwindled.[1] Differences in occupational type are also striking. The northeast region showed a heavy concentration in the professions but was relatively low in proprietary and managerial occupations. The southern and north central regions were middle range in terms of the professions and showed a higher concentration in the proprietary, managerial, clerical, and sales fields. The north central area stood out for having a high proportion of skilled labor, as shown in previous studies. Both mountain and Pacific regions had relatively low concentrations of professionals and high levels of farmers, although the mountain region exceeded the Pacific in the proportion of the latter.

The numbers are too small to permit a regional comparison of ethnicity of firm within each occupational type, but we can compare the Pacific area with the others combined. Generally, Pacific Coast Nisei were more often in the ethnic economy within each occupational type. Thus 72 percent of Pacific Coast proprietors and managers were in small business, compared to 62 percent

1. Some of the regions are combined to provide large enough figures to enable us to make comparisons. Thus we combined New England and the Middle Atlantic states and classified them as northeast; the east, central, and west central areas as north central; and the South Atlantic, east south central, and west south central regions as south. Because of the large numbers residing in the mountain and Pacific states, however, we have kept these regions separate.

TABLE 11:1

MALE NISEI PERCENT IN SMALL BUSINESS AND OCCUPATIONAL TYPE
BY REGION OF RESIDENCE (MALES AND MARRIED FEMALES REPORTING)

	North East	South	North Central	Mountain	Pacific
Professional	70%	47%	49%	26%	28%
Proprietary	11	20	20	18	20
Clerical	2	12	8	9	12
Farm	0	6	3	26	15
Crafts	12	8	19	12	12
Service	4	8	1	9	13
Total	100	100	100	100	100
	(56)	(51)	(226)	(140)	(1560)
Nisei in small business	23	29	30	47	51
	(56)	(52)	(226)	(139)	(1555)

of those in the rest of the country, while among service workers
and laborers, 86 percent of Pacific Nisei worked in the ethnic
economy, as compared to only 45 percent of non-coast residents.

Year of birth does not explain the regional variation in
concentration of Nisei in small business. The weak age variation
across regions did not follow the pattern of economic differences.
Indeed, the return to the Pacific Coast was especially prominent
among the young, and this shows up in our data. It was the north
central and southern regions that had fewest young Nisei. In
contrast, education did vary by region in the same direction as
small-business concentration. Of the northeastern Nisei, a stagger-
ing 40 percent had some postgraduate training, while only 22
percent had no college education. Among Pacific Coast residents,
on the other hand, only 14 percent had postgraduate training, and
44 percent had no college education. The mountain region was
virtually identical to the Pacific in educational distribution, while
the distributions in the two remaining regions lay between the
extremes.

The causes of regional differentiation lie, in part, in history.
The different regions attracted Issei from different backgrounds
and with different occupations, a factor that has had ramifications
into the second generation. The regions also differed in the

amount of antagonism expressed by the surrounding society to the Japanese, since hostility was at its peak on the Pacific Coast, encouraging the middleman minority's protective response of concentrating in independent businesses. Additionally, one would expect that the larger the number of Japanese Americans and/or the higher their concentration in the population, the more easily they could sustain an ethnic economy, not only because they would automatically have a base clientele, but also—and even more importantly—because the organizational and cultural ties that provide aid in building and maintaining a small business would be kept. In other words, all the factors that sustain a middleman minority, as depicted in figure 2:1, were stronger in the Pacific states.

PACIFIC REGION

Since the bulk of the Japanese American population was located in the Pacific region, we have the numbers by which we can examine breakdowns more fine than broad regional ones. In particular we will look briefly at the three Pacific Coast states and at urban-rural differences.

Japanese American small business was about equally strong in the three Pacific states, with 50 percent of the Washington Nisei, 54 percent of the Oregon Nisei, and 51 percent of the California Nisei engaged in small business. There were occupational differences, however. In particular, Oregon stood out as a farming area for the Nisei, with almost 32 percent of its second generation engaged in this line of work, more than twice the proportion found in the other two states. Washington led the way in the category of proprietors and managers, while California dominated the region in concentration of service workers and laborers.

To examine urban-rural differences in the Pacific area, we have separated Los Angeles, the metropolis of Japanese America, from other West Coast cities and from other parts of the region. Table 11:2 shows the differences in occupational type and small-business orientation for Los Angeles and for rural and urban sections of the balance of the Pacific region. The rural areas, of course, contained many farmers and hence are recorded as heavily concentrated in the ethnic economy. Rural small-business Nisei were by no means exclusively farmers, however—they also served rural communities as storekeepers and the like. Los Angeles, where the origins of the Issei community were agricultural, was now considerably less agricultural than other Pacific cities. No doubt, this was partly a function of land prices, as otherwise Nisei there tended distinctly toward the small-business economy, especially in service occupations (notably gardening). Only those living in cities served mainly Japanese American clienteles, and of these the majority were in Los Angeles.

(It is instructive here to compare occupational patterns of Chicago Nisei. Chicago was the largest area of post-1941 Japanese American settlement. Forty-three percent of Chicago's Nisei males were professionals in the mid-1960s, compared to 28 percent for Los Angeles and 32 percent for other Pacific Coast urban Nisei males. At the other end of the occupational spectrum, only 1 percent were service workers and laborers in Chicago. Thirty-four percent of the Chicago Nisei males were in small business, but this was one-third lower than the Los Angeles level of 51 percent. In areas where the urban ethnic economy was not built up before the war, it developed only hesitantly thereafter.)

TABLE 11:2

MALE NISEI OCCUPATIONAL TYPE AND SMALL-BUSINESS AFFILIATION, PACIFIC AREAS ONLY (MALES AND MARRIED FEMALES REPORTING)

	Pacific Rural	*Pacific Urban Excluding Los Angeles*	*Los Angeles*
Professional	15%	32%	28%
Proprietary	12	21	22
Clerical	8	13	13
Farm	52	15	6
Crafts	6	11	14
Service	8	8	18
Total	100	100	100
	(172)	(628)	(754)
Nisei in small business	74	46	51
	(172)	(625)	(752)

In the Pacific states, within each occupational type the concentration in small business was higher among rural Nisei than among those living in Los Angeles, the latter, however, being more prone toward small-business involvement than any other urban Nisei in the West. (Service workers and laborers were an exception, with Los Angeles leading even the rural areas in concentration of self-employment within this occupational type.)

RESIDENTIAL HISTORY

Residential mobility helps to shed light on the question of culture versus concentration. If Nisei who were raised in one area and moved to another retained the economic forms of their childhood area, we may conclude that cultural factors were in operation; but if regional shifts were accompanied by changes in economic form, the structural factors that differentiated the regions were evidently at work, affecting individuals regardless of their heritage. (Of course, a Pacific Coast Nisei may have moved elsewhere precisely to escape from the ethnic economy. Such choices, however, would perpetuate historical distinctions and point to structural roots of residential differentiation.)

The wartime evacuation was aimed exclusively at Pacific Coast residents, accompanied by an official hope that they would disperse residentially and not recongregate in the West. Looking at the principal place of residence before the war (1932-1941) and immediately after it (1946-1952) we find that about 90 percent of the male sample Nisei in the northeast, south, and north central regions remained where they were. All who moved, however, went to the Pacific region. Seventy-nine percent of mountain-state dwellers remained where they were; 14 percent moved westward. By 1946-1952, 72 percent of prewar Pacific Nisei had returned. The largest segment—19 percent—of those remaining dispersed was in the north central area, especially in Chicago.

Between the postwar period and the mid-1960s, the three easternmost regions had lost still more Nisei, some to the mountain region but most to the Pacific states. The north central area had lost eight-tenths of its postwar complement of Nisei; most of these moved to the Pacific Coast, but some had gone to the mountain states. Mountain-state Nisei, too, continued to move out to the Pacific region, 31 percent of the postwar group having done so by the mid-1960s. The overall picture is one of continuing movement to the Pacific area, not only by people who had been evacuated from there, but even by people born and raised elsewhere. A minority remained away from the Pacific region, including original residents, people who had been compelled to relocate by the war, and subsequent emigrants.

The relationship of residential history to small business is complex. For those who lived outside of the Pacific region before the war, current residence made little difference to economic form. Forty-five percent of those still living away from the Pacific region in the mid-1960s were in small business, compared to 44 percent of those who had moved to the Pacific region. This fact suggests cultural continuity, but when we look more closely, we find that 20 percent of the stable non-Pacific residents were farmers, compared to only 6 percent of those who moved from the non-Pacific areas before the war to the Pacific Coast thereafter, probably a function of the dominance of mountain-region Nisei among the nonmovers, for many of these were in farming before the war and were rarely disrupted in this enterprise.

For prewar Pacific residents, the picture is much clearer. Among those living away from the Pacific region in the mid-1960s, only 27 percent were engaged in small business, a figure far lower than the 51 percent of those who left but subsequently returned and took up small business. This suggests a pattern: escape from the ethnic economy could be achieved by leaving it geographically, while a return to the coast signified, at least for many, a return to prewar economic forms. The contrast in occupational type confirms this picture. Thirty percent of the returnees were professionals, compared to 54 percent of those who moved eastward. Professionals possessed the skills that enabled them to leave the ethnic economy geographically as well as organizationally. In contrast, those who were involved in small business appear to have found it difficult (or undesirable) to move away from the Pacific area.

These findings support a structural rather than a cultural interpretation of regional differentiation: even those raised in the cultural milieu of the Pacific Coast were differentiated according to where they lived at the time of the survey. The ethnic economy seems to have thrived in the Pacific states and not in the East, regardless of the background of the personnel who made up its residents.

LOS ANGELES

Residential differentiation raises the possibility that some of the relationships we have found so far are not real and would disappear if we controlled for region. To examine this possibility we have tried to treat residence as a constant by focusing on one place, Los Angeles. Here we have a large enough sample to do an internal analysis. We shall not repeat every relationship described so far, only a few of the more important ones.

In chapter 7 we found that income was distributed differently in the ethnic and corporate economies, with the latter providing more middle-income security and the former harboring poorer Nisei as well as providing opportunities for greater wealth. This finding persisted in Los Angeles. Forty-six percent of those in small business there earned less than $10,000, compared to 29 percent of those not in small business; but at the other end of the scale, 14 percent of the small-business people earned over $20,000, compared to 9 percent of the people in the corporate economy. (The ethnic economy was more balanced to the poor side in Los Angeles than in the rest of the country, undoubtedly reflecting the higher proportion of poorly paid gardeners in the city.)

Cohort occupational patterns among the Nisei were the same as in the rest of the nation. The youngest cohort of Nisei, born before 1935, were 45 percent professionals, compared to 42 percent of those born in 1925-1934, 16 percent of the 1915-1924 group, and 7 percent of the pre-1915 cohort. Conversely, gardening, and to a much lesser extent farming, were more likely to be engaged in by older Nisei. Younger Nisei in Los Angeles were far less often engaged in small business: 68 percent of those born before 1925 were in small business, compared to 41 percent of those born in 1925-1934 and 28 percent of those born after 1934. The greater concentration within the ethnic economy in Los Angeles was due to the number of older Nisei in the city and their unusually strong tendency to engage in this economic form.

As we saw in chapter 9, small business was much stronger among the less educated Nisei, a trend that remained strong in Los Angeles. Sixty-eight percent of Los Angeles Nisei with high-school education or less were in small business, as compared to 45 percent of those with thirteen to fifteen years of schooling, 30 percent of the college graduates, and 32 percent of the postgraduates. Similarly, the highly educated in Los Angeles were heavily concentrated in the professional fields (80 percent of the postgraduates were professionals), as in the rest of the country.

Overall, there seems little reason to believe that the major findings are spuriously due to residential differentiation. Even within Los Angeles, similar relationships were found. Our thesis, then, does not depend on a particular local ecology.

CONCLUSION

In this chapter we found that the middleman-minority form was more prevalent among second-generation Japanese Americans residing in the Pacific Coast states than among Nisei residing elsewhere. Given considerable historical reshuffling of personnel, this regional specialization was surprisingly stable, suggesting that features of the region itself contributed to it. At least two relevant characteristics present themselves: that the middleman form requires a critical mass to supply the social supports for retaining a small-business concentration, and that a history of occupying a middleman position, including a legacy of societal hostility that drives people back to the protection of the ethnic economy, may be a necessary condition for continuing the form. Both are probably important, and both help to explain the relative vitality of Japanese American small business on the coast.

Throughout part II we have examined some of the factors that divide the Nisei into those who have continued in the path of their parents by retaining a middleman-minority position and those who have not. There has been important attrition among the second generation, yet a surprising 40 percent have recreated, even after the tremendous dislocation of the wartime treatment of the minority, some semblance of prewar economic forms. Generally, second-generation middlemen are the oldest and least educated of their generation. They tend to derive from farming backgrounds, which in turn may reflect lower educations and poorer backgrounds of their parents. In addition, they tend to congregate in the Pacific region. All of these characteristics suggest that the ethnic economy may be a protective pattern for Nisei who think themselves not competitive in the general economy. There is still the possibility of doing well financially in the small-business world for a few, however, notably independent professionals and some farmers, so that the form does hold a positive attaction as well. That this positive attraction has its strongest effect among the older Nisei, including first sons, suggests a continuing cultural contribution to the form.

The route out of the middleman form seems fairly clear. Youth, education, a professional job, residence outside of the Pacific region—all spell the decline of the middleman form for second-generation Japanese Americans. The tremendous importance of age suggests the dominance of historical experience in the outcome. Most Nisei who were too young to suffer the terrible discriminations of the prewar job market were somehow freed from the middleman role. Many Nisei pursued higher education, anticipating that it would probably lead to a rewarding professional career in the corporate economy. Of course, this confidence may have been as much a product of postdepression changes in the general economy as of changes in the public's attitude toward the Japanese. Although the Japanese experienced the war as a more traumatic dividing line than did other groups, it may also be the case that other middleman groups in the United States, such as the Jews, Armenians, and Greeks, show roughly simultaneous subgenerational shifts. If so, it would suggest that changes in the general opportunity structure in the United States were more important in the decline of the middleman form among the Nisei than was the war.

Part III
CONSEQUENCES FOR ETHNIC SOLIDARITY

12

The Family

If the middleman-minority approach makes sense of Japanese American economic patterns, then participation in ethnic small business has been linked with the retention of ties to the ethnic community, and vice versa. A hypothesis that follows from this reasoning is that many of the Nisei who have moved into the broader economy should have loosened their ties to the ethnic community, while those who have continued to be involved in small business will more often have preserved bonds with the ethnic community. We argue, in other words, that even in a period when ethnic adherence is voluntary and is scarcely penalized by the outside society, a period when ethnic diversity is widely praised, attachment to the ethnic group fades when the felt economic need for it fades. Although we only consider the specific historical setting of the Nisei in the mid-1960s, the question is one of general significance for cultural pluralism under advanced capitalism.

In part III we first take up three important aspects of the ethnic community, examining the degree to which in the mid-1960s each was dependent upon the small-business focus of the modified postwar ethnic economy. These three factors proceed, as it were, outwardly from the relatively intimate to the relatively remote. Family and kin interactions are examined first, in this chapter. Acquaintances, friends, neighborhood, and ethnic-newspaper readership are then scrutinized, in the first part of chapter 13, under the general rubric of informal associations. The final theme in the associational trio concerns formal organizations and leadership, which occupies the last section of chapter 13. Under these topics, the ties that voluntarily link individuals of Japanese descent to an identifiable Japanese American community are assessed, with special attention paid to the degree to which they depend on participation in the Japanese American small-business economy.

The third and final chapter in this section explores the Japanese American community from a different standpoint: that of overt values and value-based behaviors. Here we examine parts of the meaningful basis for the Japanese American ethnicity that respondents expressed in the mid-1960s. Ideally, we would like to see whether either socialized values or attitudes and beliefs carried by religious adherence can be said to have provided a basis for Japanese American ethnicity, independent of an economic basis. We are aware, however, that our cultural data are imperfect indicators and that we must unfortunately rest content with a set of findings that lend some support to our argument, but do so more suggestively then conclusively.

The ethnic economy of the prewar period was to an important degree a family economy. Depending on unpaid labor from within the nuclear household, on cut-rate labor from other kin, and upon business connections provided by the kinship network and its kenjinkai extensions, the ethnic firm grew in the soil of familial ties of obligation. In this chapter we raise the question of the degree to which the reconstructed Nisei ethnic economy was still linked to family in the mid-1960s. Did the ethnic economy encourage familism at this late date, and did family solidarity still subserve the ethnic economy? Our questionnaire did not elicit a full account of the kinds of work-related assistance Japanese American family members provided for one another, but it does indicate something of the degree of interpenetration of the family and the ethnic economy and shows how this varied among Nisei of different age and in different geographical contexts.

The Nisei entirely removed from his or her own kin and spouse's kin in the mid-1960s was rare. Of the male Nisei in our sample, only 16 percent told the JARP survey that, apart from wife and children, they had no relatives living in the same metropolitan area or county; only 19 percent of the Nisei women were geographically removed from kin; and about one-half of both men and women were enough embedded in kin settings to be able to report five or more relatives in the area.

For the Nisei in small business, the figure was even more extreme: a mere 9 percent of those in business for themselves lived in cities or counties where they had no relatives. Thirteen percent of the employees of Japanese American firms did so, but 21 percent of those employed in the corporate economy were in this sense on their own. There was even a similar relationship for women whose husbands were in the small-business world of the ethnic economy, though the difference was not quite so strong. The questionnaire did not exclude in-laws from the classification of relatives; perhaps both the husband's and the wife's families sometimes provided support (in a broad sense) for Nisei small business.

Occupational type was also related to the presence of relatives in the same city or county as Nisei respondents. Farmers least frequently settled entirely apart from relatives, with only 8 percent of them reporting no relatives living in the vicinity. Service workers and laborers often reported local relatives in large numbers, 67 percent of them reporting five or more living in the same city. At the other end of the scale, professionals proved especially likely to have moved away from relatives. Twenty-six percent told us that none of their relatives resided in the same city; only 39 percent reported having two or more relatives present. Evidently, family ties complemented certain distinctive lines of work.

Within each occupational type, those in the ethnic economy were more prone to have relatives living in the vicinity. The difference was most striking for service workers and laborers: 92 percent of those in small business had at least one relative in the same city or county, while only 68 percent of those in the corporate economy did. Similarly, 92 percent of the ethnic-firm proprietors and managers had at least one relative in the area, compared to 79 percent of the corporate proprietors and managers. The figures for independent and corporate professionals are 82 percent and 73 percent, respectively, and for clerical and sales workers, 95 percent and 86 percent. Only in the craftsmen-and-operatives category did an equally high proportion in the two economic forms have relatives in the same city or county. It should be noted that regardless of occupational type, never did more than 20 percent of the Nisei in the small-business economy live so isolated from family ties as to have no relatives at all in the same city or county.

Certain occupational types evidently permitted Nisei more flexibility in terms of the possibility of moving away from relatives, but at the same time the organization of the firm (small business versus corporate) crosscut this dimension, with those in small business being pulled closer to their relations. (Of course it is possible that those working in small business may simply have been more free, as independents, to choose which city or county to live in, and that, if equally free, corporate employees would likewise have chosen to live near relatives.)

Among relatives, residential proximity of parents and siblings seems most closely related to small-business participation, suggesting that continuity of residence rather than the active seeking of relatives to live near may be the touchstone. Of self-employed Nisei and those working for Japanese American employers, 76 percent lived in the same city or county as did their parents and/or at least one sibling. Among the Nisei working outside the ethnic economy, 59 percent lived in the same city or county as their parents, and 64 percent had a brother or sister living in the area. Small-business members were also slightly more likely than corporate-employed Nisei to have had non-nuclear-family members in the same metropolitan area or county.

Since stochastic processes alone would make it more likely that younger Nisei would be more prone to live near relatives, the interplay of age and firm type upon this feature of ethnic life, shown in table 12:1, is especially interesting. In each age cohort, not surprisingly, the corporate-economy people were more likely to have been living away from the family. However, differences were most striking in the youngest cohort, among whom those in the corporate economy were hardly less likely to be living away

TABLE 12:1

MALE NISEI WITH PARENTS OR SIBLINGS LIVING IN THE SAME
METROPOLITAN AREA OR COUNTY BY TYPE OF FIRM
CONTROLLING FOR YEAR OF BIRTH

	Year of Birth			
	Before 1915	*1915-1924*	*1925-1934*	*After 1935*
Percent with parents present				
Small business	69	75	74	91
Corporate economy	55	60	57	63
Percent with siblings present				
Small business	67	76	74	87
Corporate economy	59	64	63	66
	(22)	(214)	(258)	(140)

from parents and siblings than were the oldest who shared their economic orientation. It is evident that the geographical break with family is an event, one that comes, if at all, rather early in the adult lives of those who have left the ethnic economy. For those pursuing the small-business route, the departure from parents and siblings was not only more rare but also considerably more gradual. One suspects that for many Nisei youth, the choice between the corporate and the ethnic economy was bound up with a choice between having the family nearby and residing at a great distance from it.

So far we have only concerned ourselves with the actual presence of relatives. We do, however, have a more obviously volitional measure of involvement with the family. Nisei with at least one relative in the same city or county were asked: "About how many times in the past month have you visited with or been visited by relatives living in the same metropolitan area or county as you?" The results indicate that Nisei in small business were more likely to have visited recently with relatives and that they were more likely also to have visited with them frequently. Four-fifths of the self-employed and three-quarters of those employed in Japanese American concerns, as compared with two-thirds of those employed outside the ethnic economy, had visited with a relative in the month preceding the survey. Four in ten of the self-employed had enjoyed five such visits, as compared with three in ten of those working in the corporate economy. Professional employment, even among those still living near relatives, seems to have been associated with considerably reduced family interaction: four in ten had had no such visits in the past month, and only 24 percent saw kin as often as five times in that period.[1]

---

1. The overall figures compare rather closely with figures for a sample of white residents of Greensboro, North Carolina, who would seem to have been roughly similar in age structure to our Nisei sample. The study, carried out by Adams (1968), does not eliminate those entirely lacking local relatives, but good proportions were lifetime Greensboro residents or, if not, had their parents living nearby. Adams is not interested in small business, but he is interested in social mobility. Among these whites, at least monthly interaction with relatives was considerably the most common (90 percent for males) among those characterized as downwardly mobile blue-collar workers and next most common (74 percent) among stable blue-collar workers. The least kin oriented (56 percent with monthly interaction) were stable white-collar workers, the group apparently most like our Nisei small-business group, who were strongly tied to kin. The difference in who seeks kin, we maintain, lies in the structural incentive for kin interaction produced by the continuing ethnic economy.

Kin interactions are a substantial part of ethnic-community life, seen broadly. Even within the Pacific Coast states, kin ties depended on elements of the ethnic context of places. Thus over three-quarters of rural Pacific Coast Nisei lived in the same county as their parents, but (leaving aside Los Angeles) only 58 percent of the urban Nisei did. Urbanization per se, however, is obviously not the key, for 80 percent of the Los Angeles Nisei had a parent nearby. In Pacific cities apart from Los Angeles, 28 percent had three or more kin of any kind in the neighborhood, but 43 percent of those in Los Angeles and 44 percent of those in the rural districts did. Rural Nisei with relatives in the vicinity depended greatly upon them for friendly contact: 49 percent of all rural Nisei reported five or more visits in the month prior to the survey, as compared with 38 percent of the Los Angeles Nisei and 33 percent of the other urban Nisei.

Living in the same city or county with one's relatives may have been a matter of chance; one may simply have a large number of relatives but have little or nothing to do with them. Living in the same neighborhood (or, in some cases, the same household), however, cannot be construed as accidental so easily; it often indicates a strong desire to maintain kinship ties or a set of friendship and institutional ties in which kin are typically embedded. By this criterion, it is evident that those Nisei who were in small business showed more attachment to their family. They were 18 percent more likely to live in the same neighborhood as relatives and typically had large numbers of relatives in the same neighborhood when they had any there at all. Employees in ethnic businesses were somewhat less likely to live close to their families than were the self-employed, but they too were substantially more likely to do so than the employees of non-Japanese concerns. One-half of those employed outside of the ethnic-small-business world were living in neighborhoods away from all other relatives. The comparable figure for the self-employed was one-third.

The two extremes among the occupational categories were, appropriately, professionals and farmers, the former being least likely to live in the same neighborhood as relatives and the latter most likely. Within each occupational type, those in small business more often lived close to relatives than did those working in the corporate economy—and this was especially true for proprietors and managers. (Indeed, corporate managers were even less likely to live near relatives than were professionals.) The professionals showed a surprising lack of differentiation in terms of familial ties. It appears that all professionals, regardless of organization of the firm, "preferred" to live apart from relatives, a unique arrangement among the self-employed Nisei (see table 12.2).

Even within a single-community context—Los Angeles, for instance—the relationship of economic form and kin embeddedness persists. Half of the Los Angeles Nisei men who were in small business or working for a Japanese American reported three or more relatives in the neighborhood. Those employed in the corporate economy lived near to this many relatives only 34 percent of the time, even in Los Angeles. Of the latter group, fully 44 percent lived in neighborhoods with no kin at all; but for those working in small business, the corresponding proportion was only 28 percent. Though in a statistical sense we could separate the interaction with kin and residence from participation in the ethnic economy, the historical and more profound truth of the matter is that our snapshot survey has captured a complex of choices that in all likelihood the particpants did not themselves separate analytically, a complex within which local milieus, family relations and economic form were tightly linked.

Living near relatives may not always have been wholly a matter of choice. In some cases Nisei might have preferred to distance themselves but lacked the economic wherewithal to make the break. In table 12:3 we look at the simultaneous effects of economic form and income on living near relatives. It is quite clear that Nisei in the two economies have been encouraged to diverge from their ethnic ties where income is greater. For those working within the Japanese American ethnic economy, there was a weak tendency to move out of family neighborhoods as income

TABLE 12:2

PROPORTION OF MALE NISEI WITH ANY RELATIVES IN THE SAME
NEIGHBORHOOD BY OCCUPATIONAL TYPE AND TYPE OF FIRM

	Professional	*Proprietary*	*Clerical*	*Farm*	*Crafts*	*Service*
Small business	39%	63%	72%	78%	65%	68%
	(72)	(141)	(36)	(147)	(23)	(87)
Corporate economy	42%	38	61		56	50
	(309)	(63)	(90)	(6)	(116)	(20)
Total	41	55	64	78	57	65
	(388)	(206)	(132)	(154)	(143)	(109)

TABLE 12:3
PROPORTION OF MALE NISEI WITH ANY RELATIVES IN SAME
NEIGHBORHOOD BY INCOME AND TYPE OF FIRM

Current Income	Small Business	Corporate Economy
To $10,000	71%	57%
	(195)	(206)
$10,000 – $19,999	60	44
	(186)	(369)
$20,000+	64	29
	(117)	(38)

increased. Among Nisei working in the general economy, though, the tendency to leave family neighborhoods when income permitted was indeed marked. The net result was that among those with a $20,000 or more annual income, over twice as many people in the small-business world lived near relatives than did those otherwise employed.

For most occupational types, increased income was associated with a decline in the proportion of those who had any relatives living in the neighborhood. Among professionals, for instance, 47 percent of those earning less than $10,000 a year had relatives in the neighborhood, compared to 38 percent of those who earned $20,000 or more. Farmers, however, provided an exception: wealthier farmers were more likely to live near relatives, the proportion with relatives in the neighborhood increasing from 73 percent for the farmers with the lowest incomes to 82 percent among farmers earning more than $20,000 annually. Nisei farmers obviously did not seek to move away from their families and may even have valued family attachments all the more as their farm enterprises increased in size.

In view of these differences in behavior, it is not surprising that there would be a difference in values consistent with the various uses that the family serves for persons differently situated economically. Thus the JARP survey found a palpable occupational difference when we asked respondents to agree or disagree with the statement "The best man is the one who puts his family above everything." Farmers, deeply connected with family, answered yes in 81 percent of the cases; professionals, however, agreed far less often: only 59 percent responded in favor of the statement. This difference is visible, though not so strongly, when we return to our small-business and corporate-economy division. The familistic statement was endorsed by 72 percent of those working in small business and by 61 percent of those otherwise employed.

This chapter has shown that economic form and family ties are related. The ethnic economy, or middleman-minority form, seems to support and to be supported by close relations with one's relatives. We should note, however, that family ties can be preserved either inside or outside a broader ethnic community. One may retain a strong bond with the family, but that family may be isolated from any contact with Japanese American community life. Therefore, in order to see the links between the middleman form and retention of an ethnic community, we must look beyond family relations. This is the subject of the succeeding chapter.

13

Informal and Formal Associations

INFORMAL FORMS OF AFFILIATION

In the previous chapter we saw that the maintenance of close familial ties among the Nisei tends to be related to participation in small business. Now we turn to the larger ethnic community to see whether small business also seems to support strong ethnic ties. In a later section of this chapter we study formal community organizations. The present section focuses on some of the more informal aspects of ethnic affiliation: the social relations surrounding the place of work, close friendship, the neighborhood, and the reading of ethnic newspapers.

WORKPLACE

Since we are concerned with the relationship between work and social relations, it seems logical to start with the social relations stemming from the work environment. The Nisei were asked, "About what proportion of people you see regularly at your present job are Japanese Americans?" and were presented with a checklist of decreasingly inclusive choices. The wording of the question left the respondent to define *people you see regularly*—they might be workmates, or clientele, or simply people who work in the vicinity of the workplace.

Married and widowed females reported about the ethnicity of their husbands' work environments, so we have combined the responses of women and men in this section. Only 4 percent of the Nisei respondents said that nearly all of those they saw at work were Japanese Americans; another 4 percent said about three-quarters were, and 6 percent replied that about half were. The vast majority, or 86 percent, worked in an environment that was less than one-half Japanese American; 14 percent said that about a quarter of those seen at work were Japanese Americans; 47 percent of the respondents told us they saw nearly none at work; and another 25 percent said they saw none whatsoever. Clearly, few Nisei could owe any sense of ethnicity they might have felt to isolation from people of backgrounds different from their own.

At the same time, some work environments had higher proportions of Japanese than others. To account for this fact, we decided to combine all those who said that at least one-quarter of the people they saw at work were Japanese Americans, making a total of 28 percent who worked with a relatively high number of Japanese.

This division turns out to be strongly related to small business. Only 13 percent of those employed in the corporate economy said that as many as one-quarter of the people they were exposed to at work were Japanese Americans. In contrast, 47 percent of those owning or working in small businesses saw this proportion of Japanese at work. Within small business, employees were more likely than owners to report a heavily ethnic work environment—67 percent of the former reported that at least one-quarter of their work associates were Japanese Americans—probably because ethnic firms with nonfamily employees were bigger than the average enterprise run by a Nisei. This is evidently something like the classic prewar situation. The owners of small businesses tended to report a less ethnic work environment, with 40 percent saying that one-quarter or more of the people they met at work were Japanese Americans.

Occupational types, too, varied considerably in terms of ethnicity of the workplace. Professionals rarely had much contact with Japanese Americans, as might be expected, with only 15 percent reporting that as many as one-quarter of the people they met were Japanese. Farmers were at the other extreme: 49 percent reported this level of contact. Proprietors and managers (36 percent), clerical and sales workers (34 percent), and craftsmen and operatives (25 percent) fell in the middle. The real surprise, however, lies with service workers and laborers: only 19 percent of them reported that one-fourth or more of the people they met at work were Japanese. Undoubtedly this is a product of the fact that gardening is a relatively isolated occupation that does not lend itself easily to building up a set of paid or unpaid employees, coupled with the fact that most gardeners work for non-Japanese families. Since most gardeners were self-employed rather than employees in small business, they tended to pull down the proportion of the self-employed who meet other Japanese Americans at work.

Table 13:1 shows, for each occupational type, the relationship between small business and contact with Japanese Americans at work. It is evident that regardless of occupational type, small business was associated with a much more heavily Japanese American work context, the only exception being gardening. Even the self-employed professionals fit the small-business mold here. While virtually all corporate occupational types showed low rates of meeting Japanese Americans at work, it is interesting to note that some individuals did not follow this pattern. This could be a product of misclassification on our part, but, more likely, it suggests that there is a certain degree of occupational clustering among the Nisei even in the corporate economy.

The Nisei were also asked how regularly they socialized off the job with those they saw at work. Such contacts were about equally frequent for those in small business and those outside of it. When we introduce the ethnicity of the work context into the equation, however, it turns out that those Nisei who worked in small business and for whom at least one-quarter of the people they met at work were Japanese Americans were more likely to report seeing people from work often. Twenty-seven percent so reported, compared to between 12 and 14 percent for the other three combinations. Generally, for Nisei outside of the ethnic economy, the tendency to socialize with people from work was not affected by their ethnicity. For Nisei males working in small

TABLE 13:1

PROPORTION OF NISEI MALES WHO MEET AT LEAST 25 PERCENT JAPANESE AMERICANS AT WORK BY TYPE OF BUSINESS AND OCCUPATIONAL TYPE
(MALES AND MARRIED FEMALES REPORTING)

	Professional	Proprietary	Clerical	Farm	Crafts	Service
Small business	42% (132)	47% (280)	56% (62)	51% (241)	67% (43)	20% (169)
Corporate economy	8 (504)	12 (122)	24 (151)	33 (18)	15 (201)	14 (37)

business (and their wives), though, the ethnicity of those they met at work made a substantial difference. The more Japanese Americans these people found in their work environment, the more likely they were to meet workmates socially. Conversely, where their work environments did not include Japanese Americans, people who worked in the ethnic economy were considerably less likely to meet work people socially than were those working outside the ethnic economy; 53 percent of the former reported they almost never saw people they met at work socially. Of those in small business who met at least one-quarter Japanese Americans at work, however, only 29 percent reported almost never or never meeting them socially. Of course, we cannot be sure that many of the people they were meeting were Japanese American, but it seems likely. Moreover, where this supposition is correct, we observe a clear instance of the characteristic Japanese American economic form sustaining a small bit of the ethnic community. A (presumably) prior decision to participate in the small-business economy has seemingly given a significance to ethnicity which was lacking for those working in the corporate world. A special kind of interpenetration between economic and social concerns exists in the ethnic economy, one supporting the informal aspects of association we have learned to think of as ethnic.

FRIENDSHIP

Members of the Nisei sample were asked about their friends in such a way that we might discern some facts about their informal patterns of contact, those potentially far removed from the world of work: "We want to know a few things about the people who are presently your closest friends outside your immediate family—that is, the people whom you see most often or feel closest to. Think for a moment of *two* people you would say are your closest friends." The respondents were then asked about the ethnicity of each of these friends and also how near to the respondent each friend lived. We have elected to cut the distribution at a particular point: between those whose two closest friends were both Japanese Americans (47 percent of the sample), and all others, whether both or one friend was non-Japanese.

Generally, friendship was not a function of neighborhood. Two-thirds of the best friends lived outside of the respondents' neighborhoods, and ethnicity of friends was unrelated to residential proximity. Economic form, however, was closely related to ethnicity of friends. When the man in the household worked in the corporate economy, both husband and wife were less likely to include only Japanese as their two closest friends. Forty-three percent of the Nisei men employed by non-Japanese concerns and 38 percent of the wives of these men reported that their two best friends were Japanese Americans. In contrast, no less than 71 percent of the employees of Japanese American firms limited their two closest friendships to fellow ethnics, as did 61 percent of the wives of men so employed. Once again, the self-employed showed a middle-range figure: 57 percent with two Japanese American friends for the men, 53 percent for their wives. While the proportion with Japanese American best friends is multiply determined (for example, by size of the local Japanese American community as well as by firm type), small-business participants in different settings continued to have more Japanese American best friends than did Nisei working outside of the ethnic economy.

Occupational type, too, was connected to ethnicity of friends, with service workers (69 percent) and farmers (61 percent) the groups who most often had two friends from the ethnic community. At the other extreme were professionals, of whom only 36 percent reported that both of their closest friends were Japanese American. The fact that service workers and laborers met few other Japanese at work yet still selected their friends from the ethnic group suggests that the link between small business and ethnic friendship goes beyond mere opportunity. Among those working in corporations and bureaucracies, income was unrelated to the ethnicity of their friends. Among those in small business, on the other hand, those with greater incomes had less exclusively Japanese American friendship patterns. The highest income group among those in the ethnic economy had hardly more Japanese best friends than those in the corporate economy. The most socially segregated, by this measure, were the employees of ethnic small business, but the low-income self-employed follow close behind.

NEIGHBORHOOD

Workplace is only one of many contexts in which social relations develop. Neighborhood is another, and it surely provides at least the potential for myriad informal associations. The relationship between neighborhood and small business, of course, may be a two-way one. People who are involved in the ethnic economy may choose to live in a more densely ethnic neighborhood; but by the same token, living in an ethnic neighborhood presents opportunities within the ethnic economy. Our Nisei respondents were asked: "Would you say that this neighborhood is made up mostly of Japanese Americans, mostly non-Japanese Americans, or is it mixed?" Four percent described their neighborhoods as mostly Japanese, another 37 percent as mixed, and the remaining 59 percent as mostly non–Japanese American. The Nisei as a group did not, then, generally see themselves as residentially segregated in the mid-1960s. Retrospective residential histories revealed the perception of a slow but steady emergence from Japanese American neighborhoods, accelerating after World War II.

Since neighborhood segregation is, in part, a function of discrimination by others in the housing market, the JARP survey inquired into the role that perceived discrimination played in Nisei residential patterns in the mid-1960s and found that despite their generally comfortable current position, 19 percent of our male Nisei sample had experienced housing discrimination in the previous ten years. Additionally, another 41 percent reported that they had heard of instances of housing discrimination affecting Japanese Americans, though they had not experienced it themselves, a fact probably not unrelated to their sense of ethnic solidarity. (A representative sample of all Californians, asked by the JARP about their willingness to sell their houses to blacks and to Japanese Americans, almost unanimously responded that if their neighbors were not opposed, they would sell to Japanese Americans. The proportion dropped to three-quarters when asked if they would sell to Japanese Americans if their neighbors opposed the sale, but only 16 percent anticipated a negative reaction if they sold to Japanese Americans. Fully 70 percent expected neighbors to object if they sold to blacks, and half said they would not sell to them in the case of such objection; indeed, 16 percent said they would not sell to blacks even if their neighbors did not object.)

The relationship of discrimination to ethnicity of neighborhood of Nisei respondents is somewhat surprising, for it was those who reported the least discrimination who lived in more heavily ethnic neighborhoods. Thirty-three percent of those who had experienced housing discrimination reported living in Japanese American or mixed neighborhoods, compared to 45 percent of those who had not experienced discrimination. By the postwar period, evidently, *experiences* of discrimination did not often push Nisei into ethnic neighborhoods, but living in a substantially Japanese American neighborhood protected Nisei from having to face discrimination. We can, for present purposes, largely discount the role of direct housing discrimination in determining the Nisei residential pattern and assume that on the whole by now Nisei have achieved something of the kind of ethnic mix in their residence patterns that they currently desire.

Nisei who worked in small business were more likely to live in relatively ethnic environments. Ethnic-neighborhood residence was even more common among the employees of Japanese-owned small businesses (52 percent) than among Nisei small-business owners themselves (46 percent). Both exceed the 36 percent of the corporate-employed Nisei who lived in ethnic neighborhoods. As we would by now anticipate, it was the professionals who led the exodus, with only 27 percent found in neighborhoods they described as relatively Japanese American.

As with living in the same neighborhood as relatives, one might expect that income would have something to do with these patterns. Generally, the poorer the Nisei male, the more likely he was to live in a substantially Japanese American neighborhood. Thus 48 percent of those who earned up to $10,000 per annum lived in a Japanese American or mixed neighborhood. This declined to 38 percent and 33 percent for those earning from $10,000 to $20,000 and $20,000 and up, respectively. When we simultaneously introduce the economic form Nisei participated in, it becomes evident that in all cases increased income is associated with leaving the ethnic neighborhood, to about the same extent as economic form is (table 13:2). This finding suggests that most people in the corporate economy start their work lives outside of an ethnic neighborhood. The process for most of them was not one of earning enough to leave their base in the ethnic neighborhood; they already lived outside of a semisegregated situation even as their careers began, and this condition may have helped direct them to corporate-economy jobs. Opportunities in the small-business economy, by contrast, must circulate much more readily in ethnic neighborhoods. Thus, it may be that ethnicity of neighborhood is the determinant of choice of economic form, rather than the other way around.

TABLE 13:2
PROPORTION OF NISEI MALES IN JAPANESE AMERICAN OR MIXED
NEIGHBORHOODS BY TYPE OF BUSINESS AND FAMILY INCOME
(MALES AND MARRIED FEMALES REPORTING)

Income	Self-employed	Employee of Japanese American	Total in Small Business	Total in Corporate Economy
To $10,000	55%	62%	56%	38%
	(337)	(48)	(385)	(347)
$10,000–$20,000	40	46	41	36
	(290)	(61)	(351)	(625)
$20,000+	38	36	38	23
	(175)	(11)	(186)	(84)

Higher income was associated with departure from the ethnic neighborhood among those in the ethnic economy no less than among those in the corporate economy. The simplest explanation is one we can only suggest, not prove: that pursuit of higher-quality housing had led the Nisei (as others) outward from the more densely ethnic, center-city neighborhoods that earlier had furnished a bridgehead for the group. If this is so, and if (to a degree) the ethnic economy grows from ethnic-residence proximity, the very prosperity of the ethnic economy may be at odds with its continuance.

NEWSPAPERS

Strictly speaking, the reading of Japanese American newspapers is not an instance of informal association. The ethnic press, however, is above all a way of keeping in touch with the affairs—formal and informal—of the community. Reading the newspapers reflects an interest in the goings-on of the ethnic community qua community; it indicates a link recognized by the group members themselves. Such newspapers not only represent a social bond but also serve economic functions, providing a communication network for people interested in conducting business matters within the small-business economy. Thus, retail dealers advertise extensively in the vernacular press. News and advertising both indicate important economic links with the general economy and with the growing import-export business. The editorial policies of the papers generally reflect their dependence upon distinctive Japanese American concentrations, particularly small business. The ethnic press is thus a kind of bridge between economic and social aspects of community life.

JARP survey data on the frequency of reading ethnic newspapers indicated that (for men and their wives) readership was rather strong among those in small business but weak among those working in the corporate world. Only about a quarter of the Nisei males who were neither self-employed nor working for Japanese American concerns—and their wives—read the ethnic press regularly in the mid-1960s. Among the self-employed, 44 percent kept in regular touch through the press, and their wives to the same degree. Employees of Japanese concerns did not read these papers as frequently as did their employers, but their wives did so somewhat more frequently. In Los Angeles, the small-business portion of the Nisei was somewhat more strongly tied into the ethnic community by regular newspaper reading (51 percent), while those not so employed trailed considerably behind, with 29 percent reporting regular readership and fully 31 percent of those lacking the economic link but living in the Japanese American metropolis hardly ever or never reading the ethnic press at all.

A low rate of readership among farmers (38 percent were regular readers) was somewhat surprising. Perhaps it can be explained by the fact that since the war and evacuation, Japanese agricultural marketing has gone mainly through conventional, non-ethnic channels. Since farm labor, apart from family labor, is now by and large non–Japanese, and since market information is no longer in any sense ethnic, the Japanese farmer has no business reason to read the ethnic press on a regular basis.

FORMAL ASSOCIATIONS AND LEADERSHIP

The classic Japanese American ethnic economy depended heavily on both manifest and latent functions of ethnic voluntary associations. Such groupings, we have indicated, were important in promoting the kinds of cooperation upon which the group's economic success depended and in facilitating the kinds of labor arrangements which were part of the Japanese American (and general middleman-minority) formula in the early days. Since the war, of course, much has changed, yet a pattern of group participation has persisted among some of the Nisei. It is our purpose in this section to investigate the degree to which such participation is associated with attachment to the modified ethnic economy. In other words, is small business conducive to the continuation of ethnic organizations?

Survey research is an imperfect technique for studying the organizations of a community. A survey weighs each individual equally, no matter how insignificant he or she may be to community life. This study does not pretend to be able to inform the reader about the structure of the formal community among the Nisei, but we do know a great deal about the distribution of membership in formal organizations within the Nisei community, and thus we can examine patterns of membership of individuals, seeing how these distributional aspects of associational life relate to economic form.

Thirty percent of the male Nisei surveyed said they belonged to no organizations whatever. Another 23 percent belonged to only one; 19 percent belonged to two, 13 percent to three, 10 percent to four or five, and 4 percent to six or more. Married women were somewhat less likely to belong to formal organizations, with 39 percent unaffiliated and 23 percent belonging to one only. With this information in hand, we then asked the Nisei: "Of the groups you belong to, about how many have mostly Japanese American members?" We were thus able to distinguish affiliation in ethnic and nonethnic organizations.

A variety of associations were popular among the Nisei, differing substantially by sex. Table 13:3 presents the organizations to which each Nisei respondent devoted the most time. Over one-third of the women were involved in child-related organizations, such as the PTA, while the men were more likely to favor work-associated memberships. In the cases of almost half of the men, their major organizational memberships were clearly identifiable as ethnic. This was less often true for their wives, 37 percent of whose favorite organizations were clearly Japanese American. Ethnicity of favorite organization varied greatly with the purpose of the organization, and once again we see a complex of preferences, partly ethnic and partly otherwise, which represented the basis according to which Nisei chose how to allocate their time. The political associations in which Nisei were active were thus virtually all Japanese American, while occupation-related organizations, especially labor unions, were less often ethnic. Recreational-

TABLE 13:3
NISEI'S MOST TIME-CONSUMING ORGANIZATIONS BY SEX OF
RESPONDENT AND APPARENT ETHNICITY OF ORGANIZATION

	Males		Females	
Type of Organization	Apparently Japanese American	Other	Apparently Japanese American	Other
Occupational; trade	13%	36%	1%	9%
Labor (union or committee)	0	3	0	1
Financial	4	5	1	1
Service; social welfare; charity	7	9	7	10
Public service	0	2	0	0
Veteran; patriotic	7	5	1	2
Political; public affairs	30	1	33	2
Religious; church related	6	3	9	5
Educational; cultural; hobby	4	5	10	7
Recreational; social; fraternal; athletic	20	17	28	13
Child related	9	14	9	50
Total	100 (366)*	100 (382)*	100 (172)*	100 (292)*

*Figure excludes Nisei who belonged to no organizations.

educational and child-based associations were fairly evenly mixed.

In the sections that follow we ask two basic questions: (1) Were people in small business more likely to be members of ethnic associations? and (2) Did their involvement tend to be restricted to ethnic organizations?

JAPANESE AMERICAN ASSOCIATIONS

Since most Nisei who belonged to Japanese American organizations were members of only one or two, we here trichotomize Nisei as unaffiliated, as members of only one ethnic organization, or as highly affiliated having two or more memberships. Economic form bore a strong relationship to membership in Japanese American associations among Nisei men in the mid-1960s. A substantial majority (61 percent) of those Nisei working in the corporate economy belonged to no ethnic association whatever; only 15 percent belonged to more than one such organization. Of those in small business, however, just 39 percent belonged to only one ethnic organization, and one-quarter belonged to two or more. Within the small-business economy, the self-employed participated considerably more actively (63 percent with at least one membership, compared to 44 percent for employees of Japanese concerns). Wives of Nisei small-business participants were more likely to affiliate with ethnic associations than were the wives of corporate and public employees: 52 percent of the women whose husbands owned or worked in small business belonged to ethnic organizations, compared to only 27 percent of the wives of corporate employees.

By far the occupational group most active in ethnic associations was that of service workers and laborers—notably gardeners—of whom over two-thirds belonged to at least one ethnic association and over one-third belonged to two or more. Farmers followed, with 66 percent belonging to at least one, and then proprietors and managers, among whom 53 percent were members. Members of the three corporate-economy occupations—and professions especially (39 percent)—were less likely to belong to ethnic organizations.

Within each occupational type, small-business orientation affected degree of ethnic-organizational affiliation in the predicted way. This was especially noteworthy for the professionals. Among professionals who worked in the corporate sector, only 35 percent belonged to at least one Japanese American organization, whereas small-business professionals had a far higher rate of membership: 54 percent. (In fact, 30 percent of this group belonged to more than one ethnic organization.)

We should recall that even in the least propitious occupational types in the corporate economy, some Nisei still belonged to Japanese American organizations. This affiliation was clearly not supported by the economic basis we are discussing. Ethnicity can stand in some cases without a direct economic link.

Other factors affected membership in formal organizations— in particular, age, education, and income. Generally, the older, the more educated, and the wealthier were more likely to belong to formal organizations, whether ethnic or nonethnic. Of these factors, age was by far the strongest. Among the Nisei born after 1934, 54 percent were not affiliated with any organization. The next-oldest cohort (born in 1925-1934) was far more often affiliated, with only 29 percent lacking any memberships. Twenty-three percent of those born between 1915 and 1924 did not belong to any organizations, while only 16 percent from the pre-1915 group were nonmembers. The same pattern obtained, but even more clearly, for membership in ethnic organizations alone. At one extreme, 76 percent of the youngest age group belonged to no Japanese American associations; at the other, only 33 percent of the oldest group did not belong to any.

Of course, this relationship with age in part explains the observed pattern of ethnic-organization adhesion by economic form. Accordingly, table 13:4 shows for the four birth cohorts of males the proportions belonging to a Japanese American organization. The findings are clear and also intriguing. Within each cohort,

TABLE 13:4

NUMBER OF JAPANESE AMERICAN ASSOCIATIONS MALE NISEI BELONGED TO BY TYPE OF BUSINESS AND YEAR OF BIRTH

Year of Birth	No. of Japanese American Organizations	Small Business	Corporate Economy
Before 1915	0	24%	45%
	1	42	50
	2+	35	5
Total		100	100
		(34)	(22)
1915–1924	0	34	53
	1	37	27
	2+	29	20
Total		100	100
		(258)	(209)
1925–1934	0	42	58
	1	36	28
	2+	22	14
Total		100	100
		(166)	(251)
After 1935	0	65	79
	1	29	11
	2+	6	10
Total		100	100
		(52)	(137)

the relationship to economic form holds: those in small business supported related activities with their association patterns, but the distinction decreased with youth. If we interpret age as a cohort phenomenon, we can project a decline in the reluctance of Nisei to move out of ethnic organizations and thereby a decline in the differential in participation depending upon firm type. If we interpret age as a proxy for maturation, we would see the increasing relevance of ethnic-economic form to participation rates as overall proneness to affiliation grew with age. Whichever the interpretation, it is noteworthy how unaffiliated non-small-business Nisei were at all ages and how thoroughly enmeshed in formal community affairs were the older Nisei who ran small businesses.

Education had a much weaker impact on overall affiliation than did economic form, the more educated on the whole participating in more organizations. Education, however, was rather sharply correlated in a negative direction with membership in Japanese American organizations. When we control for years of education, the relationship between small business and participation in ethnic formal organizations still remains. Among those Nisei who did not go beyond high school, 63 percent in small business belonged to Japanese American organizations, compared to 47 percent of the corporate employees who did. Among those with at least some college training, the corresponding figures were 58 percent and 37 percent, respectively. The effect of type of firm was stronger among the more highly educated, with the less educated more likely to belong to ethnic organizations regardless of the type of firm they worked in. In contrast, within the ethnic economy, the highly educated participated in community organizations almost as much as did the less educated.

Nisei with high family incomes belonged to more organizations overall. Of those earning up to $10,000 annually, 37 percent belonged to no organizations, while 19 percent belonged to three or more. In contrast, 22 percent of those earning $20,000 or more did not belong to any organizations, while no less than 46 percent belonged to three or more. Income was a powerful determinant of membership in general-community organizations. The relationship was considerably weaker for ethnic organizations, with only a 9 percent difference in membership between those earning less than $10,000 and those earning over $20,000.

At given levels of income, the association between small-business involvement and membership in ethnic organizations persisted. The relationship was especially strong in the highest income bracket, with those in small-business who earned over $20,000 showing a 65 percent membership rate, compared to 39 percent of corporate employees in the same income bracket. It appears that Nisei who were successful in the ethnic economy were typically active in Japanese American organizations, while those who were successful in the corporate- or public-economy worlds did not show much interest in retaining an affiliation with the organized ethnic community.

Thus, a pattern emerges. People in the corporate economy were much less likely to belong to Japanese American associations than those in the small-business world. Among the older, less educated Nisei in the corporate economy, however, there was a lingering affiliation. Within the ethnic economy, the picture was different. There was an increase in affiliation with age, and higher education was less of a deterrent. The most economically successful members of the ethnic economy were active members of ethnic organizations: for those working in a small-business world, ethnic-organizational membership was general and widespread.

NON–JAPANESE AMERICAN ASSOCIATIONS

Our Issei survey showed that the first generation tended to be exclusive (or excluded) in their memberships before World War II, when they were in their prime and the Nisei were growing up. About three-quarters of the Issei reported membership in ethnic organizations in the prewar period, but very few (less than 5 percent) belonged to nonethnic associations. The self-employed among the Issei were somewhat more prone than employees to affiliate with formal community organizations, but self-employment did not distinguish between Issei membership or nonmembership in nonethnic organizations: both groups failed to join them.

Our prediction was that for Nisei in the postwar period, participation in small business would be negatively correlated with membership in nonethnic organizations—that the ties of small-business Nisei to the ethnic community would tend to be somewhat exclusive. In fact, though, the Issei pattern continued among the Nisei in the mid-1960s, though at a far higher level of participation in nonethnic organizations. For the Nisei, too, being a part of the ethnic economy made little difference to affiliation in nonethnic organizations. In both cases, 52 percent of Nisei males belonged to no nonethnic organizations, 27 percent belonged to one, and 21 percent belonged to two or more. Within the small-business economy, employees were less likely to belong than were the self-employed (31 percent versus 50 percent), but the overall figures were identical. The ethnic economy of the mid-1960s supported Japanese American organizations, but it did not preclude participation in non–Japanese ones. Such affiliations were, of course, far more common among the Nisei in the mid-1960s than they had been among the Issei a generation before, and in this sense (but not differentially within the Japanese American population) the ethnic community had become less exclusive as those in the ethnic economy had been challenged by other, outside opportunities.

This finding covers up, to some extent, differences among the occupational types, but within each occupational type, economic form did not affect the likelihood of belonging to non-Japanese organizations. Professionals affiliated more often than did any other category with nonethnic organizations, with 61 percent belonging to at least one such organization. At the opposite extreme were service workers and laborers, with only 29 percent reporting membership. Managers and proprietors (45 percent), clerical and sales workers (34 percent), and craftsmen and operatives (also 34 percent) fell in between.

Farmers in the prewar economy had been served well by ethnic organizations and, accordingly, were particularly insulated from general-community groups. (Among the Issei in our survey, only 1 percent of the farmers belonged to nonethnic organizations!) Among the Nisei, in contrast, fully 56 percent of the farmers reported membership in nonethnic associations, and one-quarter belonged to more than one. Compared to their parents, Nisei farmers have more frequently joined the local farm bureaus. Apparently the deadly racial competition in farming, expressed in Japanese farmers' organizations and the Alien Land Laws, is over.

Year of birth was weakly related in a curvilinear manner to number of non-Japanese American organizational affiliations, with the youngest and oldest groups belonging the least often. Within each age group, however, ethnicity of firm did not significantly affect membership. Education was much more closely related to membership in nonethnic organizations than it was to affiliation with ethnic ones. The more highly educated Nisei typically belonged to more general-community associations. Within educational groups, though, no relationship between small-business participation and nonethnic-organizational affiliation appeared. Finally, high income was highly related to general-community-organizational membership, but controlling for income revealed no relationship between membership and economic form. Though membership in ethnic organizations was importantly related to economic form, membership in nonethnic organizations was independent of participation in the small-business world.

ORGANIZATIONAL OVERLAP

Now that we have looked at membership in ethnic and nonethnic organizations separately, we can look at them in tandem to discover the prevalence of various personal styles of affiliation. We examine four types: Nisei who belonged to no organizations; members only of Japanese American organizations; members only of general-community organizations; and members of both.

Table 13:5 presents the basic relationship between economic activity and these four types. Within the small-business economy, employees were much more likely to be nonmembers than were their employers or the self-employed. In addition, if they did join, their more common practice was to join only ethnic organizations. The self-employed tended to cluster in the members-of-both category, but over one-quarter of them belonged solely to Japanese American organizations; they rarely belonged to nonethnic associations alone.

Overall, of the Nisei in the ethnic small-business economy, a small plurality belonged to both types of organization, followed by those belonging exclusively to ethnic ones. Rather rarely did they belong to non-Japanese American associations exclusively. One in four belonged to no organizations at all. Nisei who were in the corporate economy were a good deal more likely to be unaffiliated. Corporate joiners were most likely to join nonethnic organizations exclusively, and only rarely did they belong exclusively to ethnic organizations. Clerical/sales workers and craftsmen/operatives (the lower corporate-economy occupations) were most likely to be unaffiliated. Contrast with these the lower

TABLE 13:5

MALE NISEI ORGANIZATIONAL AFFILIATION BY TYPE OF FIRM AND OCCUPATIONAL TYPE

Organizational Memberships	Type of Firm				Occupational Type					
	Self-Employed	Employee of Japanese American	Small Business	Corporate Economy	Professional	Proprietary	Clerical	Farm	Crafts	Service
None	22%	39%	25%	34%	27%	30%	40%	20%	41%	25%
Only Japanese American organizations	27	32	28	18	12	25	27	24	25	47
Only non-Japanese American organizations	14	17	15	26	34	17	15	14	14	6
Both	36	12	33	21	27	28	18	41	20	21
Total	100 (438)	100 (72)	100 (510)	100 (619)	100 (387)	100 (206)	100 (131)	100 (152)	100 (146)	100 (108)

ethnic-economy lines of work, farming and gardening: gardeners generally belonged exclusively to ethnic organizations, and farmers, as we have suggested, belonged most often to both ethnic and nonethnic organizations and were but rarely unaffiliated. Professionals often belonged only to nonethnic organizations and seldom exclusively to Japanese American groups. Proprietors and managers, a heterogeneous occupational category, were less likely than farmers to belong to both types of organizations, were less likely than gardeners to belong only to ethnic organizations, and were a distant second to professionals in exclusively nonethnic membership.

LEADERSHIP

We can come a bit closer to comprehending the relationship of continued voluntary ethnic-organization affiliation and the modern ethnic economy by examining ethnic-group leadership. To try to get at this elusive phenomenon, we constructed an index of leadership based on three items: (1) self-reported officership or committee membership in at least one of the organizations belonged to; (2) self-reported personal acquaintance with "the one person who stands out in your mind as the most important leader . . . of all the Japanese Americans in the communities where you have lived"; and (3) a self-report that someone outside the family had asked the respondent "for advice about politics or public affairs" in the past few months. To qualify as a leader, a respondent had to answer all three of these items affirmatively, an intentionally stringent criterion that yielded only 4.8 percent of the male sample as leaders. Two of the three items had no particular ethnic tinge, while one had; but since positive responses to all three were required of leaders, those far removed from the ethnic community were not likely to be so scored. Thus 68 percent of the leaders belonged to at least one Japanese American organization, as compared with 47 percent of the nonleaders. At the same time, the dominant quality of the leaders seems to have been wide affiliation, rather than specifically Japanese American memberships. No less than 67 percent of the leaders belonged to three or more organizations (ethnic and nonethnic), compared with 26 percent of the nonleaders.

Leaders, as might be expected, were the wealthier and more educated segment of the community. The differences were really large. Fully 39 percent of the leaders but only 12 percent of the nonleaders were in the $20,000-or-more bracket. Postgraduates constituted 36 percent of the leaders but only 16 percent of the nonleaders. Leaders were older than nonleaders, although not by very much. Even while older than the average Nisei in our sample, the leader group clearly led for relatively "meritocratic" reasons, the basis for their leadership inhering in some attribute or achievement of their own rather than in the continuity with the past they offered.

Leadership was somewhat related to participation in the ethnic economy. Half of the leaders were from the ranks of the self-employed, compared to 38 percent of the nonleaders; yet professionals, as well as proprietors/managers and farmers, were particularly prone to leadership. (Gardeners, on the other hand, were especially underrepresented in this category, although they were the major stalwarts of community-organization membership.) Among the professionals, leaders were much more likely to be in the ethnic economy than were nonleaders: 50 percent of the leaders who were professionals were in small business, compared to only 16 percent of the nonleader professionals.

Overall, the leadership group was quite varied. Occupational distributions, educational, and income figures suggest a leadership that emerged through different routes and that would lead the Nisei in different directions. While the community tended to be led by members of the ethnic economy, these were most likely to be highly educated, successful, independent professionals. Successful businessmen and farmers complemented this leadership but were not the dominating element that they were in the days of Issei leadership.

CONCLUSION

This chapter has demonstrated a consistent link between small business and informal and formal bonds of community among the Nisei, although these patterns do not overlap in any simple manner. On the whole, those Nisei who had tighter social bonds to the Japanese American ethnic group in a variety of informal and formal contexts were more likely to be participants in ethnic small businesses, and vice versa. With our imperfect indicators we cannot assert that a given percentage of ethnic solidarity is explained by economic form. We can see preferentially chosen ethnic behavior of many kinds among Nisei not now tied economically into the community, but the weave of economic and social concerns is surely strong enough to suggest that change in the vitality of ethnic small business will have an effect upon ethnicity both as it is felt and experienced and as it is structured and defined by ethnic-group organizations. The middleman-minority economic form supports ethnic solidarity, and vice versa. At least part of the model presented in figure 2:1 has received confirmation in these data.

14

Socialization, Values, and Religion

The purpose of this chapter is to explore some elements of the content of Japanese American ethnicity and its relationship to small business. We want to examine whether attachment to things Japanese or to "traditional" values supports a pattern of small-business enterprise. By no means is such an association inevitable; it is quite conceivable that members of the small-business economy developed a unique culture tied to the exigencies of American small business to the exclusion of Japanese values. Although we made no attempt to question the Nisei on all values that they might possibly hold, the survey asked several questions designed to help us determine respondents' degrees of attachment to customary Japanese beliefs and practices. In this chapter we examine socialization practices to which the Nisei were exposed as children, familiarity with the Japanese language, current expressions of values, and religious affiliation.

SOCIALIZATION

Our treatment of socialization will cover three topics. First, we shall consider the effects of a major socialization practice that some Nisei experienced—that of having been sent to Japan for a part of their formal education. Second, we shall examine the impact of a local ethnic socializing institution, the Japanese language schools. Finally, we shall look at the effect of certain values that parents taught Nisei as children. In all cases, as usual, the main concern will be to trace the relationship between these background experiences and current Nisei economic activity.

KIBEI

The practice of sending sons and daughters back to Japan for part of their education created a subgroup of Nisei known as Kibei. The practice was not uncommon before the war, despite its divergence from the Americanizing ideals of citizenship espoused by most of the Issei leadership and the sharp criticism it entailed by the enemies of the Japanese Americans. Almost 10,000 Nisei had had some education in Japan before World War II (Thomas, 1952:17). The shock of the war pretty much brought an end to the custom (Kitano, 1976b:160), so that the Kibei are now an older segment of the Nisei generation. In the JARP survey we found that 34 percent of those born before 1915 were Kibei, a proportion that declined to 15 percent of those in the 1915-1924 cohort, 8 percent of those born in 1925-1934, and 6 percent of those in the youngest group.

Before and during the war, the Kibei stood out as an unusual group. They were more likely to be Buddhist than other Nisei and less likely to speak English fluently. In economic matters they were also distinct: Thomas (1952:42) reports that "an appreciably greater proportion of them than the Nisei were working for other Japanese, and they were disproportionately [represented] in agriculture rather than in urban pursuits, in manual rather than clerical activities." Bloom and Riemer (1949:97) indicate that they were overrepresented among Nisei retail produce proprietors in Los Angeles. According to Thomas (1952:63-64), most Kibei were sent away to free the mother to work as unpaid labor in the family enterprise and were recalled when old enough to participate in the family firm. It would appear that, at least before the war, the Kibei were more likely to be in the ethnic economy than other Nisei.

The Kibei no longer seemed so distinctive in the late 1960s. According to Kitano (1976b:160): "The Kibei population has . . . remained static and is currently indistinguishable from the middle-aged Nisei population. Certain impressions suggest that a higher proportion of them remain in Japanese 'cultural activities,' such as the judo, Kendo, and akido clubs, and they may not, in general, be as well acculturated as their Nisei peers,. . . but the passage of time and the changing conditions have done much to resolve the major issues."

The JARP survey indicates that in the mid-1960s Kibei were

more likely to be self-employed and also more likely to be employees in ethnic firms. Of all Kibei, half were self-employed and another 10 percent employed in Japanese American businesses. Among the non-Kibei the corresponding figures were 39 percent and 6 percent. Kibei were much less likely to be professionals (20 percent, versus 34 percent among the non-Kibei) but were heavily overrepresented among gardeners (24 percent versus 9 percent). Within each occupational type, especially in white-collar occupations, the Kibei emphasized the small-business form, so that among professionals, for example, 30 percent of the Kibei but only 19 percent of the non-Kibei worked within the ethnic economy.

We must ask whether the relationship of Kibei background to economic form was a function of age, or, rather, whether Kibei experience may help to explain the strong relationship between age and small-business concentration. If we dichotomize (to economize on Kibei cases), we find that of the pre-1925 birth cohort, 63 percent of the Kibei but 55 percent of the non-Kibei were occupied in the small-business world. Of the 1925-and-later birth cohort, the corresponding figures were 45 and 34 percent respectively. Age thus accounts for a part of the effect of Kibei experience on current economic activity, and, conversely, Kibei experience is a part of the bundle of historical experiences of older cohorts which explains their concentration in small business.

Regardless of year of birth, Kibei were less likely to be professionals than were non-Kibei, but the younger Kibei were more often professionals than were the older Kibei. Much of the overrepresentation of Kibei in gardening is accounted for by the older group, but regardless of age, Kibei were more often gardeners than were non-Kibei.

Level of educational attainment was somewhat lower for Kibei than for other Nisei, but this did not fully explain the Kibei concentration in small business, for at all levels of education Kibei were considerably more likely to participate in the ethnic economy. Thus, among those with thirteen or more years of schooling, 36 percent of the non-Kibei but 53 percent of the Kibei were in small business. Nor did educational differences fully explain the effect of Kibei socialization upon occupational type. In particular, as already mentioned, Kibei were far more likely to be gardeners (this was especially true of the least educated). Fully 38 percent of the Kibei who had no more than high-school education were service workers and laborers, compared to 17 percent of the non-Kibei with this much education. Insofar as gardeners represented the core of the organized community, it is evident that Kibei, particularly those lacking college education, were well represented at that core.

JAPANESE LANGUAGE SCHOOLS

The Japanese language schools were also primarily a prewar institution. With 220 such schools in California by 1930 (Bell, 1935:20), they were a much more popular institution than was sending Nisei as Kibei back to Japan: about four-fifths of the Nisei in our sample had attended a Japanese language school at one time or another. The uniformity of this experience was related to cohort, with 54 percent of the youngest group, born after 1934, having attended language school, as compared to 85 percent of those born between 1915 and 1934. The oldest cohort was about as likely to have attended as the youngest cohort, reflecting the temporal pattern of growth and decline of the language-school institution.

There is some question as to the degree to which these schools taught Japanese culture. Because a considerable part of white hostility toward the Japanese Americans focused on the language schools, much of the formal content taught at these institutions concerned American citizenship. Writing in 1925, Tsuboi (1926:163) stated that "the ultimate purpose of the work of the Japanese language school teacher is the making of good American citizens out of children of Japanese parentage." The goal of teaching the Japanese language was described as being related to this purpose. Many of the Issei, especially women, did not know much English, and it was felt to be essential for socialization and the maintenance of the family that the children know and respect the language of their parents (Bell, 1935:21).

The JARP survey reveals that Nisei who attended language school as children were only modestly more often employed in the ethnic small-business world of the mid-1960s than were those who never attended. Even this effect was present only among the older Nisei. It seems to be the case that the language schools taught nothing that was critically related to whether the Nisei chose the small-business economy over the corporate economy, and also that Issei parents who chose not to send their children to language school were probably not otherwise especially deviant in their ethnic context.

PARENTAL TEACHINGS

The Nisei were asked several questions concerning the values they had been taught in the home. One of these asked: "While you were growing up, would you say that your parents wanted you to take an active part with Caucasians in their activities, or to stick pretty much with Japanese Americans?" Of course we expected that the latter upbringing would be conducive to participation in small business. Looking at males only, we found that 45 percent of those who said that their parents urged segregation were in small business, compared to 38 percent of those whose parents reportedly urged them to mix. This finding follows the expected direction but is complicated by the fact that many persons answered that their parents had urged both interaction patterns rather than only one, and those in this group were the most likely to be found in the ethnic economy, with 50 percent of them so affiliated. Either people in small businesses were in fact more likely to have had parents who urged them to get a foothold in both worlds (as their adult organizational affiliations might suggest), or they were perhaps more likely to feel that it was impolite to speak about a parental policy of this kind. Either way, we are left with the impression that parental urgings of this kind may have had only a small effect on current economic activity.

Nisei respondents were also asked whether their parents had "stressed" three notions reflecting what were commonly described as important Issei values: (1) "You must behave properly to avoid bringing shame to the family;" (2) "One must make returns for all kindnesses received;" and (3) "You must act so as not to bring dishonor to the Japanese American community." The overwhelming majority, over 80 percent of the Nisei in each instance, reported that indeed their parents had stressed these values.

We would expect that children of parents who emphasized these traditional values would be more inclined to work in the ethnic economy, if there were a clear line leading from a relatively traditional upbringing to a career in small business. This was not, however, the case, according to the JARP findings. The only one of the three values that bore any relationship to economic activity was the first one, avoiding family shame, and here the percentage difference was modest: 46 percent who said their parents had stressed this value were employed in small business, as compared with 38 percent of those whose parents reportedly did not emphasize this value. The other two value items were related in the expected direction, but even more weakly. Although the findings on parental teachings are basically negative, we hesitate to conclude, on the basis of this kind of evidence, that parental teachings arrayed along a traditional/assimilationist continuum played no part in current Nisei economic proclivities. We can, though, indicate tentatively that Nisei in and out of the ethnic economy alike recalled an upbringing in which reciprocity and family and ethnic honor were stressed. These dimensions were part of a consensus within the Japanese American community at that time (though they may no longer be). Other values may perhaps have differentiated Nisei upbringing in such a way as to incline some Nisei toward and others away from the small-business economy.

LANGUAGE

In contrast with retrospects on parental exhortations, language ability is a more closely measurable item about upbringing and culture, one that suggests a longer-lasting (and perhaps instrumental) relationship with economic behavior. Twenty percent of the male Nisei reported to the JARP survey that they could speak Japanese fluently and another 39 percent that they could speak it pretty well. Four percent said they knew no Japanese at all, and the balance knew a little. In the sample, 35 percent of the males said that they could read Japanese.

More Nisei in small business in the mid-1960s could speak Japanese well and read the language than those in the corporate economy. Seventy percent of those in small business said they could speak Japanese well or fluently, and 43 percent that they could read the language. For those outside the ethnic economy, the comparable figures were 50 percent and 27 percent. Professionals were least often able to speak Japanese, but skilled and semiskilled workers could do so only slightly more often. Gardeners were most often able to speak and read the language. Within each occupational type, those in small business were better acquainted with Japanese. Thus among professionals, 44 percent of those in small business but only 24 percent of those in the corporate economy could read it; and among service workers, 53 percent of those working in the ethnic economy but only 20 percent of those who worked in the corporate economy could do so.

As might be expected, year of birth was strongly related to Japanese language skills, as also to economic form. Thus among Nisei born after 1934, 60 percent could speak little or no Japanese, but of those born a decade earlier, a majority were comfortable in Japanese. The relationships were sharp and essentially linear. In the oldest cohort no fewer than 49 percent claimed that they could speak Japanese fluently. In table 14:1 we show the relationship of economic form to skill in the language, controlling for year of birth. Even the strong age relationship does not eliminate the effect, although age, too, retained its independent significance.

Why should activity in the ethnic economy be associated with greater ability to speak and read the Japanese language?

TABLE 14:1
MALE NISEI ABILITY TO SPEAK AND READ JAPANESE
BY YEAR OF BIRTH AND TYPE OF FIRM

	Small Business	*Corporate Economy*
Born before 1925		
Speaks fluently	33%	20%
Speaks well	44	40
Speaks little or none	23	40
Total	100 (305)	100 (236)
Reads	48 (303)	33 (236)
Born 1925 and later		
Speaks fluently	19	13
Speaks well	41	32
Speaks little or none	40	55
Total	100 (221)	100 (398)
Reads	37 (220)	23 (396)

There are a number of reasons. For one, the ethnic economy provided a more intensely Japanese environment and created an opportunity for the language to be used. Moreover, the language may have been of value in the pursuit of business, through links with Issei businesses or Japanese corporations, even to the point where some ethnic-economy businesses might specifically select or promote people who had this skill. On the other hand, it could be that language is but one indicator of closeness to Japanese culture and that it is this closeness which led Nisei to enter and remain in the small-business mode.

VALUES

The Nisei were asked various questions about their beliefs and attitudes. Table 14:2 indicates how opinions on a series of statements differed by type of firm. The first four items suggest that it was the Nisei in small business who were slightly more concerned with occupational success and making money. They were less likely to feel that occupational success is overstressed in American society. These correlations are expected. The fifth and sixth items suggest two of the reasons for their greater ambition. One very powerful motive appears to be helping one's children get ahead. Nisei in the ethnic economy were considerably more likely to have held this value than were those in the corporate economy. Again, this is expected. On the other hand, responses to the sixth item (not very commonly subscribed to) surprised us at first. As we have seen, the ethnic economy was less of a route to security than was employment by a large corporation or bureaucracy; ethnic small business was risky. Perhaps to people who chose this route, however, the risks, associated with the corporate world—of societal hostility and the like—appeared greater. In a sense, the ethnic economy can be seen as a haven against the harsh outside world. It would provide a good living without making it necessary for one to confront the possible antagonisms of the white community.

The last two items in the table give us some insight into psychological differences between participants in the two economies. Again there is an apparent contradiction. On the one hand, people in small business seem more often to take a fatalistic attitude toward life or at least to believe such fatalism to be a

TABLE 14:2
MALE NISEI SMALL-BUSINESS ORIENTATION BY PERCENT RESPONDING
AFFIRMATIVELY TO STATEMENTS ABOUT VALUES

	Small Business	Corporate Economy
The best way to judge a man is by his success in his profession	25% (520)	19% (631)
Americans put too much stress on occupational success	66 (510)	72 (631)
Next to health money is the most important thing in life	30 (518)	23 (630)
The most important qualities of a real man are determination and driving ambition	62 (513)	48 (628)
The most important thing for a parent to do is to help his children get further ahead in the world than he did	75 (513)	57 (629)
All a man should want out of life in the way of a career is a secure, not-too-difficult job, with enough pay to afford a nice car and eventually a home of his own	28 (518)	16 (631)
The secret of happiness is not expecting too much out of life and being content with what comes your way	65 (513)	56 (625)
I often worry about possible misfortunes	49 (515)	40 (629)

secret of happiness. On the other hand, they are in fact more likely to be worried about the future. This latter attitude reflects, perhaps, their greater ambition and drive toward success combined with a consciousness of the risks inherent in the route they have chosen. Again, the reader should note that the percentage differences are not great.

Political values were not tapped systematically, but one item on the questionnaire bears an interesting if oblique relationship to domestic political controversies of the 1960s. It read as follows: "In your opinion, which is more often to blame if a person is poor—a lack of effort on his own part or circumstances beyond his control?" The question distinguishes conservative from liberal assumptions about poverty. There was a slight tendency for small-business people to select the conservative alternative and blame the individual. These findings are in tune with the political-party preferences discussed in chapter 7. Although we do not have much data to support any firm conclusions, it would appear that ethnic small business supports a relatively conservative political stance.

It is interesting to note that, at least on this item, Nisei in small business did not adhere to contemporary Japanese culture. The same item was asked on several postwar surveys in Japan, revealing there a trend away from an individualistic conception of responsibility for economic failure. The Nisei respondents answered more individualistically than did contemporary Japanese respondents, with those in small business stressing this value more highly still. Perhaps Nisei in the ethnic economy were retaining values that were current in Japan at the time of emigration. While advanced corporate capitalism has progressed both in Japan and in the United States (as have its associated liberal values), the ethnic economy here remains in a more traditional mode.

RELIGION

Thorough examinations of a culture (or a subculture) typically pay most serious attention to matters of religion. As bodies of articulated doctrine, as symbol systems, as sets of regular communal practices, religions often provide much of the definition of social life as well as of cosmology. Thus the impact of the American experience upon religion is one of the most common and rewarding cultural studies. Prime among the questions within this area are the interactions of geographic mobility and religion, of social mobility and religion, and, where we have a contribution to offer, of ethnic pluralism and religion. We would, of course, share our most skeptical reader's doubts concerning how much a sample survey can teach us about the content of religion, and so we limit ourselves here to a consideration of some correlates of specific religious professions. While confining ourselves to a social-relations interpretation that is both parsimonious and satisfying, we have not forgotten that we simply have not explored the kinds of documentation that would permit us to erect a cultural interpretation.

The case of the Japanese American religion is in many ways an especially intriguing one. Most immigrants to America practiced one or another version of the dominant religion of America, Christianity, whereas most Japanese immigrants were Buddhists, and adherents, to one degree or another, of the state-centered Shinto religion as well. The Japanese in North America were viewed by Protestant missionaries, however, as an especially valuable group to proselytize, since their ties with the homeland offered potential assistance in missionizing Asia, long a goal of American Protestant Christianity. And the Japanese Americans, to a greater degree than most or perhaps any other ethnic groups, were ready and willing to be converted.

They were at the same time highly tolerant of the American style of pluralistic religion; while many Japanese Americans converted, many did not. The group was highly differentiated by religious preference, but hardly split by it. As we shall show, the patterns of differentiation remained meaningful: religious behavior corresponded to other preferential behaviors. Nevertheless, we really do not know from our survey (nor have we seen documentation that would enable us to know otherwise) whether religious decisions by Japanese Americans were initially highly freighted with meaning. We do not know, either, how far the structural choice of Buddhist or Christian affiliation had ramifications for the subsequent symbolic-meaningful concerns of the actors, though it is obvious that such choice has had social consequences as well as social antecedents.

As represented by our survey, in the mid-1960s male Nisei (including reports on husbands by married women) were widely divided in religious affiliation. Fifty-two percent were Christian, 38 percent adhered to Buddhism or other traditional Japanese religions, and 10 percent claimed no religion at all. This current religious diversity reflects a history of conversion and reconversion. The Issei, on arrival in the United States, were (according to our Issei respondents) already Christian in about 10 percent of the cases, evidently converts of Christian missionaries abroad. More Issei gradually adopted Christianity, so that by the time of the Issei interviews, 35 percent of the sample were Christians.

Nisei acquired Christianity by three routes. Thirty percent of the sample were born into a Christian family; an additional 15 percent were raised as Christians, often at a missionary or church-affiliated school, though their parents were not; and another 8 percent of the Nisei were brought up in the traditional Japanese religion, but converted to Christianity sometime later in life. For the Nisei in the mid-1960s, religious variety seems to have been less the product of hardy sectarianism than of widespread unconcern. In our sample, only 15 percent of the male Nisei who claimed any religious affiliation attended religious services weekly or more frequently. Fully 65 percent failed to attend even monthly.

Attendance varied somewhat by religious affiliation, to be sure. Christians attended services more regularly than those affiliated with traditional faiths, 40 percent of the Christian males attending at least monthly as compared to 29 percent of those in traditional faiths. This finding does not suggest that the latter were fallen-away Buddhists, however, since it undoubtedly has something to do with differences in the prescriptions of the two religious systems as well as with the lack of centrality of organized religion to Japanese culture.

Despite this lack, we find that religious affiliation was a significant differentiator of the Nisei. The difference is not, we think, at the doctrinal level. Rather, affiliation per se has a kind of symbolic meaning. The retention of Buddhist profession would seem to imply an orientation toward things Japanese and perhaps to Japan itself, or at least toward the Issei generation and things more nearly in the classic first-generation mold. Affiliation with Christianity, on the other hand, would seem to imply an alertness to American culture and society. Befu (1965:212) mentions that "Buddhism provided an important link with Japan in ways Christianity did not. Buddhism was the religion of the ancestors of the Japanese immigrants, and when a man died, his ashes were preserved in the church until ready to be taken back to Japan by one of the relatives or friends." In many ways, however, the Buddhist religion in America has moved, as a collective institution, in a direction almost parallel to that of the individual choice of conversion. As early as 1946 Paul Radin detailed many adaptations and changes in Buddhist festivals and ceremonies, while McWilliams (1944:100) points to Sunday schools, much of the apparatus of the Protestant social church, and an undisguised syncretism: "In these Buddhist churches, people sang Christian hymns with a few words changed, such as 'Buddha loves me, this I know.' "

To say that conversion to Christianity was a symbolic statement of an orientation toward the perceived culture of majority Americans is not as absolute as it might seem. Many, probably most, Nisei Christians belonged to churches the majority of whose members were Japanese Americans. (It is unfortunate that the question of ethnicity of church membership was not asked in the survey.) Thus, a decision to convert to Christianity did not necessarily imply a move in an assimilative direction, since it was a step that could be taken within the ethnic community. On the other hand, a retention of Buddhism did seem to symbolize a tie to the "homeland" of Japan, yet as an institution Buddhism had become Americanized. This apparent paradox becomes understandable if one recalls the seriousness of the Christian missionary effort with the Japanese Americans. For those who may have been relatively unconcerned doctrinally but who resisted or resented missionary efforts, an Americanized Buddhism would bear the perfect symbolic weight.

Religious preference was quite strongly correlated with economic form among the Nisei in the mid-1960s. Members of traditional Japanese religions were 16 percent more likely to be engaged in small business, with 58 percent of them, compared to 42 percent of the Christians, so employed. Nonaffiliates (who generally resembled Christians more nearly than they resembled traditionalists) were least often engaged in small business, with only 37 percent. Much, but not all, of this variation can be accounted for by differences in occupational type. While 39 percent of the Nisei Christians were professionals, only 20 percent of the Buddhists fell into this occupational category. On the other hand, Buddhists were far more likely to be farmers (21 percent versus 10 percent) and, to a lesser degree, gardeners (15 percent versus 7 percent).

A possible explanation of the relationship between religion and economic behavior might be that both were related to year of birth. It could be that the older Nisei were more likely to be affiliated with traditional religions, and we already know that they were more likely to be part of the small-business world. Surprisingly, though, the survey reveals that among the Nisei in the mid-1960s, religion and year of birth were not strongly related except that nonaffiliates were much younger than both Buddhists and Christians.

We thus have two major but independent dimensions related to participation in the ethnic economy. To discover the nature of the interaction between the two variables, we examined the relationship between religious affiliation and economic form for different birth cohorts displayed in table 14:3. It is clear that religion was a most important source of differentiation among the

TABLE 14:3
PROPORTION OF MALE NISEI IN SMALL BUSINESS BY
RELIGIOUS AFFILIATION AND YEAR OF BIRTH

| | Religious Affiliation | | |
Year of Birth	Traditional	Christian	None
Before 1925	73%	47%	41%
	(189)	(292)	(39)
1925–1934	45	35	44
	(160)	(208)	(45)
After 1934	25	31	23
	(53)	(79)	(58)

oldest Nisei but has declined in importance among younger Nisei, who were less likely to have come into contact with Protestant missionaries and for whom continued traditional adherence would thus have less emblematic meaning.

As is usual with year of birth, of course, the finding can be interpreted in one of two ways. It could mean that the youngest Nisei have not yet fulfilled their potential and that religion will eventually become a more potent differentiator; or it could mean (and we think this more likely) that religious conversion and steadfastness were once important differentiators of Nisei behavior, but because younger Nisei cohorts have not been asked so insistently to make a decision in this area, religious affiliation is now rather random among younger Nisei as a correlate of ethnic-economy involvement. (We remind the reader that this particular interaction with age is not what we have typically found elsewhere in this survey, a fact that lends support to our historical interpretation of the meaning of the religious pattern.)

Religion not only differentiated the Nisei in terms of economic activity but also was related to educational achievement. Of those affiliated with traditional religions, 44 percent had had some college education, while fully 66 percent of the Christians and 67 percent of the nonaffiliates had attained this level of schooling. Controlling for year of birth, we again find religion to have been of declining importance as a differentiator. Among the oldest cohort of Nisei, 60 percent of the Christians received at least some college education, compared to 32 percent of the traditionalists. The religious difference was also substantial for the 1915-1924 and 1925-1934 cohorts, but it had largely disappeared for the youngest group. (Young Christians, however, were still more likely to enter postgraduate study.) What may once have been a cautious attitude toward American culture and its institutions had, by the late 1960s, become dispelled to a large extent.

The fact that religion had educational consequences may explain its observed relationship to economic activity. In other words, it is possible that religion only affected the choice of continuing in school or not, which in turn channeled Nisei one way or the other in their occupational careers. Our data, however, indicate that, even if we control for education, religion and economic activity continued to be correlated. Among Nisei with a high-school education or less, Buddhists were more likely to be farmers and gardeners, while Christians were more likely to be professionals. Among those with at least some college training, Christians showed a higher preference for the professions—53 percent, versus 37 percent of the Buddhists. Similarly, holding education constant did not remove the relationship between religion and small-business concentration. Among those with a high-school education or less, 68 percent of the traditionalists were in the small-business world, compared to 50 percent of the Christians. Among the Nisei with at least some college, 37 percent of the Christians and 45 percent of the Buddhists were in small business. While educational level made a big difference in these choices, religion continued to exert an independent influence.

CONVERSION

So far we have not considered the direction of causality in the relationship between religion and economic activity. Does religion cause a particular orientation toward one's work, or does religious affiliation follow from prior occupational choices? Nisei, for instance, may have found themselves in small business, discovered this to be in some way more compatible with Buddhism, and changed their religious affiliation accordingly.

Conversion has in fact been associated with a movement toward the firm type more closely associated with the religion adopted, as table 14:4 shows. People who were born into traditional religions but became Christians were more likely to work in the corporate economy than were people who retained their traditional affiliation. Similarly, Christians who became traditionalists were much more likely to have been active or to become

TABLE 14:4
MALE NISEI TYPE OF EMPLOYMENT BY
RELIGIOUS AFFILIATION AND RELIGIOUS CONVERSION

	Traditional, *No Conversion*	*Traditional Converted to Christian*	*Christian Converted to Traditional*	*Christian, No Conversion*
Self-employed	50%	41%	48%	32%
Japanese American Employer	6	3	3	7
Non–Japanese American Employer	44	56	49	61
Total	100 (326)	100 (105)	100 (59)	100 (461)

active in the small-business world than were those who remained Christians. The religion Nisei adopted proved to be a better indicator of current economic form than religion at birth: converts *to* Christianity were, in terms of occupation, more like lifetime Christians than were converts *from* Christianity; and converts *to* traditional religions were more like lifetime adherents than were converts *from* traditional religions. At the same time, though, in the economic sphere lifetime Christians behaved less traditionally and lifetime Buddhists more traditionally than did either set of converts. From table 14:4, it would appear that religious affiliation sometimes followed occupation but that since religion was in the great majority of cases the religion Nisei were assigned at birth, the order of causality was most often from original cultural orientation to subsequent economic orientation. Each religion, even in the mid-1960s, remained firmly associated with a particular type of economic organization (though certainly not confined to it). By this finding, the voluntaristic quality of the continuing Nisei ethnic economy is emphasized, as is the cultural meaning of the choice of career.

Level of schooling shows the same relationship to religion. Those who were born and remained Christian showed the highest degree of education: 69 percent of these had at least some college education. Of those who converted to Christianity, 56 percent had attended college. Converts to traditional Japanese religions were less likely again to have had college education, indeed less than lifetime traditionalists. Of the former, 45 percent had some college training, of the latter, 49 percent.

Earlier in this chapter, we pointed out that some of the Issei brought up their children in a religion other than their own. This enables us to look separately at the effects of early religious influences from the home environment apart from youthful adherence. Not all permutations occurred in adequately large numbers, of course, but five significant groups were found among the Nisei: those whose parents had been traditionalists, who were themselves raised in a traditional religion, and who never converted (TTT); those with the same background but who converted (TTX); those lifetime Christians whose parents were traditionalists (TXX); those with a similar background who reconverted to their parents' religion (TXT); and those whose parents were Christians and who were raised as and remained Christians (XXX). The marginals point to a complex net flow of Nisei religious careers toward Christianity, owing, among other things, to the smallness of the return flow toward traditionalism. Our argument here, however, concerns the differential relationship.

The impact of these various religious-career types on a continuing commitment to the postwar version of the ethnic economy is clearly visible in the JARP data. The full historical impact of religion on Nisei small-business participation depends on entire religious careers. Three-quarters of Nisei with the XXX religious sequence were employed in the corporate economy in the mid-1960s. The XXX group was also the most prone to be employed in the professions (53 percent), and not one among our sample was a farmer, while only two were gardeners. Of Christian converts from a solid traditional background (TTX), 58 percent were in the corporate economy. The TXX, too, were more likely to be in the corporate economy (48 percent) than were current Buddhists (TTT had 45 percent, TXT, 42 percent). It is interesting to note that the reconverts to Buddhism were the group most committed to small business. Again we have evidence for the volitional quality of the differentiation of the Nisei according to economic form, one that by the nature of the distribution of religious careers points to the depletion of recruits for the ethnic economy.

RELIGIOUS INTERMARRIAGE

Why should religion be so strongly related to economic form? Has it something to do with doctrine? Should we develop a Weberian hypothesis concerning the tenets of Buddhism and Christianity, by which Japanese Buddhism appears especially well related to the kinds of ascetic and materially concerned traits appropriate to small entrepreneurship? Although there may be something relevant in the philosophies of the religions themselves, we think that this is not the critical factor. Rather, we suspect that each religion represents a system of social relations around which a particular economic form has developed. For many of those entering one or the other modal economic career, it became convenient to convert because most others with whom one interacted met in a certain church, perhaps conducting business in that context or perhaps only affirming ties that had business-related consequences.

That social relations matter more than doctrine is vividly illustrated by religious intermarriage. A small number of the male Nisei were married to women of different faiths (or of no faith). The occupational focus of these men, as table 14:5 shows, differed from that of other male Nisei of the same religious affiliation: the religion of the wife seems to have played some part in economic form. Buddhist men with Christian wives were less likely to be in the ethnic economy, more likely to have some college training, and less likely to be farmers than were traditional men with traditional wives. Conversely, Christian men with traditional wives were less educated, more often in small business, and less often professionals than were Christians married to Christians. Much in line with our social-relations interpretation of current religious affiliation, in the small-business world we find just about equal proportions of Christian men married to Buddhist women and of Buddhist men married to Christian women. This fact suggests that even when a man has not accepted the doctrine of a particular faith, if he has a close link to it socially (through a spouse in this instance) he is likely to share the economic configuration of its members. The data are open to the opposite interpretation, however: a man's activity in an economic form incompatible with his religion might have led to his having selected a wife belonging to a more compatible religion. In either case, as with the conversion pattern, the drift here is away from the ethnic economy, since there are more Buddhist men who have married Christian women than there are Christian men who have married Buddhists.

RELIGIOUS ATTENDANCE

Pursuing the social-relations rather than the doctrinal notion, we might expect that those who most often attended religious

TABLE 14:5
MALE NISEI OCCUPATIONAL TYPE, SMALL-BUSINESS INVOLVEMENT, AND EDUCATION BY RELIGIOUS INTERMARRIAGE

	Husband Traditional			Husband Christian			Husband Nonaffiliated		
	Wife Traditional	Wife Christian	Wife Nonaffiliated	Wife Traditional	Wife Christian	Wife Nonaffiliated	Wife Traditional	Wife Christian	Wife Nonaffiliated
Professionals	19%	20%	21%	25%	39%	53%	24%	42%	60%
Managers/proprietors	19	29	7	25	22	21	28	14	3
Clerical/sales workers	10	11	7	16	11	5	20	10	14
Farmers	23	11	7	7	10	16	12	7	6
Craftsmen/operatives	13	16	29	17	11	5	8	13	3
Service/unskilled laborers	16	13	29	10	7	0	8	14	14
Total	100	100	100	100	100	100	100	100	100
	(579)	(92)	(14)	(81)	(828)	(19)	(25)	(84)	(35)
Percent of males in small business	61	50	46	49	42	55	56	40	32
	(572)	(93)	(13)	(79)	(823)	(20)	(25)	(83)	(34)
Percent of males with at least some college	39	58	36	55	63	55	50	63	76
	(588)	(93)	(14)	(84)	(846)	(20)	(24)	(84)	(35)

services would have a chance to reinforce the social tie that was expressed by religious affiliation. Our data show that this is true, but only marginally. Among Buddhists, being part of the small-business economy was connected with religious attendance in the anticipated direction. For Christians, there was no correlation between small business and attendance at services, but a strong relationship with occupational type emerged. Their degree of attendance was closely related to the status of the occupational type: the higher the status, the higher the attendance. This is a different kind of phenomenon from those we have been discussing, tied in no straightforward way to the maintaining of distinct economic forms among the Nisei in the mid-1960s. Of Nisei professionals who were Christians, 47 percent attended church monthly or more often, while service workers of Christian persuasion attended that often in only 21 percent of the cases, with other types arrayed along this dimension. No such status variation was observed among the Buddhists, however. Within the two subcultures suggested by the Christian-traditionalist dichotomy, the economic realm was differently related to religious attendance. We may well speculate that in giving us a view of the ethnic economy toward what may well be its historical end, our cross-sectional view has also given us a glimpse of the organization of the realm that will take its place when and if the ethnic economy is no longer a viable alternative for young Japanese Americans entering the job market.

CONCLUSION

We have shown in this chapter that there is a weak but positive relationship between concentration in small business and the cultural content (as opposed to patterns of interaction) of Japanese American ethnicity. This might be taken as an indicator of evidence to support cultural theories of middleman minorities. The evidence is slight, however, and probably confounded by many of the other factors presented in part II.

The one exceptional factor is religious affiliation, which is strongly related to small-business concentration. Nevertheless, we hesitate to interpret this as a strictly cultural effect. Religion is not only a set of beliefs and cultural practices; it is also a set of social relations. While the particular beliefs associated with traditional

Japanese religions may have inclined their Nisei adherents to accept precapitalist economic forms readily, we are inclined, on the basis of patterns of changing membership, to believe that the practical advantages stemming from social contacts established at religious institutions are more important to the small-business mode than are specific religious beliefs. This is not to suggest that religious content is not inherently important to church members; rather, we suspect that the social bonds of trust and the information passed around within a congregation may be advantageous in the business world as well.

Regardless of how we interpret religious affiliation, the fact that Nisei in the ethnic economy were more likely to be Buddhist than Christian helped to reinforce the link between small-business affiliation and ethnic solidarity. Since Buddhism is more distinctly an ethnic religion than Christianity, the clustering of small-business participants in Buddhist churches helps to keep an ethnic institution alive. This has been the central theme of part III: that concentration in small business and the retention of ethnic ties are correlated. We now turn to the third generation, the Sansei, to assess the degree to which they are continuing a middleman-minority mode of economic adaptation and to consider the implications for a viable Japanese American ethnic community in the future.

15

The Sansei

Those Sansei who were old enough to be included in our survey (eighteen years or older) were the children of the oldest sample Nisei. Only 4 percent of the Sansei males in our sample had parents from the two youngest Nisei cohorts, but 27 percent had fathers born before 1915, and another 69 percent had fathers born between 1915 and 1924. In the population at large, there are older Sansei, but because sample Sansei had to have had grandparents alive in the early 1960s in order to be included in our study, the older ones were not contacted. Thus, the picture we draw of the Sansei may not represent the complete story of this generation. Nevertheless, we believe the children of the sample Nisei can give us a feel for important generational processes.

Only 133 male Sansei reported to us an occupation in which they were currently employed; 20 more were in the army, Peace Corps, or Vista. (Since so few Sansei women were married, and even fewer married to other Sansei, we chose to omit their reports on their husbands' activities.) Of the 133, 60 percent were professionals, 7 percent proprietors and managers, 8 percent clerical and sales workers, 2 percent farmers, 20 percent craftsmen and operatives, and 3 percent service workers and laborers. This is quite a different distribution from that of the Nisei. Sansei were already almost twice as likely to be professionals in the mid-1960s and were often working in skilled- and semiskilled-labor occupations. They were considerably less likely than the Nisei to be in any other line of work. Table 15:1 presents the specific occupations in which the Sansei were employed, together with the occupations they hoped, and expected, to enter.

The Sansei were also asked whether they were self-employed. Only 8 percent answered affirmatively, a considerably lower rate than was found among their fathers. Of the ten individuals who

TABLE 15:1
CURRENT, PREFERRED, AND EXPECTED OCCUPATIONS OF MALE SANSEI

	Current	Preferred	Expected
All occupations	133	339	315
Professional, technical, and *kindred workers*	80	270	238
Accountants and auditors	5	13	13
Airplane pilots and navigators	1	5	3
Architects	0	6	4
Artists and art teachers	3	8	10
Authors	0	2	1
College professors	3	13	13
Dentists	4	16	11
Designers	4	3	1
Dietitians and nutritionists	0	0	1
Draftsmen	6	2	3
Editors and reporters	1	2	0
Engineers	19	53	51
Entertainers	0	1	0
Lawyers and judges	0	7	3
Musicians and music teachers	0	3	0
Natural scientists	3	18	14
Optometrists	0	3	2
Personnel and labor-relations workers	0	2	1
Pharmacists	6	13	15
Photographers	0	1	3
Physicians and surgeons	1	17	15
Public-relations men and publicity writers	0	0	1
Recreation and group workers	1	1	1
Social-welfare workers, except group	2	9	8
Social scientists	0	13	7
Sports instructors and officials	1	3	3
Surveyors	1	1	2
Systems analysts	1	0	1
Teachers	5	21	25
Technicians	7	12	10
Therapists and healers	0	3	1
Professional, technical, and kindred workers (other)	6	19	15

TABLE 15:1 (Continued)
CURRENT, PREFERRED, AND EXPECTED OCCUPATIONS OF MALE SANSEI

	Current	Preferred	Expected
Managers, officials, and proprietors, excluding farm	9	32	28
Buyers and department heads, store	3	1	1
Officials and administrators, public administration	1	4	3
Eating and drinking establishments	0	1	0
Apparel and accessories stores	0	0	1
Purchasing agents and buyers (other)	1	2	1
Managers and executives (other)	0	0	2
Managers, officials, proprietors, manufacturing	1	2	1
Export-import business	0	1	0
Bankers and other financiers	2	6	5
Automobile-repair services, garages, and gasoline sales	1	1	1
Managers, officials, and proprietors (other)	0	14	13
Clerical, sales, and kindred workers	11	9	15
Agents (other)	0	1	0
Bookkeepers	1	0	0
Office-machine operators	1	1	1
Postal clerks	0	0	1
Secretaries	0	0	1
Stenographers	0	1	1
Stock clerks and storekeepers	1	0	0
Typists	1	0	0
Real-estate agents and brokers	0	3	5
Wholesale salesmen	1	0	0
Stock and bond salesmen	1	1	3
Sales clerks	3	2	2
Produce clerks	2	0	1
Farmers and farm workers	3	7	8
Farm owners, partners	0	7	7
Farm managers, foremen	3	0	1

TABLE 15:1 (Continued)
CURRENT, PREFERRED, AND EXPECTED OCCUPATIONS OF MALE SANSEI

	Current	Preferred	Expected
Craftsmen, foremen, operatives, and kindred workers	26	15	21
Carpenters	1	1	1
Decorators and window dressers	1	0	0
Electricians	1	2	1
Foremen	1	1	1
Machinists	0	1	0
Mechanics and repairmen	8	5	7
Tinsmiths, coppersmiths, and sheetmetal workers	0	0	1
Craftsmen and kindred (other)	1	1	1
Apprentices	2	0	0
Assemblers	2	0	0
Attendants, auto service and parking	1	0	0
Brakemen, railroad	1	0	0
Checkers, examiners, and inspectors, manufacturing	2	0	0
Filers, grinders, and polishers, metal	1	0	0
Painters, excluding construction and maintenance	1	0	1
Truck and tractor drivers	1	1	1
Welders and flame cutters	2	1	1
Operatives (other)	0	2	2
Service workers and laborers	4	6	5
Barbers	1	2	2
Kitchen workers, excluding private household	2	0	0
Protective-service workers (other)	0	1	1
Policemen and detectives	0	1	1
Sheriffs and bailifs	0	1	0
Gardeners, excluding farm, and groundskeepers	0	1	1
Stock boys, office boys, etc.	1	0	0

were self-employed, six were professionals (or 8 percent of all professionals), another two were proprietors, and two were farmers. Since the Sansei were not asked for the ethnicity of their employers, we cannot judge how many of them were employees in ethnic small businesses, but we do know that 16 percent of the employees said that at least one-quarter of the people they met regularly at work were Japanese Americans, which suggests that at least some of them were working within the ethnic economy.

Most of the sample Sansei males were young and had not completed their educations. (Only one-quarter were twenty-five or older.) Sixty-one percent reported that they were currently students, while another 22 percent said they were planning to reenter school. Even for those who were employed full time during the survey, their occupation did not provide an accurate picture of their probable life's work. The questions concerning the Sansei's future prospects may thus be more revealing of the future of Japanese American small business.

Table 15:1 presents the details of responses to two perspective questions: (1) the occupations they preferred, and (2) the occupations they expected to work in, even if they did not achieve their preference. Most Sansei thought they would achieve their occupational preferences, although the final distributions belie the amount of individual shifting between preferences and expectations. Overall, however, these questions revealed that no less than 80 percent of the male Sansei preferred professional occupations and that 76 percent expected to enter them. This preponderance overshadows all remaining responses. Nine percent both preferred and anticipated proprietary or managerial occupations; 3 percent preferred and 5 percent expected clerical and sales work; 2 percent both preferred and expected to be farmers; 4 percent preferred but 6 percent expected to be craftsmen or operatives; and only 2 percent preferred and expected to be service workers or laborers. Table 15:1 reveals that only one of the Sansei expected to be a gardener.

The prospective occupational distribution may lead us to anticipate the demise of the middleman-minority form with the third generation, but this prediction is not necessarily entirely correct. The Sansei were asked if they had ever worked for pay in their parents' businesses, and a remarkable 52 percent said they had. If we conjecture that a larger group than this must have worked without pay, then the majority of the generation had at least been exposed to the ethnic economy in their youth. More important, the Sansei were asked, in regard to their preferred occupation; "In this occupation, do you expect you would be working for yourself all the time, working for someone else all the time, or sometimes working for yourself and sometimes for someone else?" Twenty percent expected self-employment, 39 percent thought it would be mixed, and 41 percent expected that their preferred occupation would involve working for someone else.

Table 15:2 shows the relationship between preferred occupation and self-employment. For three of the occupational types the numbers were too small to convert to percentages, so here we simply present the raw numbers. In table 15:3, we have combined the traditional ethnic-economy occupations—proprietorships, farming, and service work/labor—for the purpose of obtaining percentages. The professionals were kept separate because there were so many of them, but clerical/sales and crafts were combined. It can be seen that the Sansei were more likely to anticipate self-employment or semi-self-employment in the traditional occupations of the ethnic economy. In addition, quite a few planned to become self-employed professionals. Among these were fourteen Sansei who planned to become dentists and eleven who wanted to be physicians or surgeons. As with the Nisei, the majority of those who wanted to be engineers (thirty-three out of fifty-three) expected to be employees, with only three prospective engineers expecting to be totally self-employed.

The mixed category appears to be more a feature of professionals than of other occupational types, and it probably includes people who may anticipate doing some consulting on the side, those who might work partly for a large firm or public institution and partly in private practice, and those who have no very clear

TABLE 15:2
MALE SANSEI PREFERRED OCCUPATION BY EXPECTED
TYPE OF EMPLOYMENT

	Professional	*Proprietary*	*Clerical*	*Farm*	*Crafts*	*Service*
Self-Employment	48	8	2	3	2	4
Mixed	112	9	3	3	5	1
Employee	110	15	4	1	8	1
Total	270	32	9	7	15	6

TABLE 15:3
MALE SANSEI PREFERRED OCCUPATION (COMBINED) BY
EXPECTED TYPE OF EMPLOYMENT

	Professional	Clerical and Crafts	Proprietary, Farm, and Service
Self-employment	18%	17%	33%
Mixed	41	33	29
Employee	41	50	38
Total	100	100	100
	(270)	(24)	(45)

view of this aspect of their expected career. Clearly, however, those in this category seem quite distant from the old Issei ethnic economy. Even with the totally self-employed we should exercise caution in interpreting this pattern as a clear indicator of a return to the middleman form. As we saw among the Nisei, self-employed professionals seemed, of all the occupational types, least to fit the mold of ethnic small business, and so strong was the hold of the professions on the young Sansei in the mid-1960s that these dominate even among the self-employed. Nevertheless, we present the findings on prospective self-employment, hypothesizing that such arrangements bear some relationship to older forms.

The eldest among the Sansei look a little more like the Nisei than do the youngest among them, from this point of view. Of the Sansei twenty-five years old and over, 72 percent preferred the professions, as compared to 82 percent of the younger Sansei in our sample. Twenty-six percent of the eldest preferred self-employment, followed by 21 percent of those twenty-one to twenty-four and 14 percent of those under twenty-one. This suggests a continuation of the subgenerational ripple from the Nisei, although it should be recalled that we are only looking at the oldest end of the generation as far as our sample is concerned but that the sample itself excludes the grandchildren of the very oldest Issei, who had died before the study was undertaken. There is no obvious reason, however, to reject the implications of the trends revealed.

The high degree of proposed concentration in the professions was commensurate with Sansei educational attainment. Only 9 percent of the 377 male respondents to this question reported that they had had twelve years of education or less; 91 percent had at least attended some college, and this proportion would surely increase as more continued in school. The majority of sample Sansei, 63 percent, had had thirteen to fifteen years of schooling, since many were college students at the time of the survey. Twenty-eight percent had completed college, of which the majority (16 percent) had had some postgraduate training.

Educational attainment was, of course, related to preferred occupation. Only 37 percent of those Sansei without college education wanted to enter the professions, while over 80 percent of those in the other three educational categories hoped to become professionals. There is a curvilinear relationship to self-employment, with the least and the most educated preferring self-employment. This reinforces the fact that we should exercise caution in interpreting the findings here to mean the survival of the ethnic economy, even in its Nisei form.

Although it appears that the Sansei, at least in our sample, had largely moved out of an ethnic economy, we can still examine the small amount of differentiation that remained. Were those who expected to be self-employed more likely to retain ties with the ethnic community? Are there patterns of this sort that might suggest among the Sansei, too, an economic basis for ethnic solidarity?

COMMUNITY

Many of the Sansei still lived with their parents. Of 376 males responding to this question, 57 percent lived in the same house as their parents, and an additional 12 percent were unmarried students who lived away from home while they attended school. Thus only about 31 percent of the Sansei males, less than one-third of the sample, were really launched as fully independent adults. This fact makes it difficult to judge their attachment to a Japanese American community and its relationship to their expected economic behavior. Many may now live in mixed neighborhoods and assiduously visit their relatives, but when they establish themselves, they might move far away from the ethnic community. Nevertheless, let us briefly look at a few of the community characteristics of the Sansei, especially those that seem least tied to direct family influence.

Two measures of informal association, friendship patterns

and the reading of ethnic newspapers, give us some indication of the attachment of the Sansei to an ethnic community. Twenty-four percent of the Sansei males reported that both of their two closest friends were Japanese Americans. This compares with a 50 percent rate for the Nisei. Eleven percent of the Sansei read Japanese American newspapers regularly, 33 percent occasionally, while the majority, 56 percent, read them hardly ever or not at all. (For the Nisei, the corresponding figures were 34, 30, and 36 percent, respectively.)

Membership in formal organizations is greatly affected by age, as we have seen in the case of the Nisei. The youth of the Sansei thus made them appear less affiliated than they might someday become. Still, that only 15 percent of the Sansei males in our sample belonged to at least one Japanese American association cannot be attributed entirely to youth, since 34 percent belonged to some organization regardless of ethnicity. (Twice as many Nisei belonged to some organization—ethnic or nonethnic—but three times as many had joined at least one ethnic organization.)

On cultural items, too, the Sansei males showed a seeming decline of ethnic traits. Thus only 20 percent of them were affiliated with traditional religions, compared to 38 percent of the Nisei. Language skills indicated an even more marked decline, with only 3 percent of the Sansei men having fluency in Japanese, compared to 20 percent of Nisei men. At the other end of the scale, while only 4 percent of the Nisei said they could not speak any Japanese at all, 38 percent of the Sansei so reported. The perpetuation of the culture of Japan was surely fading, at least in the mid-1960s.

Worst of all from the point of view of the perpetuation of a distinct ethnic community was the intermarriage rate. Almost four in ten of the ninty-four male Sansei in our sample who had married were married to non-Japanese; and among those seventy-nine who were going steady or were engaged, over half—53 percent—were involved with non-Japanese American women. This behavior was supported by attitudes. The Sansei were asked the following question: "Speaking for yourself, do you think that, on the whole, the effect of Sansei marrying Caucasians is: good for them, makes little difference, bad for them?" The bulk of the Sansei men (75 percent) felt that intermarriage made little difference. Among the remainder, 15 percent felt intermarriage was good, and 10 percent felt it was bad. The intertwining of ethnicity and kinship cannot long survive rates like these.

Still, the Sansei respondents to our survey were not totally assimilationist. Many of them expressed a desire to learn more about the Japanese heritage. Ninety-one percent of the males said that they would like to speak the Japanese language better than they now did, while 83 percent thought they ought to know more about Japanese culture. In addition, the Sansei were asked the following general question about assimilation: "Should minority groups in America try to preserve something of the culture of their own group, or blend their culture into the mainstream of American life?" Fifty-eight percent answered in the pluralist direction, favoring the preservation of a distinct culture. We wonder, however, whether these attitudes can be supported by much beyond pious hopes. (It should be recalled, on the other hand, that the Sansei survey was conducted in the middle 1960s and therefore predated much of the growth of ethnic consciousness later in that decade and in the early 1970s. It is conceivable that these new trends have drawn a higher proportion of Sansei back within the orbit of an ethnic community, leading them to avoid interracial dating, to seek within the ethnic group for more of their intimate friendships, and to strengthen ethnic ties in other ways. Our guess, however, would be that such a tendency is unlikely on more than a limited scale, in part because the economic basis for such a tendency is extremely weak.)

ECONOMY AND COMMUNITY

Let us now turn to the relationship between economic and social characteristics of the Sansei to see if the aforementioned economic basis persisted into the mid-1960s. Table 15:4 presents the findings for self-employment according to the Sansei's preferred occupation. These data are the nearest we come in our survey to a direct measure of potential involvement in an ethnic economy.

There appears to have been little relationship between prospective self-employment and ethnicity of informal social ties, at least as measured by the ethnicity of two closest friends and by the propensity to read ethnic newspapers. Membership in formal organizations, however, appears related in a positive direction. Religion shows a rather strong correlation: Buddhist Sansei were distinctly more likely to expect self-employment. Ability to speak the Japanese language, on the other hand, did not show the same

TABLE 15:4
SOCIAL CORRELATES OF PREFERRED
SELF-EMPLOYMENT OF SANSEI MALES

	Self-Employed	Mixed	Employee
Closest friends only Japanese American	25%	22%	25%
Reads Japanese American newspapers regularly/occasionally	44	53	37
Belongs to Japanese American organization(s)	19	16	13
Traditional religion	32	20	15
Speaks any Japanese	60	68	59
Japanese American wife	72	57	54
Japanese American steady date	53	41	48
Considers intermarriage bad	17	9	7
Would like to speak Japanese better	94	91	90
Would like more training in Japanese culture	53	44	33
Thinks minorities should preserve culture	58	65	52
	(73)	(144)	(150)

pattern. Those who did not anticipate self-employment were far more likely to have outmarried than the self-employed. Steady dates, too, were more often Japanese American among the self-employed than among those who anticipated being employed by others, but those who expected a mix of employment and self-employment were even more prone to have steady, ongoing relationships with Japanese American women. These behavior patterns were supported by attitudes. Thus, those who expected self-employment were more likely to disapprove of intermarriage.

The relationship of self-employment to the desire to improve Japanese language skills was extremely weak. It would appear that any linguistic basis for increased participation in the ethnic economy had disappeared by the third generation. More general cultural traits, however, were still linked to it. This was shown in the correlation with religion and was again revealed in the expressed desire for additional training in Japanese culture. The prospective self-employed were 20 percent more likely than were prospective employees to desire more training in Japanese culture.

The pluralism item showed some tendency for the prospective self-employed to be more pluralistic than the prospective employees, who were more assimilationist, but the mixed group was the most pluralistic. This may, in part, have been a function of age. The mixed group turns out to have been the youngest, and it might perhaps be the vanguard of the new ethnic consciousness. Members of this group expressed more ethnic consciousness in the form of reading the ethnic press more often and knowing the Japanese language better than the others did, but, on the other hand, they were as likely to outmarry as those in the employee group. These tendencies suggest a possible contradiction between ideals and actions.

On the whole, although the picture was mixed, it appears that there was some continuity in the relationship between economic and social forms among the Sansei. We must exercise caution in concluding anything definite about the way this generation will develop, however. Our measures were inadequate for the task, and even if they had not been, the Sansei have yet to determine their own direction.

PARENTS OF THE SANSEI

It is difficult to examine occupational transmission from the Nisei to the Sansei because the relevant numbers are so small. However, it must be evident from the marginal totals that occupational transmission was slight, since so many more Sansei than their fathers were professionals. Looking only at the Sansei who hoped to become professionals, the sole group for whom there were sufficient numbers to convert to percentages, we find that only 18 percent had fathers who were themselves professionals. Twenty-five percent were the sons of proprietors and managers, 28 percent were the sons of farmers, and the fathers of 16 percent were service workers and laborers. It would appear that in the mid-1960s the ethnic economy of the Nisei was rapidly dissolving into an almost universally professional Sansei group and that father's occupation had not much hindered this process.

Still, at the level of prospective self-employment, we did find some continuity. Those Sansei who expected to be self-employed were more likely to be the sons of farmers (42 percent) than were those who expected mixed (22 percent) or employee (32 percent) status. Those in the mixed and employee categories, on the other hand, were more likely to be sons of proprietors. In other words, a transmission from the Nisei to the Sansei was in process, much like the one we discussed in chapter 10 as characterizing occupational-inheritance patterns among the immigrants and their children. Even more striking, Sansei who expect to be self-employed were more likely than those in the other two categories to be sons of self-employed Nisei. Eighty percent of those Sansei who predicted self-employment for themselves were sons of the self-employed, compared to only 55 percent of those who predicted mixed or employee status.

In conclusion, we find among the Sansei in our sample a great shift away from the occupations of their fathers and into the professions, much as their own fathers (particularly the youngest cohort) had shifted earlier. There seems to have been some retention of the self-employment ideal of the ethnic economy, even among Sansei, and this appears to have been transmitted most often by parents who were active in small business. In addition, economic forms were found to be related to social forms, if weakly, with those Sansei most desirous of self-employment also the most likely to retain ties to an ethnic community. While our measures are too shaky to enable us to assess these issues with any certainty, they do point to the erosion of an economic basis for ethnic solidarity within the third generation of this particular ethnic group.

16

Conclusion

This book has examined the Japanese American experience from a middleman-minority perspective. In part I we described the theoretical tradition of the middleman-minority concept and examined the Issei in that light. We found that Issei economic forms did more or less correspond to the classic middleman type. They developed small businesses that depended upon noncontractual bonds of mutual obligation, even though they were located in an advanced capitalist economy.

The typical middleman-minority pattern, depicted in figure 2:1, appears to have applied fairly well to the prewar Issei. Ethnic solidarity played a critical role in helping them get established in independent business and farming, while their concentration in this type of enterprise isolated them from the surrounding community and reinforced their ethnic solidarity. The nature of Japanese immigrant enterprise put the Issei in conflict with certain segments of the surrounding society. The precapitalist form of their businesses deemphasized internal class divisions and produced an especially loyal and hardworking labor force. They clashed not only with competing businesses, which had to rely on more costly labor, but also with organized labor, which felt that low labor standards in Japanese enterprises threatened their own labor standard.

If we look at the other side of the coin, we find that the Issei were driven by the surrounding society into these very kinds of small businesses. Their opportunities for employment were severely restricted. Japanese immigrants were denied citizenship rights and therefore could not lodge complaints against discrimination. New immigrants were forced to take jobs wherever they could get them, and the fact that fellow ethnics offered them an opportunity to establish themselves was bound to produce loyalty. Societal hostility and concentration in small business thus mutually reinforced one another.

Finally, the hostility of the surrounding society helped to reinforce whatever propensities toward retaining a solidary ethnic community the Issei brought with them, while their solidarity provoked hostile reactions. They were perceived as unassimilable, a problem that was exacerbated by their growing importance in particular and often highly visible lines of economic enterprise. All of these themes, and their interweaving, are common to most middleman minorities.

We may now briefly consider what the Issei experience says about theories, outlined in chapter 2, which attempt to explain the middleman-minority phenomenon. Contextual theories suggest that middleman groups come into existence because they are needed by society, in particular by elites who require a small-business sector to deal with the masses. We have not examined evidence on the nature of the clientele of Japanese American businesses and so cannot speak to this point, although it might be a fruitful topic for further research. In particular, if Issei business catered importantly to minority and poorer white communities, such a tendency could provide support for the idea that they were acting as a kind of go-between for local elites.

On another point of contextual theory we are also completely lacking evidence: the degree to which elites helped to channel the Issei into the middleman mode. Were there links between Issei small farmers and large farming corporations such that the latter benefited from the existence of the former? Did local capitalists at least sometimes back discriminatory laws and practices in order to force the Issei into independent small business? None of the evidence we have examined suggests that this was the case. If anything, most societal action toward the Issei seems to have been aimed at pushing them out of small business. The Alien Land Laws, for instance, tried to deny them the right rather than encourage them to become small farmers.

The possibility remains, however, that anti-Japanese actions were mainly the product of local labor and small business, while corporate capital supported Issei enterprise. For corporate capitalists, a middleman group may have helped control labor, especially Japanese immigrant labor, and the Issei may have acted as a buffer group to provide services for the more "troublesome" sectors of the population as well as to absorb hostility.

For cultural and situational explanations of the Issei middleman position, on the other hand, there seems to be a good deal of positive evidence. The immigrants did come with some cultural baggage that encouraged concentration in small business, most notably their strong bonds of ethnic solidarity. These combined with their situation as a sojourning immigrant group to give them a motive for retaining ties to the ethnic community. Undoubtedly the fact that they were a separate and distinct ethnic community aided them in their ability to deal objectively with clients, though again we have no direct evidence on the point.

Regardless of its causes, the fact that the Issei were able to establish a substantially precapitalist business form in the context of modern, capitalist America demonstrates that the form does not necessarily disappear with advanced capitalism. Perhaps what is most remarkable is that these immigrant businesses, dependent upon precapitalist-type bonds of ethnic loyalty, were not only able to survive but could actually thrive within capitalist society. This paradox is resolved by the fact that under certain circumstances, notably in marginal fields of endeavor, noncontractual relations can be less expensive and more efficient than formal contractual ones. As long as there remain less-developed niches within capitalist society where this continues to be true, one can anticipate that specialized minorities with strong ethnic communities will arise to fill them.

Despite the fact that middleman minorities may perform important functions for the surrounding society, their presence also produces conflicts, as we have seen. These conflicts are, to some extent, beneficial to the small-business mode, as they reinforce the ethnic solidarity on which it is built and drive members of the ethnic community to work harder, save their money in an insecure environment, and sell their labor inexpensively to ethnic entrepreneurs who at least promise them a job. At some point, though, the hostility from the surrounding society becomes so intense that it extinguishes the form altogether. In the case of the Japanese Americans, this point was reached with the onset of World War II, when the war with Japan set in train a series of events that, not incidentally, destroyed the ethnic economy by forcing the evacuation of all persons of Japanese ancestry from their major areas of concentration.

The war marked an important turning point for the Japanese Americans. Essentially it ended the middleman-minority position of that minority. Many reasons can be adduced for the change: that the postwar social climate was, for a variety of reasons, much less racist than the one before the war; that the general economy had become far more concentrated in large corporations, leaving little room for a small-business-centered minority to gain much economic power; that the evacuation broke Issei economic power at a point in their lives when they no longer were youthful enough to recreate it; and that the war, by chance, also marked the shift from first- to second-generation dominance of the ethnic community, with important implications for the kinds of communal resources a nonimmigrant generation could mobilize.

The bulk of our study concentrates on the second generation. While there is considerable theory available regarding how the middleman-minority position is sustained, little is known about its dissolution, especially under conditions conducive to assimilation. While the Japanese American case is unique in the United States in that these people were subjected to a form of expulsion, in many ways the second generation was in a position similar to that of the second generation of other middleman-type immigrant groups in the United States, such as the Jews, Greeks, and Armenians. Our concern here has been to understand the degree to which middleman forms are retained into the second (and third) generation in advanced capitalist America, why they are differentially retained, and what the implications are for the perpetuation of strong ethnic communities.

In part I we examined the Nisei experience before the war, using historical materials. We found the Nisei to be fully enmeshed in the middleman-minority position of their parents, working as unpaid family or low-wage labor in Issei businesses or running their own businesses in the ethnic economy, tied to the ethnic community while serving the surrounding society or segments thereof. An attempt was made to disentangle the degree to which this was imposed by the outside society's discrimination and the degree to which it represented a chosen path with perceived opportunities. The dominant interpretation in the literature is the former, and while we could not prove it was not so, we at least suggested that there may have been positive aspects to the situation as well. The middleman-minority position not only was a reaction to discrimination but also afforded certain opportunities, even to the Nisei. We concluded that the Nisei were probably torn in their desires. Their American education (although this did not reflect their parents' intentions) encouraged assimilation. Nevertheless, their upbringing and the possible economic rewards of successful self-employment encouraged them to continue in the small-business mold. Regardless of their desires, however, the complex of variables that make up the middleman form combined with a major economic depression gave them little choice. They had to continue in small business.

The postwar period, as we have seen, provided a whole new social context for the Japanese minority. No longer were they excluded from participation in the surrounding economy as employees, while opportunities for ethnic small business concomitantly shrank. Despite this, some of the Nisei came back from the relocation and reestablished, in modified form, the small-business economy of their parents. Never were they to regain the kind of control over a particular economic niche that the Issei exercised in, for instance, the Southern California produce industry—that had been forever destroyed; but they were able, in important numbers, to become self-employed.

The Nisei in the mid-1960s could hardly be considered a full-fledged middleman minority. However, the fact that close to half of them were owners or employees of ethnic small businesses enabled us to examine empirically some of the factors that contribute to the retention or dissolution of the form in the second generation. This was the subject of part II of the volume. We saw that the middleman form was retained most among the oldest and least educated Nisei males, that they tended to be the sons of farmers rather than of urban proprietors, and that they tended to cluster on the West Coast. In addition, these features tended to be interrelated. For instance, the sons of urban proprietors were most likely to receive higher education, which provided them with one important means of leaving both the ethnic economy and the West Coast.

One might be inclined to conclude from this set of findings that societal hostility no longer pushed Nisei in the direction of small business. True, the postwar environment was much more conducive to Nisei participation in the general economy. No longer could it be said that Japanese Americans went into small business because there were no available jobs in the surrounding economy. Societal hostility may have played a more subtle role for the second generation, however. The fact that older Nisei were more inclined to concentrate in small business may reflect a legacy of societal hostility, which took the form of direct past discrimination that limited current job options and also existed as a more deep-seated, generalized wariness caused by prewar and wartime experiences. Nisei who reached maturity before the war had had a possibly traumatizing experience, one that may have kept them forever suspicious of white society. The ethnic economy may thus continue, serving as a refuge, even when overt hostility appears to have diminished. And the retention of a small-business mode would help to maintain for this ethnic group a "stranger" orientation and thereby perpetuate the cycle.

The decline in small-business concentration of the minority as a whole probably has contributed to the decline in societal hostility toward the Japanese Americans. There is a mutual relationship between these two phenomena, as suggested in figure 2:1. The last twenty or thirty years have seen a spiraling downward of this interaction: as societal hostility has decreased, so has the motivation to retreat into ethnic small business, which in turn has reduced the points of conflict between the minority and the surrounding society.

One of the most intriguing findings of part II was the role of education in the decline of the middleman-minority form. We believe that such education was provided by parents, not so much to allow their children to escape from the ethnic economy, as to give them a better position within it. The goal was for the sons to become independent professionals or to run the family business or farm with improved efficiency. However, education has the unintended consequence, especially when in a societal context of relatively mild hostility and discrimination, of greatly increasing job opportunities outside of the ethnic economy.

The relationship between small-business concentration and ethnic solidarity was examined in part III of this study. In general we found empirical support for a connection. Engaging in small business tended to be related to relatively high levels of attachment to the family, high rates of informal social attachments in the ethnic community, high levels of participation in Japanese American organizations, and high rates of affiliation with Buddhism. These findings provide some support for cultural and situational approaches to middleman minorities. "Hard" cultural factors, such as the passing on of particular values, received only weak corroboration, with the exception of religious affiliation, but our study hardly did justice to this complex topic. On the other hand, ethnic solidarity itself seems to be a critical factor. This can be seen either as a cultural phenomenon—the product of values brought over by the immigrants and passed on to their children— or as an outgrowth of the situation of being sojourning immigrants: through the interconnected factors expressed in figure 2:1, a hostile environment and hence a "stranger" orientation were maintained long after the period of sojourning was over.

Even the religious finding, strong as it is, lends itself more to a social-solidarity than a strict cultural-values interpretation, as does the finding of regional concentration of the remaining middleman form. All these patterns suggest that ethnic solidarity interacts significantly with small business in such a way that each sustains the other. Thus, those Nisei who have been most closely tied to the ethnic community, with its networks of mutual obligation and trust, were most likely to become firmly established in the independent small-business form, while, on the other hand, those least tied to it have tended to move into the corporate and public sectors. Needless to say, this relationship does not preclude the possibility that societal hostility helped to enforce ethnic solidarity.

Retention of the small-business mode has tended to reinforce ethnic solidarity; leaving small business has been associated with the weakening of ethnic bonds. This is perhaps our most significant finding, and one we would like to stress. It supports the work of other authors (such as Cohen, 1969; Foster, 1974; and Leon, 1970) studying very different empirical cases but nevertheless coming to a remarkably similar conclusion: that ethnicity is not an eternal verity but a variable that is responsive to societal conditions, and that one very important condition is the economic position of the group in question. Ethnic affiliation is a resource that may be called upon to support certain economic interests. When those economic interests are no longer present, ethnicity is likely to subside in importance. Our study has demonstrated this, at least to a certain extent, with the Nisei. Those who moved into the corporate economy had less material reason for retaining close ethnic ties than did those who ran small businesses, and they behaved accordingly.

This finding has important implications for the future of the Japanese Americans as a distinctive ethnic minority. Part II of our study revealed that the Nisei most likely to have resumed parental economic forms were the older, less educated members of the generation. Already the younger Nisei, who came to maturity after the war, were falling away from the ethnic economy. Our Sansei data show a marked continuation of this trend. These findings are especially poignant when we realize that our survey picked up those Sansei who were the children of the oldest segment of the Nisei generation. If these Sansei are leaving the ethnic economy, who will be left?

Our findings are supported by those of others who find astonishingly high intermarriage rates among young Japanese Americans today (Kikumura and Kitano, 1973; Tinker, 1973). On the other hand, we did find expressions of a desire to learn more about their ethnic heritage, a desire that may have increased substantially in the more ethnically conscious period following our survey. There may always be a core of individuals who keep the ethnic community alive even without an economic basis. Still, our general conclusion must be that without a retention of common and distinctive class interests, it will be increasingly difficult to keep members from defecting and disappearing into the mainstream, even if ethnic roots are honored verbally.

The decline of Japanese American small business and ethnicity spells a real loss for the richness and diversity of American life; yet there is a problem in the price that must be paid for the retention of ethnic differences, for with them goes hostility and interest-group conflict. There may be an unstable equilibrium with no point at which significant diversity can be accompanied by lack of conflict, for conflict helps to sustain the diversity, and diversity spurs on the conflict. Peaceful pluralism may indicate that group differences are really trivial. When group differences are important, will people be able to live together in harmony?

We are not trying to say that movements toward ethnic self-determination should be quelled for the sake of peace. Rather, these very movements signify that peace is not present. Interest-based differences that correspond to ethnic differences are strongly entrenched in American society. Minorities are typically exploited. Simple assimilationism of the old liberal school masks this fact and deprives minorities of a potential political base for class action—the ethnic group. The emergence of self-conscious new classes of industrial employees who are native Americans (as, for example, the Appalachian hill people in Ohio, Indiana, and

Michigan cities) and of new entrepreneurial immigrant minorities who practice many of the same thrifty and communal strategies for economic success as did the Issei (the Koreans, for instance, and perhaps the Vietnamese) indicates that the culture attendant upon advanced capitalism does not simply crush out ethnic variety, nor does it cease to create situations amenable to the formation of ethnic solidarity. Instead, as we have shown through our study of the Nisei, ethnic solidarity is a historical phenomenon, conditioned by the material situation of the group.

If, however, minorities should achieve a measure of equality (perhaps a utopian thought in most cases), would there be a reason for retaining ethnic differences? Wouldn't they disappear of their own accord? The Japanese American experience speaks to this issue, especially in the Sansei generation. It suggests that, even if they are racially distinct, when minorities become like the majority economically, it is difficult to preserve their distinctiveness. No less significant, our case study indicates that to understand ethnicity one cannot confine oneself to the examination of culture. To comprehend ethnicity fully and to gain a sense of its future, we must examine it as a dialectically changing product of concrete historical structures and processes.

Appendix A
JARP Methodology

This study is based largely on the data collected by the Japanese American Research Project (JARP) at the University of California, Los Angeles; it was designed as a broad-gauged project combining sociological and historical inquiries. The sociological project changed directors midway through and underwent revisions of purpose and procedure. A more detailed description of the history and methodology of the project will be found in a companion volume to this book, *The Japanese American Community: A Three Generation Study* (New York: Praeger, in press) by Gene N. Levine and Robert Colbert Rhodes. Levine and Rhodes ask somewhat broader questions about the Japanese American experience than those raised here.

One of the early purposes of the JARP was to sample and interview surviving members of the first generation, defined as those immigrants who had arrived in the continental United States before legislation was passed in 1924 ending further immigration from Japan, though since that year foreign-born Japanese have trickled into the country in various capacities. Hawaiian Japanese Americans have come in substantial numbers, and a wave of new immigration has arisen in recent years with the rescinding of exclusion laws. Our data, and specification of our theoretical framework, focus exclusively on the pre-1924 immigration and the Japanese American community stemming from that immigration.

An attempt was made in 1963 to list every Issei still living in the United States, excluding Alaska and Hawaii. The lists were derived mainly from membership lists of various Japanese American voluntary associations and churches, augmented by names suggested by knowledgeable local Japanese Americans who took an interest in the JARP. The lists, which included about 18,000 persons, undoubtedly were incomplete, leaving out unaffiliates and those who had drifted the farthest from the Japanese American community, though the high degree of organizational life and years of discrimination reduced the error inevitable by this method to a minimum.

Table A:1 presents the Japanese American population figures from the censuses bracketing our listing (1960 and 1970), and it is clear that the foreign born far exceeded 18,000. However, of the 101,656 foreign born enumerated in 1960 (which included those in Hawaii and Alaska), 43 percent were younger than thirty-five years of age (U.S. Bureau of the Census, 1963:8) and could not possibly have immigrated prior to 1924. Furthermore, among those who were at least born in time to have been Issei by our definition, a goodly number must have traveled as adults and thus arrived well after 1924.

A sample was selected from the Issei lists, stratified by county and designed to achieve in each county equal representation of those living in neighborhoods of six different levels of housing quality. Interviews were carried out between 1964 and 1966. Less than 1 percent refused, so we had a sample of 1,047 Issei. In their interviews, the Issei were asked for a complete listing of their children, with their addresses. This gave us a list of 3,817

TABLE A:1
JAPANESE AMERICAN POPULATION IN 1960 AND 1970

	1960	*1970*
Total Japanese American population	473,170	588,324
Mainland Japanese American population*	265,940	370,295
Total foreign born	101,656	122,500
Mainland foreign born	58,138†	101,679

SOURCES: Census of population, 1960, Subject Reports, Nonwhite Population by Race (U.S. Bureau of the Census, 1963), pp. 3, 8, 18; Census of Population, 1970, Subject Reports, Japanese, Chinese, and Filipinos in the United States (U.S. Bureau of the Census, 1973), pp. 1, 9, 11.

*For 1960, only Hawaii is excluded, while for 1970, both Hawaii and Alaska are excluded. In 1970, the Japanese American population in Alaska was 874.

†The 1960 report does not divide foreign born by state of residence; thus, we estimated this figure by assuming that the proportion of foreign born in Hawaii is the same as that in the nation as a whole.

Nisei, all of whom we attempted to contact during 1967. A respectable 60 percent response rate was achieved, yielding a Nisei sample of 2,304.

Of the original 1,047 Issei, 141 did not have any children or did not have children who responded to our questionnaire. Thus 906 Issei were parents of the people on whom the bulk of this study concentrates, the Nisei. An attempt was made to reach Issei families rather than individuals, and when the husband in the family was alive and well, he was interviewed rather than the wife. Thus 64 percent of the Issei sample was male, including seventy-five widowers and seven men who were divorced or separated. The great majority of the women (90 percent) were widows. Twenty-nine women (9 percent) had husbands living who, for various reasons, could not be interviewed, and four were divorced or separated.

The Issei were old at the time of interviewing. Twenty-two percent were eighty years old or more, another 40 percent were between seventy and seventy-nine, 20 percent were between sixty-five and sixty-nine, and 18 percent were under sixty-five years of age. The age distribution of the two sexes was fairly different, with women showing a normal curve around the modal category of seventy to seventy-four. Men, in contrast, showed a bimodal distribution, with the fewest number (10 percent) in the age range of seventy to seventy-four, and more below sixty-five and above seventy-five. These figures say less about the longevity of the sexes or about sampling error than about the peculiarities of the migration process.

Because only living Issei were sought, the sample consisted solely of families in which a member of the immigrant generation had survived into the mid-1960s. Table A:2 shows the degree to which our Issei sample is innacurate on this score, as we had a somewhat higher concentration of later immigrants than the immigration records report. This bias had an effect on the Nisei sample which omitted the children of dead Issei. In effect this meant that those in our second-generation sample were more likely to be the progeny of Issei who came in the later phases of the migration to the United States. As column 2 of the table suggests, however, our sample was considerably more nearly representative of the Japanese immigrants to the mainland who persisted there to 1930, at what might be said to be the height of the Issei generation's vigor and development.

TABLE A:2

COMPARISON OF IMMIGRATION RECORDS AND ISSEI SAMPLE ON
YEAR OF ENTRY TO THE CONTINENTAL UNITED STATES

	Immigration Records	*1930 Census*	*Issei Survey*
Male and Female			
Before 1900	6%	11%	3%
1900–1909	52	38	37
1910–1919	28	33	45
1920–1924	14	18	15
Total	100	100	100
	(275,355)	(70,477)	(1,047)
Males Only			
Before 1900	8	6	3
1900–1909	66	50	48
1910–1919	18	24	36
1920–1924	8	10	13
Total	100	100	100
	(183,120)	(45,897)	(697)

SOURCES: U.S. Commissioner-General of Immigration, Records of Immigrants Arriving in Continental United States; Fifteenth Census of the United States, 1930, Population, vol. II, General Report, Statistics by Subjects (U.S. Bureau of the Census, 1933), p. 500.

Since an attempt was made to include all the offspring of each Issei in our Nisei sample, many of the Nisei respondents were brothers and sisters. The focus on intrafamilial patterns was a methodological concentration of the JARP of which the present volume does not partake. Since the family-based sample was achieved at the cost of a bias toward members of larger families, we should consider here the extent of that bias. Table A:3 shows the degree of relatedness within those families in which there were any Nisei respondents. Each column represents a different actual family size. Thus there were 78 Issei with only 1 child, 138 with 2 children, 195 with 3, and so on. The rows represent the number of Nisei who actually responded to the interview or questionnaire. Consider 2-child Issei families, for example. For such families, we have 67 cases in which only 1 of the siblings responded and 71 cases in which both did (the latter meaning that there were 142

TABLE A:3

RESPONSE RATE OF NISEI SIBLINGS BY FAMILY SIZE FOR ALL FAMILIES WITH AT LEAST ONE NISEI RESPONDENT

Number of Nisei Responding	Number of Children Listed by Issei								Total Number of Families	Total Number of Respondents
	1	2	3	4	5	6	7	8+		
1	78	67	59	37	11	11	1	3	267	267
2		71	80	49	26	16	9	6	257	514
3			56	57	40	16	8	4	181	543
4				34	27	23	10	6	100	400
5					12	21	9	10	52	260
6						6	9	9	24	144
7							1	10	11	77
8+								9	9	72+
Total number of families	78	138	195	177	116	93	47	57	901	2277+

Nisei who shared a single brother or sister in the sample). For 3-child Issei families, of which there were 195 who appeared in our Nisei sample, in 59 cases only 1 out of the 3 responded, in 80 cases 2 out of 3 did (meaning 160 Nisei), and in 56 cases all 3 answered (making 168 Nisei). Adding these up we find that 387 Nisei in our sample belonged to 3-child families.

The most important description of the interrelatedness of the sample (as opposed to the population from which it was drawn) is to be found in the last (summation) column. Here we find that 267 persons in the Nisei sample were not related to each other as siblings. There were 257 families with 2 sibling respondents, or 514 Nisei who had a single sibling, in the sample. There were 181 3-sibling families, or 543 Nisei with 2 other siblings, in the sample. And the list goes on, until, finally, we reach the 9 families with at least 8 siblings, or at least 72 Nisei with 8 or more brothers and sisters, in our sample.

It will be noted that five families are missing from this table. Despite prodigious cleaning efforts at great expense, there were still a few errors in the data, and this represents one of them. In these five cases we have one more Nisei respondent than Issei parent claimed was in his or her family. The number of Nisei thereby omitted from the table is nineteen.

The Nisei segment of the JARP survey was conducted in three stages. First, 34 percent of the sample was interviewed by non-Japanese, professional interviewers from the National Opinion Research Center (NORC) in areas that NORC regularly covers with its samples. Second, NORC personnel conducted telephone interviews with 4 percent who lived more than fifty miles beyond NORC sampling areas. Finally, the remaining 62 percent were sent mail questionnaires, resulting in a response rate of 49 percent after three mailings.

When the Nisei were being contacted, special emphasis was placed on reaching the eldest son of the family, on the assumption that he would best represent how the family was faring in economic terms. The face-to-face and telephone-interview phases of the survey reached 95 percent of the eldest sons, while most younger sons and daughters were reached by the mail questionnaire. This emphasis on the eldest sons affected the age-sex distribution in the sample, since naturally there was a higher response rate for those contacted most directly. Thus 52 percent of the Nisei sample was male, and there was a slightly higher proportion of older (born before 1925) males than females (46 percent versus 42 percent).

Since a possible bias existed from the sampling of Nisei whose parents were still alive at the time of the survey, an effort was made to determine the extent of this error. Death records at two Japanese American mortuaries in Los Angeles were examined in an effort to locate some children of Issei who had died before the survey. By this means, thirty-eight Nisei—as well as twenty-nine of their Sansei children—were interviewed, revealing no noteworthy differences from the body of the sample, with the exception of their greater age.

An attempt was made to compare some of the characteristics of our Nisei sample with corresponding data in the census, to gauge the extent of sample bias. An age-distribution comparison is not possible because the census did not divide the Japanese American population by generation. However, we were able to compare regional dispersion and educational attainment. Table A:4 shows the former and demonstrates that while the sample Nisei were slightly more concentrated in the West than was the case for the total Japanese American native-born population, the difference was small. In view of the organizational basis for the original Issei sample, this was indeed comforting.

The 1970 census did not divide educational attainment by sex for the Japanese Americans, nor did it provide separate figures

TABLE A:4

REGION OF RESIDENCE ON MAINLAND, NATIVE-BORN JAPANESE, 1960 AND 1970 CENSUSES AND NISEI SAMPLE

	1960	*1970*	*Nisei Sample*
Northeast	4%	7%	3%
North Central	10	11	11
South	4	6	3
West	82	77	84
Total	100	100	100
	(207,802)	(268,616)	(2,299)

SOURCES: Census of Population, 1960, Subject Reports, Nonwhite Population by Race, Final Report PC(2)–1C (U.S. Bureau of the Census, 1963), pp. 7, 18 (uses an estimate of foreign-born Japanese in Hawaii); Census of Population, 1970, Subject Reports, Japanese, Chinese, and Filipinos in the United States, Final Report PC(2)–16 (U.S. Bureau of the Census, 1973), pp. 1, 9–11.

for the foreign born which could be subtracted from the total to give us a reasonable comparison. Hence we restricted the comparison to the 1960 census. There were problems here too: the census gave separate figures for those in Hawaii and for the foreign born, but not figures for both together, so that we could only subtract one or the other contaminating population, both of whom showed lower levels of educational attainment than native-born, mainland dwellers. In addition, the census gave education figures for those fourteen years of age or older, meaning that it included many Sansei, a goodly number of whom had not completed school. Table A:5 presents this comparison, and it is evident that our Nisei sample had a higher proportion of persons who went beyond eighth grade than the Japanese American population at large. Other than this, the sample did not appear to be grossly unrepresentative on this dimension.

The sample was probably the best that could be obtained under the circumstances. Any attempt to get representative Nisei lists would have been infinitely more difficult than the already arduous task of obtaining Issei lists. Nisei were less likely to belong to Japanese American organizations, and thus even this route would have been closed. At least we have managed to reach some of the nonmember children of Issei organizational members. In short, we have a sample of Nisei which does not perfectly repre-

TABLE A:5

YEARS OF EDUCATION COMPLETED BY MAINLAND AND NATIVE-BORN
JAPANESE AGE FOURTEEN OR OLDER, 1960, AND BY NISEI SAMPLE

Years of Education	Mainland (including foreign born)		Native born (including Hawaii)		Nisei Sample	
	Male	Female	Male	Female	Male	Female
0–8	18%	19%	17%	20%	6%	4%
9–11	16	16	21	19	32	43
12	33	44	37	42	27	34
13–15	17	14	13	12	17	10
16+	15	7	12	7	17	9
Total	100 (87,451)	100 (100,416)	100 (121,664)	100 (118,872)	100 (1,198)	100 (1,099)

SOURCE: Census of Population, 1960, Subject Reports, Nonwhite Population by Race, Final Report PC(2)–1C (U.S. Bureau of the Census, 1963), pp. 1, 18, 90.

sent population parameters among all living children of mainland Issei but surely does capture the variance along important dimensions which existed within the Nisei in the mid-1960s. If there are systematic biases affecting the correlates of these dimensions, we cannot discern them.

The JARP survey is unique. To our knowledge, no ethnic group in the United States has been surveyed so thoroughly, in a study using a national sample and a three-generational design. Whatever the shortcomings of the survey, these data surely provide a remarkable opportunity for the study of ethnic-group processes.

Appendix B

Groups Treated as Middleman Minorities by Several Authors of Comparative Studies

Groups	Authors
Jews	
Jews in Europe	Blalock; Foster; Jiang; Shibutani and Kwan; Wertheim; Zenner
Jews in Poland	Andreski; Eitzen; Hamilton
Jews in Rumania	Spulber
Jews in Germany	Becker; Stryker
Jews in Mediterranean countries	Cohen
Jews in Spain	Hamilton; Shibutani and Kwan
Jews in North Africa	Jiang
Jews in the United States	Rinder; Shibutani and Kwan
Chinese	
Overseas Chinese in general	Fallers; Hamilton; Shibutani and Kwan; Zenner
Chinese in Southeast Asia	Blalock; Cohen; Foster; Jiang; Schermerhorn; Wertheim
Chinese in Singapore	Fallers
Chinese in Indonesia	Andreski; Becker; Rinder; Spulber
Chinese in Thailand	Rinder

Chinese in the Philippines	Eitzen; Hamilton; Hunt and Walker; Schermerhorn; Shibutani and Kwan
Chinese in Madagascar	Fallers
Chinese in Fiji	Shibutani and Kwan
Indians and Pakistanis	
Overseas Indians in general	Hamilton; Shibutani and Kwan; Zenner
Indians in Africa	Schermerhorn
Indians in British Central Africa	Van der Laan
Indians in East Africa	Cohen; Foster; Jiang; Shibutani and Kwan; Wertheim
Indians in Kenya	Hunt and Walker; van der Laan
Indians in Uganda	Van der Laan
Indians in South Africa	Andreski; Blalock; Cohen; Jiang; Rinder; Wertheim
Indians in Madagascar	Van der Laan
Indians in Southeast Asia	Wertheim
Indians in Burma	Blalock; Jiang; Wertheim
Indians in Afganistan	Jiang
Indians in Fiji	Shibutani and Kwan
Arabs	
Overseas Arabs in general	Shibutani and Kwan
Overseas Lebanese in general	Hamilton
Arabs, Syrians, and Lebanese in Africa	Schermerhorn; Shibutani and Kwan
Syrians in West Africa	Cohen; Wertheim
Lebanese in West Africa	Cohen; Fallers; Jiang; van der Laan
Lebanese in French Africa	Van der Laan
Lebanese in Guinea	Van der Laan
Coptic Christians in Egypt	Hamilton
Arabs in China	Hamilton
Arabs in Indonesia	Shibutani and Kwan
Greeks	
Overseas Greeks in general	Jiang
Greeks in Africa	Shibutani and Kwan
Greeks in Egypt	Becker
Greeks in Russia	McElroy
Greeks in the United States	Blalock; McElroy

Armenians
  Overseas Armenians in general   Hamilton
  Armenians in Turkey   Becker; Stryker; Wertheim
  Armenians in India   McElroy
  Armenians in the United   Blalock; McElroy
    States

Parsis
  Parsis in India   Becker; Jiang; Rinder; Stryker

Japanese
  Japanese in Brazil   McElroy
  Japanese in the United States   Blalock; McElroy

Miscellaneous
  Americans in Latin America   Rinder
    and the Middle East
  Eurasians in Dutch East Indies   Blalock; Shibutani and Kwan
  Hausa in Nigeria   Cohen
  Ibo in Calabar   Fallers
  Ibo in Nigeria   Waterbury
  Ijebu in Nigeria   Shibutani and Kwan
  Jains in India   Becker
  Mestizos in Brazil and the   Blalock
    Caribbean
  Mestizos in Mexico   Shibutani and Kwan
  Metics in Greece (Athens)   Blalock
  Mizabites in Algeria   Jiang
  Mons in Thailand   Foster
  Nyssalese in Tibet   Jiang
  Portuguese in China   Hamilton
  Scots in general   Becker; Rinder
  Soussis Berbers in Morocco   Jiang; Waterbury
  Tajiks in Afghanistan   Jiang

SOURCES: Andreski, 1963; Becker, 1956; Blalock, 1967:80-81; Cohen, 1969:191; Eitzen, 1971; Fallers, 1967; Foster, 1974; Hamilton, 1978; Hunt and Walker, 1974:93-127; Jiang, 1968; McElroy, 1977; Rinder, 1958-59; Schermerhorn, 1970:74-76; Shibutani and Kwan, 1965:189-197; Spulber, 1966:89-151; Stryker, 1959; van der Laan, 1975; Waterbury, 1972; Wertheim, 1964; Zenner, 1976a.

References

Adams, Bert N.
  1968   *Kinship in an Urban Setting*. Chicago: Markham.
Aldrich, Howard
  1977   "Testing the Middleman Minority Model of Asian Entrepreneur-
          ial Behavior: Preliminary Results from Wandsworth, England."
          Paper read at Annual Meeting of American Sociological Associa-
          tion, Chicago, August.
Andreski, Stanislav
  1963   "An Economic Interpretation of Antisemitism." *Jewish Journal
          of Sociology* 5 (December):201-213.
Aris, Stephen
  1970   *The Jews in Business*. London: Jonathan Cape.
Barth, Fredrik, ed.
  1969   *Ethnic Groups and Boundaries*. Boston: Little, Brown.
Becker, Howard
  1940   "Constructive Typology in the Social Sciences." In *Contemp-
          orary Social Theory*, ed. Harry Elmer Barnes, Howard Becker,
          and Frances Barnett Becker, pp. 17-46. New York: Appleton
          Century.
  1956   "Middleman Trading Peoples: Germ Plasm and Social Situa-
          tions." In *Man in Reciprocity*, pp. 225-237. New York: Praeger.
Befu, Harumi
  1965   "Contrastive Acculturation of California Japanese: Comparative
          Approach to the Study of Immigrants." *Human Organization* 24
          (Fall):209-216.
Bell, Reginald
  1935   *Public School Education of Second-Generation Japanese in Cali-
          fornia*. Stanford: Stanford University Press.
Benedict, Burton
  1968   "Family Firms and Economic Development." *Southwestern
          Journal of Anthropology* 24 (Spring):1-19.

Blalock, Hubert M., Jr.

1967　*Toward a Theory of Minority Group Relations.* New York: John Wiley.

Bloom, Leonard, and Ruth Riemer

1949　*Removal and Return: The Socio-Economic Effects of the War on Japanese Americans.* Berkeley and Los Angeles: University of California Press.

Blumer, Herbert

1965　"Industrialisation and Race Relations." In *Industrialisation and Race Relations,* ed. Guy Hunter, pp. 220-253. London: Oxford University Press.

Bogardus, Emory S.

1945　"Resettlement Problems of Japanese Americans." *Sociology and Social Research* 29 (January-February):218-226.

Bonacich, Edna

1972　"A Theory of Ethnic Antagonism: The Split Labor Market." *American Sociological Review* 37 (October):547-559.

1973　"A Theory of Middleman Minorities." *American Sociological Review* 38 (October):583-594.

1976　"Advanced Capitalism and Black/White Race Relations in the United States: A Split Labor Market Interpretation." *American Sociological Review* 41 (February):34-51.

Bonacich, Edna, Ivan Light, and Charles Choy Wong

1976　"Small Business among Koreans in Los Angeles." In *Counterpoint: Perspectives on Asian America,* ed. Emma Gee, pp. 436-449. Los Angeles: University of California Asian American Studies Center.

Broom, Leonard, and John I. Kitsuse

1956　*The Managed Casualty: The Japanese American Family in World War II.* Berkeley and Los Angeles: University of California Press.

Cahnman, Werner J.

1957　"Socio-economic Causes of Antisemitism." *Social Problems* 5 (July):21-29.

1965　"Role and Significance of the Jewish Artisan Class." *Jewish Journal of Sociology* 7 (December):207-220.

California State Board of Control

1922　*California and the Oriental.* Sacramento: California State Printing Office.

California State Bureau of Labor Statistics

1911-12　Fifteenth Biennial Report. Sacramento: California State Printing Office.

Caudill, William, and George De Vos

1970　"Achievement, Culture, and Personality: The Case of Japanese Americans." In *Minority Response,* ed. Minako Kurokawa, pp. 179-186. New York: Random House.

Chiu, Ping
  1963   *Chinese Labor in California, 1850-1880: An Economic Study.*
          Madison: State Historical Society of Wisconsin.

Cohen, Abner
  1969   *Custom and Politics in Urban Africa: A Study of Hausa Mi-
          grants in Yoruba Towns.* Berkeley and Los Angeles: University
          of California Press.

Cohen, Abner, ed.
  1974   *Urban Ethnicity.* London: Tavistock.

Conroy, Hilary, and T. Scott Miyakawa, eds.
  1972   *East Across the Pacific.* Santa Barbara: American Bibliographic
          Center, Clio Press.

Corbally, John E.
  1931   "Orientals in the Seattle Schools." *Sociology and Social Re-
          search* 16 (September-October):61-67.

Coser, Lewis A.
  1972   "The Alien as a Servant of Power." *American Sociological
          Review* 37 (October):574-581.

Cox, Oliver C.
  1948   *Caste, Class, and Race.* New York: Modern Reader.

Dahya, Badr
  1974   "The Nature of Pakistani Ethnicity in Industrial Cities in
          Britain." In *Urban Ethnicity*, ed. Abner Cohen, pp. 77-118.
          London: Tavistock.

Daniels, Roger
  1966a   *The Politics of Prejudice.* Gloucester: Peter Smith.
  1966b   "Westerners from the East: Oriental Immigrants Reappraised."
          Pacific Historical Review 35 (November): 373-383.
  1971   *Concentration Camps USA: Japanese Americans and World War
          II.* New York: Holt, Rinehart, and Winston.

Davey, Frank
  1920   *Report on the Japanese Situation Investigated for Governor Ben
          W. Olcott.* Salem: Stage Printing Department.

Davis, Allison, B. B. Gardner, and M. R. Gardner
  1941   *Deep South.* Chicago: University of Chicago Press.

Decker, Peter R.
  1977   "Jewish Merchants in 19th Century San Francisco: Social
          Mobility on the Urban Frontier." Paper read at Western Jewish
          History Center Conference, San Francisco.

Dotson, Floyd, and Lillian O. Dotson
  1975   "Ethnic Group and Division of Labour: The Case of the Indians
          of British Central Africa, ca. 1960." In *Asian Minorities in
          Africa: Indians and Lebanese*, ed. H. Laurens van der Laan,
          pp. 206-218. Leiden: Kroniek van Afrika.

Eitzen, D. Stanley
  1971   "Two Minorities: The Jews of Poland and the Chinese of the Philippines." In *Majority and Minority: The Dynamics of Racial and Ethnic Relations*, ed. Norman R. Yetman and C. Hoy Steele, pp. 117-138. Boston: Allyn and Bacon.
Fallers, Lloyd A., ed.
  1967   *Immigrants and Associations*. The Hague: Mouton.
Fauman, S. Joseph
  1941   "The Jews in the Waste Industry in Detroit." *Jewish Social Studies* 3 (January):41-56.
Fisher, Lloyd H.
  1953   *The Harvest Labor Market in California*. Cambridge: Harvard University Press.
Foster, Brian L.
  1974   "Ethnicity and Commerce." *American Ethnologist* 1 (February):437-448.
Furnivall, J. S.
  1956   *Colonial Policy and Practice*. New York: New York University Press.
Gordon, Milton M.
  1964   *Assimilation in American Life*. New York: Oxford University Press.
Greeley, Andrew M.
  1974   *Ethnicity in the United States: A Preliminary Reconnaissance*. New York: John Wiley.
Grodzins, Morton
  1949   *Americans Betrayed*. Chicago: University of Chicago Press.
Hagen, Everett E.
  1962   *On the Theory of Social Change: How Economic Growth Begins*. Homewood, Ill.: Dorsey.
Hamilton, Gary
  1978   "Pariah Capitalism: A Paradox of Power and Dependence," *Ethnic Groups* 2 (June):1-15.
Howells, J. M.
  1920   "Remarks." Transactions of the Commonwealth Club of California 15 (August):210-211.
Hunt, Chester L., and Lewis Walker
  1974   *Ethnic Dynamics: Patterns of Intergroup Relations in Various Societies*. Homewood, Ill.: Dorsey.
Ichihashi, Yamato
  1932   *Japanese in the United States*. Stanford: Stanford University Press.
Iriye, Akira
  1972   *Pacific Estrangement: Japanese and American Expansion, 1897-1911*. Cambridge: Harvard University Press.

Iwata, Masakuzu
    1962   "The Japanese Immigrants in California Agriculture." *Agricultural History* 36 (January):25-37.

Jiang, Joseph P. L.
    1968   "Towards a Theory of Pariah Entrepreneurship." In *Leadership and Authority: A Symposium*, ed. Gehan Wijeyewardene, pp. 147-162. Singapore: University of Malaya Press.

Kataoka, W. T.
    1929   "Occupations of Japanese in Los Angeles." *Sociology and Social Research* 14 (September-October):53-58.

Kawai, Kazuo
    1926   "Three Roads, and None Easy: An American-born Japanese Looks at Life." *Survey* 56 (May):164-166.

Kikumura, Akemi, and Harry H. L. Kitano
    1973   "Interracial Marriage: A Picture of the Japanese Americans." *Journal of Social Issues* 29 (November):67-81.

King, Cameron
    1908   "Asiatic Exclusion." *International Socialist Review* 8 (May): 661-669.

Kitano, Harry H. L.
    1976a   "Japanese Americans: The Development of a Middleman Minority." In *The Asian American*, ed. Norris Hundley, Jr., pp. 81-100. Santa Barbara: American Bibliographic Center, Clio Press.
    1976b   *Japanese Americans: The Evolution of a Subculture.* 2nd ed. Englewood Cliffs, N.J.: Prentice Hall.

Koenig, Samuel
    1942   "The Socioeconomic Structure of an American Jewish Community." In *Jews in a Gentile World*, ed. Isacque Graeber and S. H. Britt, pp. 209-242. New York: Macmillan.

Kuper, Leo, and M. G. Smith, eds.
    1969   *Pluralism in Africa.* Berkeley and Los Angeles: University of California Press.

LaViolette, Forrest E.
    1945   *Americans of Japanese Ancestry.* Toronto: Institute of International Affairs.

Leon, Abram
    1970   *The Jewish Question: A Marxist Interpretation.* New York: Pathfinder.

Light, Ivan H.
    1972   *Ethnic Enterprise in America: Business and Welfare among Chinese, Japanese, and Blacks.* Berkeley and Los Angeles: University of California Press.
    1977   "The Ethnic Vice District, 1890-1944." *American Sociological Review* 42 (June):464-479.

Loewen, James W.

1971   *The Mississippi Chinese: Between Black and White.* Cambridge: Harvard University Press.

Maxwell, William Edgar

1975   "Modernization and Mobility into the Patrimonial Medical Elite in Thailand." *American Journal of Sociology* 81 (November): 465-490.

1977   "American Theories of Ethnic Identity and the Assimilation of Chinese Males into the Thai Medical Profession." Unpublished paper.

McElroy, David

1977   "Middleman Minorities: A Comparative Analysis." Ph.D. Dissertation, University of California.

McWilliams, Carey

1944   *Prejudice: Japanese Americans, Symbol of Racial Intolerance.* Boston: Little, Brown.

1971   *Factories in the Field.* Santa Barbara: Peregrine.

Meister, Dick, and Anne Loftis.

1977   *A Long Time Coming: The Struggle to Unionize America's Farm Workers.* New York: Macmillan.

Melendy, H. Brett

1972   *The Oriental Americans.* New York: Twayne.

Meyer, Henry J.

1940   "The Economic Structure of the Jewish Community in Detroit." *Jewish Social Studies* 2 (April):127-148.

Millis, H. A.

1915   *The Japanese Problem in the United States.* New York: Macmillan.

Miyamoto, Shotaro Frank

1939   "Social Solidarity among the Japanese of Seattle." *University of Washington Publications in the Social Sciences* 11 (December): 57-130.

Miyamoto, S. Frank, and Robert W. O'Brien

1947   "A Survey of Some Changes in the Seattle Japanese Community since Evacuation." *Research Studies of the State College of Washington* 15 (June):147-154.

Modell, John

1969   "Class or Ethnic Solidarity: The Japanese American Company Union." *Pacific Historical Review* 38 (May):193-206.

1977   *The Economics and Politics of Racial Accommodation: The Japanese of Los Angeles, 1900-1942.* Urbana: University of Illinois Press.

Modell, John, ed.

1973   *The Kikuchi Diary.* Urbana: University of Illinois Press.

Murphy, Thomas D.
1954   *Ambassadors in Arms: The Story of Hawaii's 100th Battalion.* Honolulu: University of Hawaii Press.

Ogawa, Dennis
1971   *From Japs to Japanese: An Evolution of Japanese-American Stereotypes.* Berkeley: McCutchan.

Okimoto, Daniel I.
1971   *American in Disguise.* New York: Weatherhill.

Oregon Bureau of Labor Statistics and Inspector of Factories and Workshops
1919-20 Ninth Biennial Report.
1923-24 Eleventh Biennial Report.
1925-26 Twelfth Biennial Report.
1927-28 Thirteenth Biennial Report.

Park, Robert E., and Herbert A. Miller
1921   *Old World Traits Transplanted.* New York: Harper.

Patterson, Orlando
1977   *Ethnic Chauvinism: The Reactionary Impulse.* New York: Stein and Day.

Petersen, William
1970   "Success Story, Japanese American Style." In *Minority Responses*, ed. Minako Kurokawa, pp. 169-178. New York: Random House.

Platkin, Richard H.
1972   "The Role of Ethnic Groups in Urban Real Estate: The Case of the Jews." Master's thesis, University of Washington.

Poli, Adon, and Warren M. Engstrand
1945   "Japanese Agriculture on the Pacific Coast." *Journal of Land and Public Utility Economics* 21 (November):352-364.

Portenier, Lillian G.
1947   "Abilities and Interests of Japanese-American High School Seniors." *Journal of Social Psychology* 25 (February):53-61.

Rademaker, John A.
1945   "Consequences of Evacuation of Japanese Americans from the Pacific Coast of the United States." *Social Process in Hawaii* 9-10 (July):98-102.

Radin, Paul
1946   "Japanese Ceremonies and Festivals in California." *Southwestern Journal of Anthropology* 2 (Summer):152-179.

Rinder, Irwin D.
1958-59 "Stranger in the Land: Social Relations in the Status Gap." *Social Problems* 6 (Winter):253-260.

Ryder, Norman B.
1965   "The Cohort in the Study of Social Change." *American Sociological Review* 30 (December):843-861.

Saxton, Alexander
  1971   *The Indispensable Enemy: Labor and the Anti-Chinese Movement in California.* Berkeley, Los Angeles, London: University of California Press.
Schermerhorn, R. A.
  1970   *Comparative Ethnic Relations.* New York: Random House.
  1976   "Parsis and Jews in India: A Tentative Comparison." *Journal of Asian Affairs* 1 (Spring):119-122.
Schmid, Calvin F., and Charles E. Nobbe
  1965   "Socioeconomic Differentials among Nonwhite Races." *American Sociological Review* 30 (December):909-922.
Schwartz, Audrey J.
  1971   "The Culturally Advantaged: A Study of Japanese American Pupils." *Sociology and Social Research* 55 (April):341-353.
Sengstock, Mary C.
  1974   "Iraqi Christians in Detroit: An Analysis of an Ethnic Occupation." In *Arabic Speaking Communities in American Cities.* ed. Barbara C. Aswad, pp. 21-38. New York: Center for Migration Studies.
Shibutani, Tamotsu, and Kian M. Kwan
  1965   *Ethnic Stratification: A Comparative Approach.* New York: Macmillan.
Shirey, Orville C.
  1946   *Americans: The Story of the 442nd Combat Team.* Washington, D.C.: Infantry Journal Press.
Simmel, Georg
  1950   "The Stranger." In *The Sociology of Georg Simmel*, ed. Kurt H. Wolff, pp. 402-408. Glencoe, Ill.: Free Press.
Siu, Paul C. P.
  1952   "The Sojourner." *American Journal of Sociology* 58 (July): 34-44.
Sjoberg, Gideon
  1960   *The Preindustrial City.* Glencoe, Ill.: Free Press.
Smith, M. G.
  1965   *The Plural Society of the British West Indies.* Berkeley and Los Angeles: University of California Press.
Sombart, Werner
  1951   *The Jews and Modern Capitalism.* Glencoe, Ill.: Free Press.
Spicer, Edward H., Aseal T. Hansen, Katherine Luomala, and Marvin K. Opler
  1969   *Impounded People.* Tucson: University of Arizona Press.
Spulber, Nicolas
  1966   *The State and Economic Development in Eastern Europe.* New York: Random House.

Stone, Russell A.
  1974 "Religious Ethic and the Spirit of Capitalism in Tunisia." *International Journal of Middle East Studies* 5 (June):260-273.

Strong, Edward K.
  1933 *Japanese in California.* Stanford: Stanford University Press.
  1934 *The Second-Generation Japanese Problem.* Stanford: Stanford University Press.

Stryker, Sheldon
  1959 "Social Structure and Prejudice." *Social Problems* 6 (Spring): 340-354.

Svensrud, Marian ,
  1933 "Attitudes of the Japanese toward Their Language Schools." *Sociology and Social Research* 17 (January-February):259-264.

Tachiki, Amy
  1971 Introduction to *Roots: An Asian American Reader*, ed. Amy Tachiki, Eddie Wong, and Franklin Odo, pp. 1-5. Los Angeles: University of California Asian American Studies Center.

TenBroek, Jacobus, Edward N. Barnhart, and Floyd W. Matson
  1954 *Prejudice, War, and the Constitution.* Berkeley and Los Angeles: University of California Press.

Thomas, Dorothy Swaine
  1952 *The Salvage.* Berkeley and Los Angeles: University of California Press.
  1956 "The Japanese American." In *Understanding Minority Groups*, ed. Joseph B. Gittler, pp. 84-108. New York: John Wiley.

Tinker, John N.
  1973 "Intermarriage and Ethnic Boundaries: The Japanese American Case." *Journal of Social Issues* 29 (November):49-66.

Toennies, Ferdinand
  1971 *On Sociology: Pure, Applied and Empirical*, ed. Werner J. Cahnman and Rudolf Heberle. Chicago: University of Chicago Press.

Tsuboi, Sakao
  1926 "The Japanese Language School Teacher." *Journal of Applied Sociology* 11 (November-December):160-165.

U.S. Bureau of the Census
  1933 Fifteenth Census of the United States, 1930, Population, vol. II. Washington, D.C.: U.S. Government Printing Office.
  1943 Census of Population, 1940, Characteristics of the Nonwhite Population by Race. Washington, D.C.: U.S. Government Printing Office.
  1963 Census of Population, 1960, Subject Reports, Nativity and Parentage, Final Report PC(2)-1A. Washington, D.C.: U.S. Government Printing Office.

U.S. Congress, House

1956   *Amendment of Japanese American Evacuation Claims Act, as Amended, to Provide Expeditious Settlement of Remaining Claims*, 84th Cong., 2nd Sess., House Report 1809. Washington, D.C.: U.S. Government Printing Office.

U.S. Congress, House, Select Committee Investigating National Defense Migration

1942   *Findings and Recommendations on Evacuation of Enemy Aliens and Others from Prohibited Military Zones*, 77th Cong., 2nd Sess., Fourth Interim Report. Washington, D.C.: U.S. Government Printing Office.

U.S. Congress, Senate

1951   *Compromise and Settlement of Japanese Evacuation Claims*, 82nd Cong., 1st Sess., Senate Report 601. Washington, D.C.: U.S. Government Printing Office.

U.S. Temporary National Economic Committee

1941   *Problems of Small Business.* Investigation of Concentration of Economic Power, monograph no. 17. Washington, D.C.: U.S. Government Printing Office.

U.S. War Agency Liquidation Unit

1947   *People in Motion: The Postwar Adjustment of Evacuated Japanese Americans.* Washington, D.C.: U.S. Government Printing Office.

U.S. War Relocation Authority

n.d.   *The Evacuated People: A Quantitative Description.* Washington, D.C.: U.S. Government Printing Office.

Uyematsu, Amy

1971   "The Emergence of Yellow Power in America." In *Roots: An Asian American Reader*, ed. Amy Tachiki, Eddie Wong, and Franklin Odo, pp. 9-13. Los Angeles: University of California Asian American Studies Center.

Van den Berghe, Pierre L.

1975   "Asian Africans before and after Independence." *Kroniek van Afrika* 6:197-205.

Van der Laan, H. Laurens, ed.

1975   "Asian Minorities in Africa: Indians and Lebanese." *Kroniek van Afrika* 6:193-296.

Varon, Barbara F.

1967   "The Japanese Americans: Comparative Occupational Status, 1960 and 1950." *Demography* 4/2:809-819.

Waterbury, John

1972   *North for the Trade: The Life and Times of a Berber Merchant.* Berkeley, Los Angeles, London: University of California Press.

Weber, Max
    1968   *Economy and Society*, ed. Guenther Roth and Claus Wittich. New York: Bedminster Press.

Wertheim, W. F.
    1964   "The Trading Minorities in Southeast Asia." In *East-West Parallels*, pp. 39-82. The Hague: Van Hoeve.

Wong, Charles Choy
    1977   "Black and Chinese Grocery Stores in Los Angeles Black Ghetto." *Urban Life* 5 (January):439-464.

Wong, Morrison G.
    1977   "The Japanese in Riverside, 1890-1945: A Special Case in Race Relations." Ph.D. Dissertation, University of California.

Yancey, William L., Eugene P. Ericksen, and Richard N. Juliani
    1976   "Emergent Ethnicity: A Review and Reformulation." *American Sociological Review* 41 (June):391-403.

Yoneda, Karl
    1971   "100 Years of Japanese Labor History in the USA." In *Roots: An Asian American Reader*, ed. Amy Tachiki, Eddie Wong, and Franklin Odo, pp. 150-158. Los Angeles: University of California Asian American Studies Center.

Young, Charles H., and Helen R. Y. Reid
    1938   *The Japanese Canadians*. Toronto: University of Toronto Press.

Zenner, Walter P.
    1976*a*   "Ethnic Solidarity in Three Middleman Minorities." Paper read at the Annual Meeting of the American Anthropological Association.
    1976*b*   "Middleman Minority Theories: A Critical Review." Paper read at the Conference on the New Immigration, Smithsonian Institute, Washington, D.C.
    1977*a*   "American Jewry in the Light of Middleman Minority Theories." Paper read at the Annual Meeting of the Southern Sociological Society, Atlanta.
    1977*b*   "Middleman Minority Theories: Historical Survey and Assessment." Paper read at Yiddish Studies Colloquium, Columbia University, New York.

Index

DATE DUE